GW00320478

Irish Speakers and Schooling in the Gaeltacht, 1900 to the Present

Tom O'Donoghue · Teresa O'Doherty

Irish Speakers and Schooling in the Gaeltacht, 1900 to the Present

palgrave
macmillan

Tom O'Donoghue
Graduate School of Education
University of Western Australia
Perth, WA, Australia

Teresa O'Doherty
Marino Institute of Education
An Associated College of Trinity
College Dublin
Dublin, Ireland

ISBN 978-3-030-26020-0 ISBN 978-3-030-26021-7 (eBook)
https://doi.org/10.1007/978-3-030-26021-7

Cover credit: Radharc Images/Alamy Stock Photo

This Palgrave Macmillan imprint is published by the registered company Springer Nature Switzerland AG
The registered company address is: Gewerbestrasse 11, 6330 Cham, Switzerland

For
Gearóid Ó Crualaoich & Muiris Budhlaeir (RIP)

Contents

Prologue

There was a time when Irish was the language most commonly used throughout all of Ireland. That, however, was over 1200 years ago.[1] By 1841, only about half of the population of the country was Irish speaking.[2] Furthermore, ten years later, in 1851, the first year in which a country-wide census of population documented information on language usage, the total number of Irish speakers recorded was now only about one-and-a-half million out of a total population of six-and-a-half million.[3] Even allowing for some adjustment to the figures due to the possibility that the number of Irish speakers was significantly underestimated, the decline in language use over the previous ten years was still very substantial. This situation can be attributed primarily to the impact of the Great Famine of 1845–49; while the effects of the tragedy were experienced all over the country, they were particularly devastating amongst the monoglot Irish-speaking communities residing on marginal agricultural land in the north-west, west, south-west and south of Ireland. Over succeeding decades, rapid emigration resulted in what remained of this cohort of the population declining further.

By 1891, the number of native speakers of Irish had declined to just over 700,000, while the concentration of these in Irish-speaking communities was probably below 500,000.[4] The census of 1891 revealed also that while about 14.5 per cent of the population of Ireland were bilingual, over 85 per cent were monoglot English-speakers, leaving less than one per cent monoglot Irish speakers. Within another decade, those areas in which Irish was the dominant vernacular contracted to such an extent that they became clearly identifiable from the majority English-speaking parts of Ireland. Now also, language activists constructed them as being a collective, with the title of An Ghaeltacht, or "the Gaeltacht".

In the mid-1920s, the new Irish State outlined the broad parameters of the boundaries of the Gaeltacht. These were re-drawn, and in more detail, on a number of occasions. Furthermore, by the time we, the present authors, were born, the term "the Gaeltacht" had become so much part of regular discourse throughout Ireland that very few, if any, realised it was a construct of recent origin.

At the same time, no full-length treatise has appeared to date on the history of various aspects of life in the Gaeltacht. This work is one contribution to rectifying the deficit. Specifically, it is concerned with the schooling of Gaeltacht students from 1900 to the present. This took place primarily in State-funded primary schools (generally known as national schools) and, to a much lesser extent, in State-funded secondary schools and vocational schools.

There is a sense in which it is not surprising that we, the authors, cooperated in writing this book as we both have intimate family connections to particular Gaeltacht districts. We also deemed it appropriate to clarify these connections for our readers so that they might have some idea as to how we initially arrived at our research focus. Thus, the next section details how each of us is positioned *vis-à-vis* the Gaeltacht.

Our Positioning vis-a-vis the Gaeltacht

I was born in the town of Lismore, County Waterford, in 1953, and was christened as Thomas Anthony O'Donoghue in the local Roman Catholic Church. The town has long been the Irish seat of the Duke of Devonshire. However, the census returns for 1901 and 1911, show that, at that stage, many residents, far from being English speaking only, were bilingual. This I attribute to individuals moving into the town from the Irish-speaking rural communities within walking distance in all directions.

My paternal grandfather fitted the latter profile, having arrived in the early 1900s, from nearby Bualadh Uí Chadladh. My father was insistent I should know about this aspect of our family background. He also made sure I became acquainted with some of the native speakers of Irish who still lived close to the town. These included Bríd Ní Ghadhra from Móin

Mhóir, which is in Cam Thíar, south of the town, on the old road known as Bóthar a' Loingsigh that connects Coill na hAile to Eó Choill and runs close to the River Blackwater. I also spent many hours north of the town, listening and speaking in Irish to Micheál de Leondra who lived at Gleann Ghairid.

The connection I had with Irish speakers was even stronger through my mother than it was through my father. She was born in the parish of An Seana Phobal, which, along with the nearby parish of Rinn Ua gCúanach (An Rinn) and a small part of the parish of An Áird Mhór, collectively constituted (as they still do) the County Waterford Gaeltacht. She lived there for the first 16 years of her life and attended the local school at Baile Mhic Airt. Not long after she was born, her father, Padraig Ó Catháin, who had also been born in An Seana Phobal, and who had originally been landless, bought a small landholding when he married my grandmother, Ellen Nic Craith, from An Rinn. This farm was in the townland of Móin Fionn in a part of An Seana Phobail known as Barra na Stuaic.

In 1939, my grandfather, along with some others, decided to leave the area. Because of government policy of the day, some in his situation were able to surrender their small plots to the State and receive a farm of good land somewhere else. As a result, three families moved a distance of 27 miles to Ballymote in the Parish of Kilwatermoy, not far from the town of Tallow. This meant they continued to live in County Waterford, albeit now in an English-speaking district. Here, my mother, along with her three brothers and nine sisters, found herself in very different surroundings. Yet, later on, she made sure that from the time I came into the world, I knew about the Irish language and Gaelic culture background of her earlier years.

My father used to bring my siblings and I to our mother's parent's house each time she was about to give birth. We also spent many summer weeks there. What I remember most was my grandfather calling out to my uncles at the height of his voice early in the mornings, to arise and milk the cows. His order was always prefaced by a t'anam 'on diabhal (your soul to the devil).

At evening time, when our aunts and uncles had gone their separate ways, we used to listen to our grandparents recalling in Irish those they termed "na rí sean-daoine" (the real old people). At the time, we could not relate to their focus, but later I came to understand that these were the monolingual Irish speakers who came after them and who saw the world through lenses very different from those of their own generation. Furthermore, because of her age, my mother only spoke of the later generation, who were bilingual and so had one foot in the old world and another in the new one when she was a primary school student.

The Irish language, which my mother inherited from her parents, was certainly not our first language at home in Lismore. Yet, as far as I know, there was much more of it to be heard around our house than in any other house in our immediate vicinity, apart from that of Muiris Breathnach, the local sergeant in the Garda Síochána (the national police force), which was only about 50 metres away. Muiris hailed from Baile an Fheirtéaraigh, in the West Kerry Gaeltacht, and he and Pad Vaughan, my father's friend since childhood, gave us the opportunity to improve our spoken Irish when they established a youth branch of the Irish language revival society, Connradh na Gaeilge (the Gaelic League) for boys and girls in the town. We also learned about the society itself, including that it was established in 1893 as the successor of several nineteenth-century groups aimed at reviving Irish amongst the majority of the Irish population, and that it spearheaded a national Gaelic revival movement over the next two decades.

Muiris and Pad, following the lead of the original founders, held true to the League's apolitical roots. Thus, we only became aware in later years that, like the Gaelic Athletic Association (which also consumed much of our lives during our adolescent years), it had attracted many nationalists of different persuasions in the early 1900s. Later academic study revealed to me that various members of the Irish Volunteers established during the same period, some of whom sought Home Rule for Ireland within the UK and others who sought total separation as an independent nation state, were also in the League, as were most of the signatories of the Proclamation of the Republic issued by the Volunteers and the Irish Citizen Army during the Easter Rising of 1916.

At primary school at the Irish Christian Brothers' school in Lismore, we spoke the Irish language in a very natural way, thanks to the commitment and good humour of Brother Blake and Brother Murphy. As a result, it was difficult for some time to comprehend what peers attending neighbouring primary schools were complaining about when they spoke of difficulties they had with learning and using the language. Later, however, I came to empathise with them on listening attentively to their stories. Equally, I came to appreciate the opportunities I received to listen to Irish being spoken in a natural setting when my parents used to take me back to my mother's home district to visit her uncle, Tomás, and his wife, Bríd.

As a young undergraduate student in England in the early 1970s, I paid little attention to much of the family background I have related so far and totally fell out of practice of speaking Irish. The situation changed a little when I returned to what is now the University of Limerick, to finish my degree. There I was enthused in particular by An Dr. Gearóid Ó Crualaoich (one of the two people to whom this book is dedicated) who, prior to moving to University College Cork, headed up the "Irish Studies" programme in which I enrolled. He was one of the most inspirational teachers I have ever had and he re-awoke in me a great interest in the Irish language, although it was to be quite a few more years before my ability to speak it improved. Equally important, I have long realised, was the new appreciation he instilled in me of Irish culture in its multifaceted dimensions, including Gaelic and non-Gaelic, Catholic and Protestant, republican and unionist.

Gearóid also broadened out my connections with the Gaeltacht, ensuring that my classmates (Bríd Ní Chonaill, Noel Kelly, Michael Burke and Tom Conway) and I spent time in the Corca Dhuibhne Gaeltacht in West Kerry and the Cois Fharraige Gaeltacht in County Galway. I also have memories of developing a close psychological contact with these areas through conversations with students in other groups who hailed from there, including Breandán Ó Beaglaoich, a wonderful player of traditional music, from Baile na Boc in Corca Dhuibhne, and Conchubhair Ó Máille, a talented athlete from Ceantar na nOileán in Connemara. Further, it was during these years as a young student I heard for the first time the strange-sounding-to-me, yet enchanting dialect of the Donegal Gaeltacht when Cathal Ó Searcaigh joined our class. This was prior to his rise to fame as one of the best Irish language poets of the late twentieth century.

In my early 20s, I returned to my native West Waterford to work as a secondary school teacher. At that point, I became determined to improve the quality of my spoken Irish. Very soon, this brought me on weekly visits back to An Rinn, where I befriended many outstanding Irish speakers who have since passed away. They included Dónal Ó Cionnfhaolaidh and his brother Seán, Tomás Ó Gríofa and Nioclás Mac Craith. The highlight of an evening spent in their company was when we were joined by Muiris Budhlaeir (RIP) (the other person to whom this book is dedicated), the principal of the nearby Scoil na Leanaí, a long established and nationally renowned all-Irish boarding school for primary school students in their final year and coming from all over Ireland. Muiris was originally from An Fearan in Corca Dhuibhne and we all appreciated the quality of his conversation, his great humour, and the manner in which he connected us to an extended Gaeltacht community. Little wonder then that when I first met my co-author and discovered that Muiris was her husband's uncle, our mutual interests resulted in engagement in academic work like that which led to the writing of this book.

There is a need also to relate how my own specific academic interest in the topic that is the focus of this book arose. It started on a wet Saturday during the winter in 1984, in Fred Hanna's bookshop on Nassau Street, alongside Trinity College Dublin. I remember browsing through an issue of The Crane Bag, a publication that marketed itself as a journal of Irish culture, literature, philosophy, anthropology and politics. This was a special issue devoted to various aspects of the Irish language. As I read the essay in it on education, one sentence leapt out at me, namely that back in 1904 the education authorities of the day introduced a bilingual programme for schools in Irish-speaking districts. I went back to the secondary sources to try to find out more about it, but to no avail. I then developed my own research agenda on the matter, the results of which constitute sections of this book. Soon, I became enthralled on realising that, commencing in 1906, which was 16 years prior to the advent of Irish independence, a host of primary schools in the Gaeltacht (239 by 1922) were involved in the teaching of what was officially termed the Bilingual Programme of Instruction (the Bilingual Programme). The aim of this innovation was to ensure that students who spoke Irish as a first language would be numerate and literate in both Irish and English at the point of leaving school.

Following the advent of national independence, the new Irish government abandoned the Bilingual Programme. In its determination to use the schools for nation building and to revive the Irish language amongst the dominant English-speaking population, it ignored ideas on the possible value of continuing with the separate education policy for the Gaeltacht established under the previous administration. Instead, teachers throughout the nation now had to teach the same almost totally Irish language-focused curriculum to all children, regardless of their language background. Indeed, it was not until over 90 years later, in 2016, that the independent Irish State introduced its very first policy specifically on the education of Gaeltacht children. Realisation of this and related matters brought me to work with Teresa in producing this book.

Growing up in the town of Kilmallock, County Limerick, in the 1960s, the O'Doherty family, of whom I, Teresa, am one of three daughters, inhabited a built environment that boasted a long and prosperous history. While the town was a faint shadow of its former glory, we were aware that it had been a Norman town, a stronghold of the Geraldines, with its own charter and mint. Also, a number of cut-stone town houses and castles, an original town gate, and extensive tracks of the town wall, were, as they still are, visible to inquisitive children's eyes. Situated on the bank of the River Lubagh, the settlement had grown up around the monastery of Naomh Mocheallóg, founded in the sixth century and was still in existence until the twelfth century.

The establishment of the Collegiate Church in 1251 and the Dominican Friary in 1291 marked Kilmallock as a thriving centre of religious and economic activities in the Middle Ages. In later times, it was also the birthplace of two of those classified as belonging to Filí na Máighe (the group of poets associated with the nearby River Maigue). One of these, Aindrias Mac Craith, better known as An Mangaire Súgach (the merry pedlar) was born in Fanstown, outside Kilmallock around 1708, lived his final years in the town and is buried in the local cemetery. The other, Seán Ó Tuama, while associated with the nearby town of Croom, was also born at Fanstown, Kilmallock, in 1709.

My awareness of the Maigue Gaelic poets when I was growing up was fostered through attendance at the annual festival of culture, Féile na Máighe, which was held during the 1970s in County Limerick, and I attended, as a member of our primary school choir to sing the beautiful lament, Slán Cois Máighe. Our primary level teachers also schooled us in the Ó Riada Mass, and Irish song, poetry, language and dance held dominant positions in our curriculum. Our teachers taught Gaeilge (Irish) first thing in the morning and, while they embraced the "new 1971 curriculum" that offered a broad and holistic education, the prominence given to Irish culture of previous decades persisted.

Although my parents could not speak Irish, our everyday conversations evidenced a rich tapestry of history and language that we took for granted at the time. Words such as caipín (cap), cipín (twig), gabháil (an armful), luathdramán (an idiot), óinseach (a female fool), mi-ádh (misery), cruth (appearance) and spailpín (a wandering landless male labourer) peppered our chats, and we knew many plants only by their Irish names. These included copóg sráide (dockleaf) and buachallán buí (ragwort).

My maternal grandfather's people, the Horgans were from Carraig an Ime and Baile Bhúirne in the County Cork Gaeltacht, and our grandfather (born in 1886), who came by train to our area as a young boy to work on a farm, told us stories of St Abby of the Bees, and of his life as a spailpín (travelling farm labourer). His wife, Kate Mangan, was one of the "Cooper Dennehy family" from Lough Gur, who had come originally from Gneevguilla, in the Sliabh Luachra region in County Kerry. They both could "trace" their families backwards for generation and they told us stories of the 1880s and 1890s that brought nineteenth-century lives and events into our lived reality.

My parents acquired a television in the late 1960s and, once broadcasting of Buntús Cainte, a foundation course in the Irish language, commenced, my mother, Chris, tuned in each week to learn some Irish so that she would be able to help my sisters and I with our homework. When my sister, Siobhán, went to secondary school in 1973, we became aware that to improve our fluency in Irish we could attend three-week summer programmes in "Irish colleges". From 1974 onwards, when I was just 10 years old, my sisters and I attended such a college each year, initially in Ballybunion, in County Kerry, and then in the Baile Mhúirne Gaeltacht, in County Cork. Our parents never considered they could afford to go on a holiday, either at home or abroad, yet each year they saved the cost of sending my two sisters and I to Irish college. While they had no career plans for us, the first generation of the family receive a second-level education, thanks to the State having making it "free" from 1967, they knew instinctively that academic success at the time was intimately connected to competence in the Irish language.

We thoroughly enjoyed our annual courses in Baile Mhúirne and our love for and competence in the Irish language blossomed. Following her success in the Leaving Certificate examination, Siobhán, got "the call" (as it was termed) to "train" as a primary school teacher at Mary Immaculate College in Limerick, where having competence in Irish was essential. As part of her course, attendance at a three-week course in the West Kerry Gaeltacht was compulsory. While accompanying my dad as he drove her to the host family house, the beauty and isolation of the Kerry landscape enthralled me. Although still only in secondary school, I resolved that in future I would attend Irish language courses there and stay in family homes, rather than continue to attend the courses offered in County Cork, which were conducted in a boarding-school environment.

Thereafter, I visited the West Kerry Gaeltacht, on the Dingle Peninsula, each summer, and when I became a student at Mary Immaculate College myself, I worked there each summer as a ceannaire (leader) on teenagers' Irish college programmes, teaching Irish songs and dances, organising sporting activities and overseeing cycle trips to historic sites. On free days, I often took the boat to the Great Blasket Island to explore the landmarks that were so well ingrained in my mind from reading in Irish the autobiography of one of its most famous, inhabitants, Peig Sayers. Occasionally, I cycled the length and breadth of the Peninsula to breathe life into my learning about the history and traditions of the area.

After graduating, becoming a primary school teacher, and taking up a position in an English-medium primary school back in my home town, I discovered that I loved teaching Irish, writing short plays in the language for the children, and bringing them to the féile (regional Gaelic culture event) in Limerick City, where they competed in Irish poetry competitions. Each summer also, I continued to teach on Irish language courses in the West Kerry Gaeltacht, primarily because I enjoyed it so much, but also to supplement my income and pay postgraduate-study fees. I met my husband when set dancing—many miles from the Gaeltacht—but I feel sure the fact he is a native Irish speaker from West Kerry added to his allure. It is said in his home district that when you marry a person from the Gaeltacht you marry the Gaeltacht in its entirety. For me, at least, this became reality, with my husband, my boys and I spending our annual holidays in the West Kerry Gaeltacht over many decades and being privileged we are able to deem the place to be our second home.

This book, it will have been noted, is in part dedicated to Muiris Budhlaeir, my husband's uncle, who, as has been indicated already, taught at Scoil na Leanaí in An Rinn, Co Waterford, in total, he spent 43 years as headmaster in that position. He also was the headmaster of the summer Irish language courses at Coláiste na Rinne (which contained Scoil na Leanaí within it), from 1953 to 1993, and thereafter he was a member of the Board of the school and the Board of the Coláiste until his death in 2009. It is very important to my co-author and I that we express our recognition of the extent to which the memory of his *mórtas cine* (pride of ancestry) and that of his generation, was influential in providing us with a major stimulus to write this book.

The Positioning of the Book

The specific focus of the book is the history of schooling of children in the Gaeltacht, especially from 1900 to the present. It opens by detailing the origin of "the Gaeltacht" as a term and provides an overview on life in Gaeltacht districts at the beginning of the twentieth century. It also gives an account of the Irish colleges established by the Gaelic League in these districts from 1900 for the teaching of adults and promoted from then onwards, partly to encourage enrolment and partly to help to highlight the existence of the Gaeltacht in the public mind nationally. An outline of the broader historical background within which these developments sit, follows, the emphasis being on the fate of the Irish language in Ireland, and specifically in education, up to the last decades of the nineteenth century.

Our decision to commence the central part of our exposition at 1900 was dictated by the fact that this was when it started to become clear that the Bilingual Programme of Instruction, already mentioned, and drawn up in 1904, was about to become a reality. Its advent represented a radical departure from the policy and practices adopted in relation to the Irish language during the history of the *longue durée* not only for minority-tongue schooling in Ireland, but also within the British Empire more broadly. Indeed, throughout much of the nineteenth century a lack of accommodation of minority cultures in education was a characteristic of British imperialism, with Anglicisation being adopted as a policy in schools in Ireland, Scotland, Wales, Cyprus and Malta.[5] British imperialists also seem to have had little appreciation of the possible educational value of hundreds of local languages on the Indian subcontinent.[6]

By the end of the nineteenth century, English was the first language of the majority of the population throughout the UK, with Welsh, Scottish Gaelic and Irish continuing to be spoken only in the more remote areas of "the Celtic fringe". Nevertheless, the different authorities had made various concessions by now to facilitate the use of bilingual teaching approaches. These commenced with native speakers of Welsh in Wales so that they might become numerate and literate in both Welsh and English.[7] Similar developments followed for Irish-speaking children in Ireland, as noted already, and for Scottish Gaelic-speaking children in the Highlands and the Western Isles of Scotland.[8]

In examining these policy changes, it is useful to consider a distinction made by the sociolinguist, Bernard Spolsky, namely that between bilingual programmes aimed at seeking "to salvage the child" and those aimed at seeking "to salvage the language".[9] Fishman elaborated on this distinction:

> The former ["salvaging the child"] is compensatory and aims at providing familiarity with "the language of mainstream society" (the language of wider political, economic and cultural participation) for children whose communities have not provided them with such familiarity, and that are characterisable as disadvantaged but culturally intact. "Salvage the language" programs, on the other hand, are language maintenance rather than compensatory in orientation.[10]

The bilingual programmes mentioned above introduced by the various authorities for Welsh-speaking, Irish-speaking and Scottish Gaelic-speaking children were certainly of the "salvage the child" type.

The Gaelic League authorities were favourably disposed towards the syllabus outlined for the Bilingual Programme of Instruction when the National Board introduced it in 1904, a matter that is not surprising given that its members had been most active over the previous decade in demanding it be drawn up. Concurrently, they were active in promoting a "salvage the Irish language" policy in relation to the great majority of the population of Ireland who, by now, were monolingual speakers of English. Further, within a decade, and in tandem with other national organisations and groups, it began to reorient its goals from being purely cultural nationalist in nature, to also being political nationalist. One consequence was that it shifted its focus so much towards directing most of its activities towards "salvaging the Irish language" throughout the whole country that it lost sight of the initial importance it placed on "salvaging the child" in the Irish-speaking districts.

Following national independence, the new Irish government introduced a largely "save the Irish language" policy by promoting it as a subject in all primary and second-level schools in the State. It also encouraged the use of Irish as the medium of instruction in schools and permeating the curricula with a study of the country's Gaelic past. Subsequent developments were such that, by 1934, the whole thrust of government policy resulted in Irish being the language of teaching, of school-based recreation and of general school life. Furthermore, the new nation's "Gaelicisation" policy, as it came to be known, was starting to become entrenched in nearly all government departments under the control of the State.[11]

In contrast to the situation that existed between 1904 and 1922, no differentiation was made in the early years of independent Ireland between the curriculum and teaching approaches prescribed for schools where students spoke Irish as a first language and for those where students spoke English as a first language. This might seem a little surprising, given the success of the Bilingual Programme of Instruction in the Irish-speaking districts in the final decades of the British administration. The situation becomes understandable, however, when one considers that maintaining a memory of what was involved would not have been consistent with the nationalist and anti-British narratives dominating in Irish political discourse and in the nationally prescribed curricula.[12]

Early enthusiasm for the nation-wide "Gaelicisation" process began to wane during the lengthy economic depressions in Ireland from the 1930s to the late 1950s. These brought into disrepute official government policy holding that national morale would be raised and economic development would follow as more and more people who were first-language speakers of English, would become proficient in the Irish language. A decline in the role of Irish in the education system followed and continued up to the 1980s. Baker summarised this situation as follows:

> By 1960...16% of pupils [throughout the State] were in All-Irish schools, 14% in schools whereas much Irish as English was being taught and 19% in schools where at least one subject apart from Irish was taught through Irish. [However], by 1980, only 3% of students received any Irish medium education in secondary schools. The number of secondary schools offering bilingual education had descended from 156 schools in 1960 to just two in 1980.[13]

Further, by the late 1980s, the maintenance of Irish in the Gaeltacht districts in the north-west, west, south-west and south of the country was under severe pressure, with the population of speakers of the language living there accounting for less than 2 per cent of the national population.

Within 10 years, a new upsurge in pride in all things Irish, including the Irish language, was beginning to reveal itself within the nation. Carnie[14] has suggested this was due to a number of influences, including the increased stature of Ireland within the European Community and improved relations with the UK. Accompanying the shift in associated attitudes was an increase once again in Irish language-medium schools outside of the Irish-speaking districts and especially in urban areas. This and related developments continue and they hold out new hope for those committed to trying to ensure the survival and further revival of Irish.

How the Gaeltacht will feature in what eventuates, however, is not at all clear. Certainly, it will be difficult to erase the collective memory there of its population being eulogized by the State from its establishment in 1922, but simultaneously being marginalized by it socially and economically. On this, successive governments, as Ferriter has pointed out, argued that the Gaeltacht inhabitants held "the nation's reserves of piety, heroism and the ancient characteristics of the race". Yet, their Irish language crusade "failed to regenerate the Gaeltacht or to ensure Gaeltacht children would enjoy equality of opportunity, or that the State apparatus in the Gaeltacht would be marked by competent Irish speakers".[15] A form of schooling could have been devised to provide the people in the Gaeltacht with the knowledge, skills and confidence to maintain their native language and traditions while simultaneously continuing to be bilingual, and, concurrently, to help them in their efforts to achieve economic advancement and improved social conditions. Instead, for much of the period under consideration in this book, those in the Gaeltacht, with certain notable exceptions, received an education that served to maintain them as one of a number of marginalized populations in Irish society. This is the central theme elaborated on throughout the work.

To conclude, it needs to be impressed on readers that this is the first book to appear that deals with the history of schooling in the Gaeltacht since 1900. They are encouraged to view it as providing the broad parameters to guide the development of a comprehensive research agenda for the field rather than constituting the last word on the subject. Our hope is that others will respond and take up the challenge. Finally, we spell place names in English throughout the work, except for places that are still officially located in the Gaeltacht. We use this approach even when referring to these places before they were ever officially categorised as being in the Gaeltacht. At the same time, where they were spelt in English in reports of various kinds, we have done the same.

Notes

1. A. Doyle. *A History of the Irish Language: From the Norman Invasion to Independence* (Oxford: Oxford University Press, 2015).
2. G. Fitzgerald. *Estimates for Baronies of the Minimum Level of Irish Speaking amongst Successive Decennial Cohorts: 1771–1781 to 1861–1871* (Dublin: Royal Irish Academy, 1981), p. 129.
3. Ibid.
4. For an overview on these and related statistics see T. A. O'Donoghue. *Bilingual Education in Ireland, 1904–22: The Case of the Bilingual Programme of Instruction* (Perth: The Centre for Irish Studies, Murdoch University, 2000).
5. N. Atkinson. 'Educational Construction in Malta', *The Irish Journal of Education*, Vol. 3, No. 1, 1969, pp. 32–39.
6. V. E. Durkacz. *The Decline of the Celtic Languages* (Edinburgh: John Donald, 1983).
7. N. Thomas. 'Education in Wales'. In R. Bell, G. Fowler, and K. Little (Eds.). *Education in Great Britain and Ireland* (London: Routledge and Keegan Paul, 1973), pp. 70–80.
8. G. Lewis. *Bilingualism and Bilingual Education* (Oxford: Pergamon Press, 1981).
9. B. Spolsky. 'Speech Communities and Schools', *TESOL Quarterly*, Vol. 8, 1974, pp. 17–26.
10. J. Fishman. 'The Social Science Perspective in the Centre for Applied Linguistics', *Bilingual Education: Current Perspectives* (Arlington: Centre for Applied Linguistics, 1977), p. 11.
11. G. Ó Tuathaigh. *The Development of the Gaeltacht as a Bilingual Entity* (Dublin: Linguistics Institute of Ireland, 1990).
12. T. O'Donoghue. *The Catholic Church and the Secondary School Curriculum in Ireland, 1922–62* (New York: Peter Lang, 1999).
13. Ibid., p. 129.
14. A. Carnie. 'Modern Irish: A Case Study in Language Revival Failure'. In J. D. Bobaljik, R. Pensalfini, and L. Storts (Eds.). *Papers on Language Endangerment and the Maintenance of Linguistic Diversity* (New York: The MIT Working Papers in Linguistics, 1996), pp. 101–116.
15. D. Ferriter. *The Transformation of Ireland 1900–2000* (London: Profile Books, 2005), p. 351.

CHAPTER 1

The Gaeltacht: Constructed, Located and Promoted

A central term introduced already is that of "the Gaeltacht". In 1926, the Irish State established the boundaries of the districts to which this anglicised collective noun referred. By then, however, it had only been in use in the sense of referring to defined geographical areas for about 25 years. Accordingly, it is apposite to present in this chapter an outline of its evolution as a construct. A brief overview follows of the social, economic and education realities of the lives of the people of the Gaeltacht at the turn of the twentieth century, which was a time when Irish language preservationists and revivalists were showing mounting concern that children residing there were not benefiting from education because English was the medium of instruction. Equally, these preservationists and revivalists came to highlight for the majority English-speaking population the actual existence of the Gaeltacht as a distinct place and to involve them in the learning of Irish, including in new "Irish colleges" that largely were located in Gaeltacht districts, and that came to give these a particular defining property in succeeding decades.

The Construction of "the Gaeltacht" as a Term Referring to a Defined Set of Places

In a pioneering work published in 2005, Ó Torna detailed the results of an in-depth investigation she had conducted on the use of the term An Ghaeltacht (the Gaeltacht) in Ireland.[1] In it, she argues that while today

T. O'Donoghue and T. O'Doherty, *Irish Speakers and Schooling in the Gaeltacht, 1900 to the Present*,
https://doi.org/10.1007/978-3-030-26021-7_1

we use the term to denote the geographical location of communities whose normal everyday language is Irish, matters were not always thus. Rather, she points out, the term was for long associated largely with such notions as "lucht labhartha na Gaeilge" and "an dúchas Gaelach".[2] The former referred to speakers of Irish regardless of location and the latter referred to those who had a Gaelic nature or a Gaelic outlook on life shaped by the fact that they made sense of the world through the prism of the Irish language.

The lexicographer, Fr. Ó Duinnín, in the original 1904 edition of his Irish-English dictionary, implied in the following definitions that the "modern" version of the term "the Gaeltacht", or An Ghaeltacht, had still not come into common usage in Ireland by this point in time:

> Gaedhealcht, -a, f., the state of being Irish or Scotch: Gaeldom, Irishry, the native race of Ireland; bean de'n Ghaedhealcht, a woman of the Irishry (Art MacC.); G. Alban, the Highlands of Scotland.[3]

The situation was different in Gaelic-speaking Scotland and had been so since the beginning of the eighteenth century. There, the term An Ghaeltacht had long been in use, not only in the sense outlined by Ó Duinnín in the extract presented above, but also to refer to geographical areas where those who spoke Scottish Gaelic resided.

Ó Torna identified the following extract as being the first instance in print of use of the term in Irish to refer to a geographical area:

> ….whether the object be to see beautiful scenery or to obtain a period of salutary rest, there are no places within reach better worth visiting than those which the Gaodhaltacht [sic] of Ireland abundantly provides.[4]

This statement appeared in an article written in the English language and entitled "The Gaelic League", that was published in an issue of the League's magazine, Irisleabhar na Gaedhilge. Ó Torna also went on to say that the first time the term An Ghaeltacht may have appeared in an Irish language piece of writing in the sense of referring to a geographical area, was in a note in a 1902 issue of the Gaelic League's newspaper, An Claidheamh Soluis. This contained an announcement that a branch of the organisation had been established in the Bóthar Buí (Boherbue) district in County Cork, which was described as being "istigh i gceart lár na Gaedhealtachta"[5] ("located in the heart of the Gaeltacht").

Over the next 25 years, speakers of both Irish and English came to use the term An Ghaeltacht, or "the Gaeltacht", to refer almost exclusively to a particular place or set of places. Indeed, acceptance in this sense was such that, by 1927, Fr. Ó Duinnín, in a new edition of his dictionary published that year, felt confident enough to offer the following definition, which was different to the one he gave in 1904:

> Gaedhealcht, -a, f., the state of being Irish or Scotch: Gaeldom, Irishry, the native race of Ireland; Irish-speaking district or districts; the Gaeltacht; bean de'n Gh, a woman of the Irishry (Art MacC.); G. Alban, the Highlands of Scotland.[6]

The extension of meaning in this definition over the earlier one was inspired by international as well as national developments, including the European-wide "Romantic movement", that had grown as a counterforce to the Industrial Revolution and that led to individuals from urbanised areas visiting the countryside to experience the beauties of nature.

A particular aspect of the "Romantic movement" in Ireland led to Irish-speaking communities along the western seaboard and its adjacent islands having "their image bolstered through the work of antiquarians, academics and novelists" and by artists seeking to depict the "unspoilt scenery and rural life".[7] A related influence, that had its origins in the idealisation by the French intellectual, Jean Jacque Rousseau, perceived "the peasant", as one who leads a simple yet noble rural life, but was worthy of study so as to reveal the possibilities of improving human nature. In considering associated developments, Nowlan elaborated as follows:

> The French Revolution and the Romantic Movement had helped to give a new significance to long neglected languages and popular traditions in many parts of Europe. Men [sic] began to look on the traditions and languages of the forgotten nationalities, especially among the Slavs and the Baltic peoples, not as quaint survivals but as fresh, creative contributions to European culture, somehow morally better than the offerings of a tired, cosmopolitan civilization.

The Celtic fringe was one of the areas influenced. On this, Jones[8] has drawn attention to the rise of the idea of the Eisteddfod or national festival of Welsh language-based culture in Wales from the 1860s.

From the latter half of the nineteenth century, a growing interest also emerged in Scotland in relation to literary and antiquarian connections with Scottish Gaelic. In a similar vein, Irish-speaking districts in Ireland, partly because of their geographical isolation, came to be the focus of related interest, especially following the visits of European scholars. These individuals believed they would be likely to witness in the districts in question "the most ancient features of Gaelic culture".[9] In particular, German and Scandanavian researchers who were contributing to the flowering academic fields of descriptive and comparative linguistics came to see them as reservoirs of fascinating speech.[10]

Equally influential from about the 1870s onwards were the debates of the Irish intelligentsia on establishing a nation state in Ireland. By 1905, the year when D.P. Moran crystalised these ideas in his "Irish-Ireland" treatise,[11] the overriding notion being promoted was that Irish identity rested upon "Gaelicism" and Catholicism. In relation to Gaelicism, a number of organisations concerned with restoring imagined Gaelic elements of a previous identity eroded through Anglicisation were well rooted by now. As indicated already, both the Gaelic Athletic Organisation,[12] established in 1884, and the Gaelic League, established in 1893,[13] were chief amongst these.[14]

A significant portion of the work conducted by the Gaelic League focused on the Irish-speaking districts scattered throughout the country. Branches of the organisation established there generated a perspective in the minds of their populations that culturally they constituted a unique group in Ireland. This perspective was amplified when speakers from the predominantly English language speaking parts of the country arrived to spend time living in the Gaeltacht in order to learn the language.

From 1926, "the Gaeltacht" became an official term of the independent Irish State following the publication of a report entitled Coimisiún na Gaeltachta (the Commission on the Gaeltacht).[15] This report was the product of the work undertaken by a special government commission established in 1925, to examine the economic and social conditions in the Gaeltacht districts. While it did not delineate exact geographical areas, it did define Irish-speaking or semi-Irish-speaking districts as ones where 25 per cent, or more of the population, were native speakers of Irish. This resulted in a recognition that such districts existed in 15 of the newly independent State's 26 counties.[16]

In the 1950s, the State decided that the nation's Gaeltacht boundaries as laid down in the 1920s no longer reflected the reality of the language situation in the country due to the rapid decline that had taken place in the number of native speakers of Irish in the interim.[17] It also decided that the strength of language use in a district should form the basis for granting Gaeltacht status, and consequently it laid down clear geographical boundaries to define Gaeltacht districts and to exclude areas in which the number of Irish speakers had declined since the 1920s. The eventual outcome was that the Gaeltacht as an officially defined geographical area was now confined to Irish-speaking districts in counties Donegal, Galway, Mayo, Kerry, Cork and Waterford.

Since 1956, only minor changes have taken place in the Gaeltacht boundaries. This involved the inclusion of a few small districts in County Kerry and County Cork. In 1967, the State added the small Baile Ghib (Gibstown) and Ráth Chairn (Rathcarran) districts in County Meath. These had become Irish-speaking districts when a number of families from the West of Ireland settled there from the 1930s, on land acquired for them by the government of the day.

Currently, the State's Department of Community, Rural and Gaeltacht Affairs, under the leadership of the Minister for Community, Rural and Gaeltacht Affairs, is responsible for overall Irish Government policy with respect to the Gaeltacht. Raidió na Gaeltachta is the State's radio station serving both the Gaeltacht and Irish speakers generally. A state-funded television station, TG4, also focuses on promoting the Irish language.

In 2002, the members of yet another commission established to examine the position of the language in the Gaeltacht districts concluded that, based on the patterns of bilingualism amongst their communities, English was becoming the dominant language.[18] They also argued that a new language reinforcement strategy that would have the confidence of the Gaeltacht people was required. Informed by the results of the 2006 national census indicating that 91,862 people lived in the official Gaeltacht,[19] a comprehensive linguistic study of the usage of Irish in the Gaeltacht was undertaken in 2007.[20]

A major response by the government was the introduction of The Gaeltacht Bill 2012.[21] All areas at that point within the Gaeltacht maintained their Gaeltacht status. Furthermore, the legislation ensured that revocation of such status in relation to any area could take place only if its population failed to prepare a language plan. Some of the final chapters of the book consider related developments. At this point, however, it is instructive to draw attention to the results of the most recent national census, namely, that of 2016, showing that the population of the Gaeltacht had risen 4.5 per cent over the previous 10 years.[22] The major concentrations of these Irish speakers were located in the western counties of Donegal, Mayo, Galway and Kerry, with smaller concentrations in counties Cork and Waterford in the south and in County Meath in the east.

An Overview of the Social, Economic and Education Realties of the Gaeltacht Around the Turn of the Twentieth Century

Fitzgerald,[23] in his research on Irish in the nineteenth century, concluded that, by 1871, only in a small number of areas in the country was the speaking of Irish by the young not declining. Amongst the number of unaffected areas were the Aran Islands, north-west County Galway and parts of County Galway east and north of the city itself, as well as the Barony of Erris in north-west County Mayo. The only areas where 60 per cent or more of young people spoke Irish were the western portion of County Waterford, the Beare Peninsula in County Cork, west County Kerry, north-west and south-west County Clare, west and mid-County Galway, Erris in County Mayo, the baronies of Gullen and Claremorris in east-County Mayo, and the Rosses in County Donegal.

Those living in the areas detailed above were largely the remnants of the lower class who had been so prominent in Ireland prior to the advent of the Great Famine of 1845–48. A complex rural society composed not just of landlords and tenants had evolved over the previous century.[24] The number of middling farmers, both Catholic and Protestant, with farms on long leases and living in fine houses, continued to increase. Beneath them were the smallholders, each holding from one to 15 acres. At the bottom were the cottiers or labourers, who received their wages from the farmers in the form of tiny strips of land that they held for less than a year at a time and on which they grew potatoes and grazed a cow to feed themselves and their families. By the time of the Famine, the number of labourers, cottiers and smallholders outnumbered farmers by two to one.

The Great Famine devastated the cottier and smallholding classes, and many of their tiny holdings were absorbed into existing farms. Those who survived and who were primarily Irish speakers also had their cultural and spiritual worlds come under severe attack, including from the Catholic Church (the Church), to which they gave allegiance. By the mid-nineteenth century, with the political situation no longer hostile, a new generation of Catholic "reforming" bishops was able to bring a unified approach and a high degree of organisation to what had hitherto been a somewhat chaotic structure of ecclesiastical administration. The international background has been aptly summarised as follows:

> By the mid-nineteenth century, Catholicism throughout Europe was reacting to the challenge of an increasingly pluralist and rationalistic society by a vigorous assertion of its exclusive claims to truth and authority. The Syllabus of Errors (1864), the determined defence of the Pope's temporal possessions against the movement for Italian unification, and the proclamation of papal infallibility (1970), were all reflections of this mood of intransigent defiance in the face of a hostile world.[25]

The Catholic bishops, led by Paul Cullen, Ireland's first Cardinal, embraced this position. A major consequence was the reshaping of popular religious practice, including in Irish-speaking Ireland.

Up to the early-to-mid-nineteenth century, Irish Catholicism, and particularly in Irish-speaking districts, had diverged from orthodox Catholicism in a variety of ways. On the one hand, it was very much intertwined with magical beliefs, while on the other hand, "Sunday mass, confession and communion other than at the point of death, were considered less significant".[26] By the 1870s, however, the situation had changed dramatically, revealing a new pattern in which

> ....attendance at Sunday mass for the first time became almost universal, while confession and communion became more regular and more frequent. The same period saw the widespread dissemination of a range of auxiliary services – benedictions, stations of the cross, novenas, processions and retreats – as well as the routine use of scapulars, medals, religious images and other aids to private devotion....Meanwhile the psychological impact of Catholic religious worship was increased by a transformation of its physical setting, as new or improved church buildings, more elaborate vestments and lavish altar furnishings allowed services to be conducted with a new emphasis on external magnificence and display.[27]

A result of this "devotional revolution" in what remained of Gaelic Ireland, as Harris has put it, was a major attempt to drive out "the remnants of Irish folk culture".[28]

At the same time, material conditions began to improve in many of those communities where their members continued to speak Irish, and especially from 1891, when the British administration established the Congested Districts Board.[29] As part of government policy of trying to "kill desires for Home Rule by kindness",[30] this Board attempted to resolve some of the economic problems of the western seaboard, which it regarded as being a product of remoteness from central markets, a lack of natural resources and population pressure. A major action was to provide special assistance to people in the region who were living on holdings with very low rateable valuations. A great number of these were native speakers of Irish.

At the end of the nineteenth century, those speakers of the Irish scattered around the country, and particularly in the areas noted above, also did not collectively "constitute any kind of coherent society".[31] Neither did they speak a standardised language. Rather, there were three main dialects, namely, those popularly known as Munster Irish, Connaught Irish and Ulster Irish. Each of these dialects also had a number of sub-dialects.

Most of the districts in which Irish language speakers were located contained considerable areas of upland, bog land or otherwise poor agricultural land that forced the people to live in settled bands along the coast and along valleys. On this, Hindley noted that, with the exception of a large section of County Waterford, and nearby in the east of County Cork and in the extreme south of County Tipperary, all came within the remit of the Congested Districts Board which, as has been made clear already, was established to provide them with "special economic assistance".[32] This included the building of harbours and piers, making improvements to housing, providing instruction by agricultural and fishery instructors, purchasing and redistributing large grazing farms, and "transplanting of better-off tenants to still better holdings farther east, so that their vacated land could be used to enlarge neighbouring uneconomic holdings".[33] Further, Hindley highlighted the Board's conclusion that, notwithstanding the great improvements made over 20 years, congestion was still "so severe in the heartlands of West Donegal, Erris [north-west Mayo], and Connemara, that no amount of migration or resettlement would make the bulk of the holdings economic".[34]

The situation specifically in the Irish-speaking areas in County Donegal towards the end of the nineteenth century was one of great distress. In 1890, Kelly highlighted the lack of employment there and the reality of people forced into "precarious and peculiar ways of living" despite emigration and seasonal migration to Scotland.[35] The same year, *The Times* of London conducted a survey in the west of County Donegal.[36] This extensive Irish-speaking district was "in very poor circumstances" economically, particularly at Gartan, Church Hill and Seacoe in the centre, and by the coast around Gaoth Dobhair (Gwedore), where each family, on average, cultivated only three acres of land.

The comparative situation across the various other "congested districts" was summarised by Ó Danachair. He stated that the reports of the inspectors of the Board tell us that the least distressed areas were those of West Munster. Even here, however, on the Dingle Peninsula, "what was regarded as a good farm produced a total return in money of no more than sixty pounds in a year" from which, "by strict economy, the farmer might save a couple of pounds".[37] He went on as follows:

> Further north, in the Aran Islands, the average small farmer could not expect more than forty pounds to pass through his hands in a year, and only by very frugal living could he effect a saving of two or three pounds. Across Galway Bay, in Cois Fharraige [the south Co. Galway coastline] and Connemara the average man was hard put to make twenty pounds a year, and could make ends meet only from some outside source, such as a remittance from America, selling turf to North Clare or the Aran Islands, or labour on the roads or other public works; for him the saving of a little capital was a dream very seldom realised. In parts of Mayo... conditions were even worse. In Achill [in Co. Mayo], for instance...there was no hope of winning a livelihood from the land or sea, and it had for many years been customary that some or all of the men of the family spent a good half of the year away from their homes as migratory labourers in the east of Ireland, or in England or Scotland, and the wages which they brought home, although amounting to only eight or ten pounds each, meant the difference between starvation and survival for them and their families.[38]

From 1831, government aspiration was that children from these districts, as well as students from all other parts of Ireland, would acquire the necessary skills to improve their lot in life through the primary school curriculum prescribed following the establishment of the National School System. For some time, scholars have highlighted the extent to which this system's dominant English language-based curriculum disadvantaged those who spoke Irish as a first language. Recently, however, Wolf has also drawn attention to another negative influence, namely, the very high under-representation of schools of any kind in Irish-speaking districts relative to the situation throughout much of the rest of the country up to the middle of the 1850s.[39]

When national schools eventually became prevalent throughout the Irish-speaking districts, they were usually small one or two-teacher establishments. The indications also are that conditions in them were very basic indeed and continued to be so for decades. For example, in the early 1900s, the national school for the Irish-speaking community at Coomhola, County Cork, was, according to a visiting inspector, one "of unfavourable circumstances as regards accommodation".[40] A similar description of the national school for Irish-speaking pupils at Ros Muc (Rosmuck) in County Galway was recorded in 1911, with a visiting inspector noting the work there was "carried on under great difficulties owing to the usually overcrowded state of the classroom".[41] At the same time, the situation in these and in other schools in Irish-speaking districts was often no worse than that in equally poor English-speaking districts in the north-west, west, south-west and south of Ireland at the time.

The Promotion of Irish Language Colleges to Highlight and Promote the Gaeltacht

A number of forces operated at the end of the nineteenth century and the beginning of the twentieth century to generate a perspective in the minds of those living in the Gaeltacht that culturally they belonged to a distinctive part of Ireland. The establishment there of specialist colleges for the teaching of Irish to adults and for the preparation of teachers of Irish was one of these. Within these "Irish colleges", as they came to be known, native speakers of Irish were regularly employed as storytellers so that learners could come to appreciate the level of fluency to which they themselves might aspire.

By 1919–20, the National Board gave recognition as institutions providing appropriate courses for the preparation of teachers of Irish and as being eligible for receipt of State financial assistance for this task to the colleges established by the Gaelic League. Those established in the Gaeltacht and the English names given to them at the time were as follows:

The Ulster College—Cloghaneely, Co. Donegal
The Connacht College—Tourmakeedy, Co. Mayo
The Munster College—Ballingeary, Co. Cork
The Ring College—Dungarvan, Co. Waterford
The Spiddal College—Galway, Co. Galway
The Dingle College—Dingle, Co. Kerry
The Glandore College—Glandore, Co. Cork
The O'Curry College—Carrigaholt, Co. Clare
The Rathlin College—Rathlin Island, Co. Antrim
The Glengarriff College—Glengariff, Co. Cork
The Omeath College—Omeath, Co. Louth

By now also, a number of similar officially recognised colleges were operating in major centres outside of the Irish-speaking districts.[42] These were the Presentation College in Cork, the Belfast College, the Leinster College in Dublin, the Ballinasloe College in County. Galway, the Castlebar College in County. Mayo, and the Dublin College.

The first Irish college opened was at Béal Átha'n Ghaorthaidh (Ballingeary), in County Cork, in 1904. A former teacher there recalled that while its main purpose was to train competent teachers of Irish, "the old method"[43] of requiring of pupils that they learn a series of rules and exceptions from grammar books and getting them to translate short sentences illustrative of such rules and exceptions from one language to another was rejected.[44] He went on to state that, as a result of adopting a new system of instruction in Béal Átha'n Ghaorthaidh, namely, "the direct method",[45] a child should be able to articulate the sounds of the new language (Irish) and from there proceed to simple conversation about everyday things. The associated expectation was that the teachers would confine themselves entirely to the use of Irish when teaching. A similar account of practices in operation at the Irish college at Túr Mhic Éadaigh (Tourmakeedy) in County Mayo was given.[46]

Overall, the establishment of the Irish colleges was an expression of the enthusiasm and determination of the Gaelic League. They were not, however, permanent colleges that functioned all-year round. Rather, they were institutions that taught intensive courses, usually in summer time. At Coláiste na Mumhan, in Béal Átha'n Ghaorthaidh, for example, there were two sessions annually, each of one month's duration, with one taking place in July and the other in August, and with students divided into two types, namely, "the candidate teacher" and "the beginning teacher".[47]

The Irish college concept, while somewhat radical in Ireland as an innovation in adult education, was not a peculiarly Irish creation. The Welsh Language Society, which paid considerable attention to the task of preparing teachers to teach Welsh, had already adopted such an approach, largely as a response to a lack of provision for appropriate preparation in existing state teacher training colleges.[48] The Society held its first "summer school" at Aberystwyth in 1903, and over the years university scholars and schoolteachers gave of their time in order to give practising teachers a sound knowledge of the Welsh language, literature and history, and of the methods of teaching these subjects in the schools.

The Welsh Language Society placed a great emphasis on language teaching methods. In 1900, William Edwards, a government inspector of schools, led the way when he advocated the use of "the direct method" in teaching Welsh to non-Welsh speakers.[49] Thomas Darlington, government inspector of schools for the counties of Cardigan, Merioneth and Montgomery, also promoted the adoption of this method, as did the Gaelic League.[50]

Different Irish colleges also developed a reputation for having their own particular practices. For example, the college at Ballingeary was considered to be the mecca of the phonetician, with the emphasis being primarily on spoken Irish above all. Concurrently, Ring College was known for its promotion of "literary purity" and taking "the more precious view of the language"; and the college in Omeath was held in high regard for advancing Fr. Toal's new phrase-method of Irish teaching.[51]

Conclusion

The term and geographical concept of An Ghaeltacht was solidified and gained public acceptance during the early part of the twentieth century. It referred to rural parts of the country, which experienced great poverty, and where the majority of the people still spoke Irish as their first language. With a preponderance of cottier and tiny holdings, with fewer schools per capita than the average across the country, and with high levels of emigration, the survival of Irish as a spoken language in these areas was under major threat. The founding of the Gaelic League, and the later establishment of Irish colleges in the Gaeltacht regions, however, proved to be significant steps in preserving it. The identification of geographical regions as the reservoir of the language, and the initiation of a flow of young teachers to Irish colleges located in the Gaeltacht districts, with the intent to develop their competence and fluency in the language, began a tradition which still perseveres.

Notes

1. C. Ó Torna. *Cruthú na Gaeltachta 1893–1922* (Baile Átha Clíath: Cois Life Teoranta, 2005).
2. Ibid., pp. 42–43.
3. Ibid.
4. *Irisleabhar na Gaedhilge*, Samhain 1893, p. 228.
5. Quoted in C. Ó Torna. *Cruthú na Gaeltachta 1893–1922*, p. 43.
6. Ibid.
7. N. C. Johnson. 'Building a Nation: An Examination of the Irish Gaeltacht Commission Report of 1926', *Journal of Historical Geography*, Vol. 19, No. 2, p. 159.
8. W. R. Jones. *Bilingualism in Welsh Education* (Cardiff: University of Wales Press, 1966).
9. S. R. Fischer. *A History of Language* (London: Reaktion Books, 2018).
10. E. Hovdhaugen, F. Karlsson, C. Henriksen, and B. Sigurd. *The History of Linguistics in the Nordic Countries* (Helsinki: Nordic Research Council for the Humanities, 2000), p. 285.
11. D. P. Moran. *The Philosophy of Irish Ireland* (Dublin: University College Dublin Press, 2016).
12. M. De Búrca. *The G.A.A.: A History of the Gaelic Athletic Association* (Dublin: Gilland Macmillan, 1980).
13. P. Mac Aonghusa. *Ar Son na Gaeilge: Conradh na Gaeilge 1893–1993* (Baile ÁthaClíath: Conradh na Gaeilge, 1993).
14. R. Foster. *Vivid Faces. The Revolutionary Generation in Ireland* (London: W. W. Norton, 2014).
15. Coimisiún na Gaeltachta. *Coimisiún na Gaeltachta Report* (Dublin: The Stationery Office, 1925).
16. J. Walsh. *Díchoimisiúnú Teanga. Coimisiún na Gaeltachta 1926* (Dublin: Cois Life, 2002).
17. M. A. G. O. Tuathaigh. *The Development of the Gaeltacht as a Bilingual Entity. Occasional Paper 8* (Dublin: The Linguistics Inst. of Ireland, 1990).
18. https://web.archive.org/web/20131017090003/; http://www.ahg.gov.ie/en/20YearStrategyfortheIrishLanguage/Publications/Report%20of%20Coimisi%C3%BAn%20na%20Gaeltachta.pdf.
19. http://www.cogg.i.e./wp-content/uploads/Linguistic-Study-of-the-Use-of-Irish-in-the-Gaeltacht.pdf.

20. https://www.cso.ie/en/census/census2006reports/census2006-volume9-irishlanguage/.
21. https://www.chg.gov.ie/gaeltacht/20-year-strategy-for-the-irish-language-2010-2030/gaeltacht-act-2012.
22. https://www.cso.ie/en/releasesandpublications/ep/p-cp10esil/p10esil/ilg/.
23. C. Ó Torna. *Cruthú na Gaeltachta 1893–1922*, p. 44.
24. This account is based on that in S. Connolly. *Religion and Society in Nineteenth Century Ireland* (Dundalk: Dundalgan Press, 1985).
25. S. Connolly. *Religion and Society in Nineteenth Century Ireland*, p. 27.
26. Ibid., p. 49.
27. Ibid., p. 54.
28. E. Harris. 'Prince Charles Not the Only One Who Needs a History Lesson', *Sunday Independent*, 17 June 2018.
29. C. Breathnach. *The Congested Districts Board, 1891–1923* (Dublin: The Four Courts Press, 2005).
30. This policy, which was based on the term used by Mr. Gerald Balfour, the Irish Secretary, was analysed at the time in J. E. Redmond. 'The Policy of Killing Home Rule by Kindness', *The Nineteenth Century: A Monthly Review*, Vol. 38, No. 226, 1895, pp. 905–914.
31. D. Greene. 'The Founding of the Gaelic League'. In S. Ó Tuama (Ed.). *The Gaelic League Idea* (Cork and Dublin: Mercier Press, 1972), p. 12.
32. R. Hindley. *The Death of the Irish Language: A Qualified Obituary* (London: Routledge, 1990), p. 28.
33. Ibid.
34. Ibid., p. 29.
35. R. J. Kelly. 'The Congested Districts', *Journal of the Statistical and Social Inquiry Society of Ireland*, Vol. IX, 1891, p. 445.
36. This account is analysed in W. J. P. Logan. An Aspect of Rural Reconstruction: The Work of the Congested Districts Board, with Specific Reference to County Donegal, 1981–1923 (Unpublished M.A. Thesis, Queen's University, Belfast, 1976), p. 73.
37. C. Ó Danachair. 'The Gaeltacht'. In B. Ó Cuív (Ed.). *A View of the Irish Language*, p. 113.
38. Ibid.
39. N. Wolf. 'The National-School System and the Irish Language in the Nineteenth Century'. In J. Kelly and S. Hegarty (Eds.). *Schools and Schooling: 1650–2000: New Perspectives on the History of Education: The Eight Seamus Heaney Lectures* (Dublin: Four Courts Press, 2017).
40. *Inspectors' Report Book, Coomhola N.S., County Cork.* This book was examined in the school in question by the first-named author in June 1987.

41. *Inspectors' Report Book, Rosmuck N.S., County Galway.* This book was examined in the school in question by the first-named author in June 1987.
42. S. Mac Mathuna agus R. Mac Gabhann. *Conradh na Gaeilge agus An t-Oideachas Aosach?* (Contae na Gaillimhe: Cló Cois Fharraige, 1981).
43. K. Magner. 'Ballingeary', *Catholic Bulletin*, Vol. 11, 1912, pp. 640–645.
44. This method was also termed "the translational method" and the Govin Method.
45. "The direct method" was termed "the módh díreach", "the módh réidh cainnte" and "the Berlitz Method".
46. E. Devine. 'The Connacht Irish College at Tourmakeady', *Catholic Bulletin*, Vol. 11, January 1912, pp. 9–14.
47. M. Wall. 'The Decline of the Irish Language'. In B. Ó Cuív (Ed.). *A View of the Irish Language*, p. 97.
48. N. Thomas. 'Education in Wales'. In R. Bell, G. Fowler, and K. Little (Eds.). *Education in Great Britain and Ireland*, p. 75.
49. Ibid., p.76.
50. A. E. Cleary. 'Gaelic Colleges', *Studies*, Vol. 6, No. 23, 1917, pp. 470–475.
51. K. Magner. 'Ballingeary', *Catholic Bulletin*.

CHAPTER 2

Education and the Irish Language in the Longue Durée

Introduction

Nationalist-minded historians have long argued that the "golden era" for the Irish language was, as they have tended to put it, when Ireland's monastic schools "served as 'lights of the north' during Europe's dark ages".[1] They have also been wont to point out that, concurrently, the Bardic Schools worked at preserving and transmitting the associated literary tradition. Successive invasions resulted in the introduction first of Norse, then Norman French and, finally, English, to the country. Nevertheless, Irish was still by far the most dominant language by 1500.[2]

In order to contextualise developments in relation to both education and the Irish language since then and specifically for the period under consideration in later chapters, this chapter opens with an account of the fate of Irish in Ireland up to advent of the independent Irish Free State in 1922.[3] A consideration of Irish and education from the Reformation until the establishment of the National School System in 1831 follows. The final section of the chapter provides an overview of the place of the language within the national school system until 1904, the year in which National Board of Education introduced a bilingual programme for Irish-speaking districts.

T. O'Donoghue and T. O'Doherty, *Irish Speakers and Schooling in the Gaeltacht, 1900 to the Present*,
https://doi.org/10.1007/978-3-030-26021-7_2

The Fate of the Irish Language in Ireland up to Advent of the Independent Irish State in 1922

Irish is a Celtic language. This means that it belongs to a specific group of Indo-European languages. Linguists divide this group into two branches, namely, the Continental Celtic languages and the Insular Celtic languages.[4] On the European continent, the Continental subgroup, which included Gaulish, Celtiberian and Lepontic, existed up until 1000 years ago. The Insular subgroup has two branches, namely, Brythonic and Goidelic. The Brythonic languages consist of Welsh, Cornish and Breton, while the Goidelic languages are Irish, Scottish Gaelic and Manx. By the end of nineteenth century, Cornish had been dead for over 100 years and Manx was on death's door. Welsh, Scottish Gaelic and Irish were now also very much the languages of minority populations amongst whom the English language continued to make major inroads and to accelerate a trend towards bilingualism.

Archaeologists and historical linguists date at about 200 BC the arrival in Ireland of speakers of a language that formed the roots of modern Irish.[5] From about the beginning of the sixth century to the end of the twelfth century, this language underwent significant change, one that was characterised later as being a shift from "Old Irish" to "Middle Irish". Old Irish, or An tSean-Ghaeilge, which dates from around 600 AD to 900 AD, is the name given to the oldest form of the Goidelic languages for which extensive written texts are extant. Middle Irish, or An Mheán-Ghaeilge, is the Goidelic language which was spoken in Ireland, most of Scotland and the Isle of Man, from around 900 AD to around 1200 AD.

It was also between the ninth century and the twelfth century, with the Viking invasions and the establishment of the Norse-speaking Viking towns of Dublin, Cork, Waterford and Galway, that the first major challenge came to the Irish language. Norman French then entered the country in 1169, with the first of the Anglo-Norman invasions. The Normans conquered the towns and much of the Irish-speaking countryside. Those who lived in the towns became largely English speaking. Those who lived in the countryside, however, learned Irish and quickly became assimilated into Gaelic culture. As a result, they became níos Gaelaí ná na Gaeil féin ("more Irish than the Irish themselves"), to use a term that was used to characterise their outlook.

During the period 1200–1600, there were various attempts by the English to suppress the Irish language. The Statutes of Kilkenny, passed in 1366, resulted in the banning of the language from the court system and from use in commerce.[6] The Tudors took similar steps in the early sixteenth century as part of their attempts to "unify" their realms.[7] These measures were generally a failure outside of the towns and the area around Dublin known as the Pale. Indeed, over the whole period, "Modern Classical Irish" thrived as a highly standardised language supported by the Gaelic chieftains and characterised by a significant literary output, particularly in the form of bardic poetry.

In the late 1500s, the first of a number of what came to be known as "crown plantations" of Ireland was established. These involved the confiscation of land by the English crown and its resettlement with loyal settlers from Great Britain. One of the guiding aims was to attempt to pacify and anglicise the country under English rule so that it could develop as a peaceful and reliable possession. The largest and most successful of the settlements was the Ulster Plantation, when Irish-speaking Catholic landowners lost much of the rich farmlands of the north-east of the country and English-speaking Protestant settlers, mainly from the Lowlands of Scotland, replaced them.[8] This plantation area became almost exclusively English speaking, although a small number of speakers of Scottish Gaelic also settled there.[9]

Within a few decades, the Cromwellian army drove most of the Irish-speaking nobility out of Munster and Leinster and replaced them with settlers from England.[10] These unlike their counterparts in the north-east had by 1700, assimilated with the native Irish and had begun to speak the language of the common people, or what linguists later came to term "An Nua-Ghaeilge" or "Modern Irish". Nevertheless, this language was soon to enter a period of major decline, while English began to grow in popular use. On this, Ó Loingsigh[11] has argued that the first major impulse towards the language shift from Irish to English on a national scale dates from the relaxation in the second half of the 1700s, of the anti-Catholic Penal Laws passed in the seventeenth century and eighteenth century to remove all rights to property, religion and education from the Catholic Irish.[12]

Concurrently, the Catholic and mainly Irish-speaking community began to acquire a new social mobility and aspire to being an English-speaking class. The eighteenth-century County Armagh poet, Art Mac Cubhthaigh, expressed his deploring of this situation as follows:

Tá mo chroí-se réabtha ina míle céad cuid
's gan balsam féin ann a d'fhoirfeadh dom fhían,
nuair a chluinim an Ghaelige uilig a tréigbheáil
is caismirt Bhéarla i mbeól gach aoin.

(My heart is torn in a hundred thousand pieces,
And no remedy will soothe my pain,
When I hear Irish being abandoned,
And the din of English in everyone's mouth).[13]

What Mac Cubhthaigh was alluding to was that those who spoke Irish appeared to desire the demise of the language, notwithstanding that it had a literary heritage extending back over many centuries. Overall, it seems that while many may have been reluctant to give up the language, they did so because they saw English as being advantageous to the economic advancement of their children within the new social and political order.[14]

The decline in the overall number of Irish speakers accelerated around 1780, with the beginning of Ireland's version of the much more extensive Industrial Revolution that was taking place in parts of England, Scotland and Wales. Carnie has summarised what eventuated regarding Irish was as follows:

> The resultant change in demography and social structure perhaps marks the beginning of the end for the primacy of the Irish language in Ireland. There was in Ireland, as in England, widespread movement of the populous from the countryside to the cities and towns. Not only was the language of the cities and towns English, but so was the technology that brought the people there. There was thus a widespread switch from Irish to English in much of the population. Irish came to be spoken primarily by the peasantry in the countryside.[15]

Similarly, Wall[16] has argued that by the time of the Act of Union, anyone with educational, professional or commercial aspirations needed to learn English, with the result that the middle and upper classes came to speak it.

The next 100 years brought great changes. The passing of the Act of Union in 1800 meant that Ireland was now subject to the parliament at Westminster. The most prominent issue over the next 30 years was the demand of middle-class Catholics for the repeal of the remaining Penal Laws that forbade them from sitting in parliament, from being judges, from being colonels in the army or captains in the navy and from holding senior positions in the civil service. Catholic Emancipation was achieved in 1829, through the leadership of Daniel O'Connell and his mobilisation of great masses of supporters, although a subsequent national effort by him to repeal the Act of Union failed.[17]

In 1841, on the eve of the Great Famine, Ireland's population was over 8 million, of whom 1.5 million were Irish speakers.[18] The great majority of the latter, as already pointed out, constituted the poorer section of the community, whose members lived largely in rural areas. Between 1845 and 1848, famine struck the entire country and the Irish-speaking districts fared particularly badly. High mortality, coupled with accelerating emigration, resulted in the total population of the country in 1891, being half of what it had been in the mid-1840s. The decrease in the number of Irish speakers was even more precipitous, with only a little over half a million remaining.

Economic and social pressure, as already indicated, also played a major part in bringing about the major language change in Ireland during the nineteenth century.[19] Thus, it is incorrect to see the Great Famine as an event that marked a sharp division between a formerly predominantly Irish-speaking Ireland and a new English-speaking country. Rather, it acted to accelerate a major language shift that had been occurring over the previous 120 years. On this, Fitzgerald[20] noted that there had been a sharp decline in the level of Irish speaking amongst the young in many parts of the country in the 30 years between 1811 and 1841. Commenting on this decline, Durkacz drew attention to the general attitude of the people at the time.[21]

The advantage of having a command of English before emigrating to Britain, America or Australia was also clear to many. Another influence was the impact on listeners of stories coming back from emigrants and from those who had moved to the wealthier English-speaking parts of Ireland:

> Comparison between the depressed Gaeltacht [Irish-speaking district] areas and the materially richer world outside produced the inevitable psychological reaction. The traditional way of life came to be seen as old fashioned, poor, unworthy, while that of the outside world appeared affluent and desirable.[22]

A consequence was that "in many homes the vernacular changed from Irish to English in one or two generations", with Irish-speaking parents speaking "such English as they had to their children while using Irish with one another".[23]

In considering the nature and extent of language change in Ireland up to this point, one significant question has not been addressed, namely, why did the acquisition of English mean, overwhelmingly, the abandonment of Irish, and why did this happen within a few generations? Ó Tuathaigh articulated this question when stating it is puzzling why "more sustained forms of bilingualism did not take hold".[24] He also posed various answers not detailed here, since to do so would cause one to stray too far from the principal focus of interest. At the same time, it is important to highlight that cogitation of the conundrum and of associated questions opens up a major field of research for others to address.

The nature and rate of the decline in the Irish language in Ireland in relation to that of the other Celtic languages still spoken in the UK in the nineteenth century, namely, Welsh and Scottish Gaelic, also needs to be considered. In Wales, in 1848, over two-thirds of the total population still spoke Welsh, and more than half of these were monolingual speakers. At the same time, the Industrial Revolution and associated migration from the English border counties was acting to promote greatly the spread of English, particularly in the south of the country.

The number of speakers of Scottish Gaelic also continued to decline. Lewis has summarised the general trend as follows:

> Speakers of Scots Gaelic have been confined to the Highlands and Islands of Scotland for several centuries. When Anglicisation was institutionalised by the Act of Union in 1707, the majority of Scots were unaffected either linguistically or culturally. But the Gaelic-speaking minority were still firm in their adherence to a traditional way of life and their language. In 1745, however, the Highlands were transformed forcibly – the clan system was destroyed and the language forced to retreat still farther. A hundred years later, in the middle of the nineteenth century, the Gaelic-speaking areas had been defined: the populous Lowlands were entirely English, but the Gaelic language remained strong in the sparsely populated Highlands and Islands.[25]

By 1911, the total number of Gaelic speakers in Scotland was 202,398, of whom only 18,400 were monolingual speakers of the language.[26]

Fundamental aspects of political life had also been changing in Ireland. During the four decades following the Great Famine, it was dominated by two great movements, namely, that to do with the land and that to do with the political relationship of Ireland with Britain.[27] The "land question" centred on the demands of the tenant farmers for fair rent, fixity of tenure and the right to sell one's interest in one's holdings. After much agitation, a series of land acts was introduced which facilitated the transforming of Ireland into a nation of farmers through a system of State-aided land purchase. An equally tenacious movement aimed at securing home rule for Ireland, however, did not yield its desired outcome. Instead, it got bogged down in the party politics of the Liberal and Conservative parties of the day, the intransigent opposition of the Ulster unionist population, and acrimony surrounding the private life of Charles Stewart Parnell, the leader of the Irish National Party at Westminster.

The final 30 years before Irish independence in 1921 also witnessed a radical move towards a demand for total political separation of Ireland from the UK.[28] Alongside this, the cultural nationalist movement considered in the previous chapter was equally thriving, one arm of it being manifested in the flowering of Anglo-Irish literature and the other being aimed at the revival of Gaelic culture, including the Irish language and Gaelic games. The Sinn Féin political and economic movement, inspired by the manner in which the Hungarians had won their independence from Austria, also began to plant its roots and disseminate its view that the Irish MPs at Westminster should withdraw and partake in a government located in Ireland that would pursue a policy of political and economic self-sufficiency. On this, it is instructive to keep in mind Foster's point that, by now, Ireland had already had its social revolution through the Land War and the Land Purchase Acts, which led to the transfer of holdings from landlords to tenant farmers.[29] If the Land War had not taken place earlier and had coincided with the nationalist campaign for independence, he has argued, a social revolution could possibly have taken place later. The turning point in the other direction was when the Catholic Church came on board with Sinn Féin in the campaign against conscription to the British Army in 1918. This changed the social agenda to a conservative one. In relation to economic policy, it also meant that, on Independence in 1922, the concept of a free-market society that showed little concern for trade union rights won out.

To make the latter points is not, of course, to downplay the significance of the activity by the Irish Volunteers, whose members sought to arouse public opinion through an armed insurrection following the abortive Easter Rising of 1916. Eventually, the Sinn Féin organisation and a number of the cultural nationalist groups converged in the movement that led to the dissolution in 1922 of the Act of Union of 1800. Concurrently, as Irish nationalist sentiment continued to increase, the Irish-speaking regions came to be represented as being an illustration of Britain's neglect of the Irish people, their dispossession of property and their subsequent transportation away from the rich pasturelands of the east and south to the poorer land in the west of the country. This, in turn, led to an increase in demands by nationalist politicians and cultural nationalists for an elevated place for the Irish language in the education system of an independent Ireland. The next two chapters detail the background to the evolution of this situation.

Irish and Education from the Reformation to the Establishment of the National School System in 1831

By the early 1500s, involvement by the State in education in Ireland was as follows:

> The earliest schools established under Act of Parliament were the parish schools of Henry VIII, the avowed purpose of which was to introduce a knowledge of the English language among the native Irish. The inevitable result of such a policy was that in time the English language became associated with power, influence and affluence; it became the language of legal, political, cultural, liturgical and economic life.[30]

Later, in the 1650s, the Cromwellian Commissioners in Dublin Castle enforced the Tudor and Stuart statutes forbidding Catholic education in the country.[31] Then, by the Act of Uniformity of 1665, all teachers were obliged to take the Oath of Allegiance and to subscribe to the (Anglican) Church of Ireland. Another act, passed in 1709, forbade Catholics from instructing youth. While wholesale conversion of the Irish people to Protestantism did not follow, the various pieces of legislation did hasten the replacement of Irish with English as the language of instruction of the small numbers able to avail of some formal schooling.[32]

A "wide-ranging, if rather haphazard, system of unofficial schools that became known as hedge schools"[33] was, concurrently, being encouraged, and particularly, though not exclusively, by the Catholic clergy. By 1731, there were at least "145 such schools in the province of Cashell alone".[34] Within them, the teachers no doubt used Irish as a medium of instruction when it was necessary to do so. However, there were very few textbooks available in the language.[35] Jones has also suggested that by the early nineteenth century, it was not usual to teach literacy in Irish in the hedge schools.[36] Here also, it is appropriate to highlight Kelly's point that the hedge schools were not schools that operated in nature. The word "hedge", he makes clear, denoted "lowly, unofficial and/or poor". Usage in this sense, he says, was the same as the way that, in the sixteenth century and seventeenth century in Europe, a 'hedge priest' referred to an individual in [holy] orders who had not the benefit of a university education".[37] Further, Catholics did not have a monopoly in the conducting of hedge schools.

Specifically regarding Protestant schools other than hedge schools, there were some notable cases of the Irish language being promoted in education by the (Anglican) Church of Ireland (the Established Church), even though the overall effort was minimal. In 1567, Queen Elizabeth turned down a request from Sir Henry Sidney, Lord Deputy of Ireland, for some Gaelic-speaking preachers from the Reformed Church in Scotland.[38] For a while, though, it seemed as if Trinity College Dublin was going to play an active part in promoting the language. An expectation from its foundation in 1592 was that it would assist in the development of a vernacular ministry.[39] To this end, Bishop Bedell, who became Provost of the University in 1627, made it a rule that Irish students had to learn to read and write in the Irish language; for this they received an extra scholarship of three pounds per annum.[40] Then, in the 1690s, the Provost, Dr. Narcissus Marsh, established an Irish lectureship at his own expense and attempted to settle Irish-speaking ministers in Irish-speaking congregations. Further, by 1684, there was a move underway to translate the entire Church of Ireland liturgy into Irish and have it adopted in churches with Irish-speaking congregations. All of this effort, however, largely came to nothing. Thus, in 1815, when Christopher Anderson, a Scottish Baptist, set about writing *Ireland, But Still Without the Ministry of the Word in Her Own Language*,[41] he found that, except in one or two isolated cases, the Church of Ireland had, over the previous 100 years, made no major attempt to provide its Irish-speaking adherents with religious instruction in Irish.

By contrast, evangelical Protestant groups had become active in relation to the language towards the end of the eighteenth century. In 1797, the Association for Discountenancing Vice, established five years previously, produced a bilingual version of St. Luke's Gospel,[42] and it contributed to the publication in Irish of the Four Gospels in 1805.[43] The establishment of the London Hibernian Society followed, in 1806. Its aim was the spreading of "religious knowledge in Ireland... by the dispersion of the Holy Scriptures and religious tracts, by the formation and support of schools, and by every other lawful and prudent measure".[44] Then, in 1809, it organised "circulation schools" in anticipation of a flow of its recently published Bibles written in Irish, and in 1812, its committee reported that the New Testament in Irish was taught in its schools and that it had produced an Irish language spelling book.[45]

Not all evangelicals found the move at the beginning of the nineteenth century towards extending Irish in the education of the peasantry to be acceptable.[46] For example, in 1807, the Association for Discountenancing Vice claimed that Irish was dying rapidly and that there should be no attempt to inhibit progress in English.[47] In Scotland, by the end of the 1700s, the adoption of a more positive attitude towards the Gaelic language was evident. Here, the Scottish Society for the Propagation of Christian Knowledge (SSPCK) came to consider it futile to persist with its policy of using English as the teaching medium in its schools in the Highlands. Its argument now was that unless teaching was based on students' knowledge of the Gaelic language, they would be unable to learn English or benefit from religious training. This led to the instruction of teachers on how to teach both English and Gaelic in the Gaelic-speaking areas.[48] Then, in 1810, Christopher Anderson founded the Edinburgh Gaelic School Society to teach Gaelic speakers "to read the Scriptures in their Native Tongue".[49]

In Wales, an even stronger link between the evangelical movement and the promotion of Welsh existed. This was due to "the activities of the Welsh Methodists and Nonconformists who had no vested interest in the Anglicisation of the principality".[50] Underpinning the link was the "fervently held belief in the right of every man [sic] to read the scripture in his mother tongue".[51] Scholarly interest in the Welsh language as a national movement had also commenced earlier in Wales than in Ireland and Scotland, with professional and middle-class people engaging in academic studies of Welsh customs, traditions and antiquities from the mid-eighteenth century, and with the first Cymmrodorion Society being established in 1751.

It was to be another 20 years before a similar movement began to manifest itself in Scotland and it was to be over 50 years before Ireland's Celtic awakening commenced with the foundation of the Gaelic Society of Dublin in 1806. The establishment of the Iberno-Celtic Society in 1818, and the Irish Archaeological Society in 1840, followed. None of these societies, however, had any great commitment to promoting the use of Irish in the education system. Rather, the interest of their members was largely in Gaelic literature written in previous centuries and in studying the content of Irish historical documents and annals.

The Ulster Gaelic Society, established in 1830, was an exception as it included amongst its aims the provision of teachers of Irish in districts where the language was most prominent[52] and also the publication of works in the language. The members, mostly Belfast Presbyterians, succeeded in persuading the (Presbyterian) Synod of Ulster to pass resolutions aimed at making the study of Irish essential for candidates taking holy orders and to establish a professorship of Irish at the Presbyterian Church's Academical Institution. After a number of years, however, the Society went into decline and ceased functioning about 1843.

Christopher Anderson was one of the very few at the time to provide an education-based rationale for instruction through the medium of the Irish language. In 1814, he toured the country in order to determine the state of popular education nationally. Two years later, in his Native Irish,[53] he argued that learning for understanding required the use of the home language of students in instruction. Otherwise, he concluded, what would eventuate would be meaningless learning and dull and listless students.

Shortly after Anderson's visit, The Baptist Society for Promoting the Gospel in Ireland was established. By 1816, it had 20 peripatetic teachers and around 1500 scholars.[54] It focused firmly on teaching students how to read scripture in the mother tongue, as did the Edinburgh Gaelic School Society, which it modelled. In 1821, it employed over 90 teachers.[55] This progress prompted the Church of Ireland to consider religious and educational opportunities that might promote mass literacy in Irish.

A result was the formation of the Irish Society for Promoting the Education of the Native Irish (the Irish Society). By the 1830s, this

Society had established a number of small congregations of converts from Catholicism in the south and west of the country.[56] In 1822, in London, an affiliated board was set up to organise for conducting classes in bible reading in Irish for the city's Irish community.

The Society for Promoting the Education of the Poor in Ireland (The Kildare Place Society), founded in 1811, also held that teaching reading in Irish was the best course to follow with Irish language speakers. In 1820, it appointed a subcommittee to examine the education practices of the Baptist Society, the Irish Society and the London Hibernian Society. It concluded that there was a need for schoolbooks in Irish for all of these societies and it produced a bilingual spelling book designed for rote learning of letters and syllables in Irish.

Catholics and Protestants alike supported the Kildare Place Society for some time, largely because it set out to be neutral on matters of religion, having a policy on reading the bible without any accompanying comment. This approach found favour with the government, which provided annual financial grants during the period 1816–1831. From about the 1820s, however, Catholics began to claim that the Society was proselytising.[57] A Royal Commission upheld this accusation in 1825.[58] As a result, the government withdrew the Society's grants in 1831. In their place, and in the same year, some 30 years since the passing of the Act of Union, the Board of Commissioners for National Education (the National Board), on which both Catholics and Protestants had representation, was established.

The Irish Language in the National Schools from 1831 to 1904

The National School System, which developed under the National Board, was a major development within the context of the UK, especially when one considers the reluctance in England at the time to involve the State in the provision of education. One of the main objectives was to establish primary or "national" schools as they were termed, across the island, where children of all religious denominations would be united for literacy and numeracy instruction in English, while separate religious instruction would be provided in line with children's particular denomination. A specific expectation of the Board was that it would "exercise the most entire control over all the books to be used in the schools".[59]

However, no consideration was given to the possibility of teaching the Irish language, or using it as the medium of instruction amongst Irish-speaking children.

In the early nineteenth century, Catholics constituted over 80 per cent of the population of Ireland. Their bishops were now beginning to reconstitute the Church into a strong and effective organisation. By the second half of the century, it had become a powerful interest group making its demands in matters of education with great determination. It had a commitment to the principle of denominational education at all levels and objected vigorously to the government's aim to draw a distinction between secular and religious education. The authorities of the Church of Ireland and the Presbyterian Church adopted a similar position. The resulting disputes with the State ensured that within a short period, national school attendance was mainly by students from one particular denomination and management was usually by local clergymen.

Within a relatively short time frame, the network of national schools grew impressively. There were 6800 national schools throughout Ireland by 1870 and student-enrolment was about one million.[60] While initially only 3 per cent of enrolled children attended daily, attendance improved incrementally and had increased to 65 per cent by 1899, and 69 per cent by 1919.

Contrary to the bilingual policy of the Kildare Place Society, the National Board did not allow instruction in the medium of Irish in Irish-speaking districts. Rather, from 1831 until the late 1870s, Irish, both as a subject and as a teaching medium, was not permitted in any schools attached to the Board. This led to severe criticism being voiced by some, most notably Dr. MacHale, the Catholic Archbishop of Tuam,[61] but to no avail. In considering this point, however, it is also important to be cognisant of Wolf's argument that there are good grounds for claiming as follows:

> The first two decades of the national system did not witness the emergence of a permanent educational environment where the attendance of Irish-speaking students was a constant and therefore challenging presence to the English-only curriculum that the schools implemented.[62]

In other words, there was a great lack of sustained participation by students for whom Irish was their regular language of conversation in the national school system up until the middle of the nineteenth century.

In a somewhat similar vein, Akenson concluded that the Commissioners were not hostile to the use of the language so much as unaware of it.[63] On this, the Board's minutes for the period 1831–70 contain only two entries relating to the teaching of Irish.[64] The first of these refers to an application in 1834, from a Mr. Thaddeus Conlon, seeking employment as a teacher of Irish. The Board's reply was that such an arrangement did not come within the plan of education as contemplated by the Commissioners. The other note relates to an unsuccessful request from a clerical manager for permission to teach Irish during the hours of secular instruction and to use the spelling and reading books of the London Irish Society.

The requests to the Board noted above do not necessarily indicate it forbade the teaching of Irish in the schools. There was also no rule forbidding the use of the language to aid in instruction in English. Concurrently, pleas for bilingual education for cultural and education reasons were being made, especially through the writings of members of Young Ireland, the romantic nationalist group active during the period 1842–48. Thomas Davis, a Dublin barrister, member of the Church of Ireland, and an influential member of Young Ireland, he expressed his views primarily through *The Nation* newspaper. In 1843, he outlined his position as follows:

> If an attempt were made to introduce Irish, either through the National Schools or the courts of Law, into the eastern part of the country, it would certainly fail, and the reaction might extinguish it altogether. But no one contemplates this save as a dream of what may happen in a hundred years hence. At present the middle classes think it a sign of vulgarity to speak Irish – the children everywhere are taught English, and English alone in the schools – and what is worse, they are urged by corporal punishment to speak it at home… Simply requiring the teachers in the National Schools in these Irish-speaking districts to know Irish or supplying them with Irish translations of the school books would guard the language where it now exists.[65]

He also argued that the publishing of a weekly newspaper, partly or wholly, in Irish, would help in extending the use of the language throughout the country.

Davis and the other members of Young Ireland had little popular support. Nevertheless, their ideas influenced successive generations.

So also did those of Philip Barron of County Waterford,[66] whose objectives included the teaching of Irish in every school and college in the country, and the teaching of the classics and other subjects through Irish. He produced elementary books of instruction in Irish and founded an Irish college at Bunmahon, County Waterford. However, he lacked any great support and later emigrated. Richard Dalton from Tipperary also sought to restore the Irish language through the provision of classes throughout the country and through publishing a newspaper, *An Fíor Éireannach* which was launched in 1862. Dalton also lacked support and eventually his newspaper ceased circulation.

It was Sir Patrick Keenan more than anyone else who, in the middle of the nineteenth century, highlighted the plight of Irish-speaking children who did not understand English and yet were receiving a primary school education through that language. He was born into a Catholic, English-speaking home in Dublin in 1826. In 1841, he became a school monitor, and between 1851 and 1871, he was a Head Inspector of the schools under the National Board in the northern part of Ireland. During his trips to the west coast of County Donegal, he became concerned about the efficiency of the schools in the Irish-speaking districts in teaching English. In one of his first reports, he argued that "the Irish-speaking people ought to be taught the Irish language grammatically; and schoolbooks in Irish should be prepared for that purpose. English should be taught to all Irish-speaking children, through the medium of Irish".[67] Although the school on Tory Island, off the west coast of the county, had been in existence for 17 years when he first visited in 1856, it had "scarcely produced one English-speaking pupil for each year it was in existence".[68]

Keenan attributed much of the inefficiency he witnessed to ignorance of Irish amongst the majority of teachers who arrived to teach in schools in the West of Ireland and argued that even in places where all social communication was in Irish, English was the language of the school and of all of the schoolbooks. He went on to agitate for the introduction of a bilingual education policy, stating that it would quickly lead to the people being better educated and the English language being spoken more widely. In arguing thus, his motivating force does not appear to have been a patriotic love of the Irish language. Rather, his belief was that the best way to teach English to Irish-speaking children was through using Irish as a medium of instruction. He was consistent in his promotion of the use of the vernacular to aid the acquisition of English as evidenced in a review of the education in Malta which he conducted in 1880, where he encouraged the use of Maltese in schools.[69]

At the same time, Keenan does not appear to have had a desire to see the Irish language disappear.[70] His position was that Irish-speaking students should learn the alphabet of their native language before they learned the vocabulary and grammar of English. He tried to impress this point on the members of the National Board and expressed annoyance when they ignored him. Then, in a report of 1857, he stated that the situation in the schools in the Irish-speaking districts was worse than ever:

> Not only is Irish not taught grammatically in such quarters, with a view to using it afterwards in the teaching of English, but it is not even used as an instrument of interpretation for the new words in English the pupils are being required to add daily to their vocabulary.[71]

He placed much of the blame on the teachers, stating that "their fatuity and negligence on this matter was most astonishing" for…the large majority of them, in parts of the country to which I refer, speak Irish fluently; and although they feel the difficulty of imparting English to their pupils by the system which they are pursuing, they yet never dream of using the only language which the pupils understand, and which they themselves could employ with most didactic ease and effect.[72] He also presented evidence on what he perceived to be the damaging effect of teaching Irish-speaking children through the medium of the English language:

> I was frequently engaged in the examination of classes of children who exhibited neither intelligence nor smartness, nor even ordinary animation whilst being questioned in English; but when the questions were given or the answers required in Irish, at once their eyes flashed with energy, their voices became loud and musical, and their intellectual faculties appeared to ripen up and to delight in being exercised.[73]

The following year, 1858, he suggested that every teacher who, on passing an examination in the Irish language, would have "legitimate occasion to employ it in tuition", should receive a supplemental salary of four-to-five pounds.[74] The proposal, however, was not accepted.

Ten years later, with several groups in Ireland pressing for a reappraisal of the national school system, the Royal Commission of Inquiry into

Primary Education 1868–70 (Powis) was established. Keenan, in giving evidence on bilingual education to this Commission, stated:

> I think those who desire that the people should speak English (and every lover of his country must be desirous that they shall), should teach them in the first instance to read Irish, in order that they all the more readily and naturally soon afterwards, learn to read English.[75]

Schoolbooks in Irish, he also argued, should be prepared. Another inspector, Cornelius O'Mahony, supported him, stating that using Irish when teaching Irish-speaking students would be very helpful in teaching pupils to understand what they read and that it would "assist materially in developing their intellectual training".[76] The Commissioners, however, chose to ignore such arguments.

The national schools, then, did play a part in accelerating the decline of the Irish language, even if unwittingly rather than by design. As outlined previously, however, it would be remiss to overlook Wolf's thesis, which has been informed by extensive statistical data. This thesis holds that the under-representation of Irish-speaking students in national schools in the Irish-speaking districts during the first two decades of the national school system is likely to also have contributed significantly to the establishment of an English language-based curriculum for schools in Gaeltacht areas up until 1904.[77]

Nevertheless, a real education dilemma continued to exist for those students living in Irish-speaking districts who were able to attend a primary school as the language of instruction continued to be English solely. Micí Mac Gabhann, who attended the national school at Machaire Rabhartaigh (Magheroarty) in West Donegal in the remote north-west of Ireland in the 1870s, gave expression in his autobiography to his memory of this dilemma:

> Cha raibh focal amháin Béarla agam féin ná ag aon duine den teaghlach ach cha raibh mé abalta freagra a thabhairt ar an mháistir nuair a chuir sé cheist orm cárbh ainm dom. Ach mura raibh focal Béarla agamsa sílim nach raibh focal amháin Gaeilge ag an mháistir.[78]

> (Neither I nor anybody in my family could speak English and I could not answer the teacher when he asked me what was my name. But if I could not speak any English he did not know a word of Irish.)

Peig Sayers, who attended Dún Chaoin (Dunquin) national school in West Kerry, at the other end of the country, also in the 1870s, recalled in her autobiography the following conservation she had with another student on her first day at school:

> 'An bhfuil i bhfad ag teacht ar scoil?' arsa mise. 'Nílim, mhuise, ach le trí seachtain. Bhí an-eagla orm ar dtúis ach anois níl pioc orm de, agus ná bíodh aon eagla ortsa leis. Beadsa i do pháirti. Tá Béarla agam agus inseoidh mé duit cad a bheidh ag an mhaistreás a rá'. Is mĕ a bhí go sásta nuair a chuala an méid sin a rá.[79]
>
> ('Have you been coming to school for some time?' I said. 'I have not, only for three weeks. I was very scared at first, but now I am not at all frightened and you need not be either. I will be your companion. I can speak English and I will tell you what the teacher is saying.' I was very happy to hear that.)

Ten years later, Fr. Geoghegan, the parish priest in the area, in a letter to the National Board, described the situation in the nearby Blasket Islands as follows:

> Teaching such children English is like teaching them Chinese. The same observation holds generally for all that portion of the promontory lying west of Dingle. It is absurd to place the same programme before these children and the children of Dublin or Belfast.[80]

This and similar pleas, however, were ignored by the Board, even though the problem became more acute following the introduction of a "payment-by-results" policy in 1872. This policy created a particular difficulty for those teaching in Irish-speaking districts, namely, having some of their income dependent on their ability to prepare students to be assessed by inspectors of the National Board through the medium of a second language since the examinations for results-fees were conducted in English.[81]

At the same time, the possibility of teaching Irish as a school subject and the likely value in adopting a bilingual approach to education in Irish-speaking schools were now matters for more open debate and consideration than had previously been the case. The Irish National Teachers' Association (which was formed in 1868 to facilitate teachers in addressing their grievances and which was later renamed the Irish National Teachers' Organisation), at its annual conference in 1874, called for the inclusion of Irish amongst the subjects for which results-fees had been paid since 1872. The following year, at the annual general meeting of the Royal Historical and Archaeological Association of Ireland, a resolution was passed, the essence of which stated:

> In order to raise up scholars to translate their priceless Irish manuscripts and to preserve the Irish language from being entirely lost, we the members of the Royal Historical and Archaeological Association of Ireland, strongly recommend to the Commissioners of Education the importance of paying for the teaching of Irish by National School Teachers, similar to Latin and French.[82]

The Association seemed to accept that the death of Irish as a spoken language was inevitable, but that the study of the language needed to be cultivated for literary and academic purposes. Within a year, however, a group of enthusiasts established the Society for the Preservation of the Irish Language, their objectives being the conducting of classes for the teaching of Irish wherever possible, encouragement of the speaking of it and the exertion of pressure to introduce it as a subject in all schools in the country.

The payment-by-results system noted already, while concentrating on reading, writing and arithmetic, also permitted examination in two "extra subjects" for senior students. Included were Greek, Latin and French. A number of groups and individuals also pressed the National Board to designate Irish as an "extra" subject. In 1879, they were successful in their efforts.[83] This resulted in 304 students being examined in the subject later in the same year, of whom 143 passed; in 1880, only 68 were examined and 32 passed; in 1881, 29 were examined and 17 passed.[84] From then onwards, the numbers presenting themselves for examination annually increased steadily, reaching 1026 by 1890. By 1899, it had grown to 1825, and by the time of the advent of the new Irish State in 1922, a quarter of the national schools in the country were teaching Irish.

From 1883, teachers in Irish-speaking districts, if acquainted with the Irish language, could use it "as an aid to the elucidation and acquisition of the English language".[85] Further, from 1900, teachers had permission to teach the language as a primary school subject within normal school hours.[86] Additionally, Irish (entitled Celtic) became a subject for examination by the Board of Intermediate Education established the previous year to oversee secondary school education in Ireland.[87] The associated course was three years' duration and a school received a fee of 10 shillings per student per annum for every student who obtained a pass in it. Initially, however, the scheme did not meet with great success.

Meanwhile, Ireland's new Gaelic cultural nationalist consciousness, as already highlighted, was finding expression in the activities of the Gaelic Union (1882), the Gaelic Athletic Association, the Irish National Literary Society (founded in 1892) and the Gaelic League. Nevertheless, the Commissioners of National Education still clung to the view that it was impossible to make Irish the "normal" language of the schools in any part of the country. The Gaelic League, as the next chapter demonstrates, set out to persuade them to adopt a contrary one.

To conclude: During the first half-century following the establishment of the National School System in 1831, the Irish language was ignored as both a medium of instruction and as a language which might be usefully taught in the schools. In response to the social movements which emerged during the final decades of the century and which promoted the native language, music, sports and traditions, the national school system slowly embraced the concept of teaching Irish in schools. By the early years of the twentieth century, schools were permitted to become bilingual and although only the most remote areas of the country were by then exclusively Irish speaking, a significant minority of schools adopted bilingualism and the speaking and teaching of Irish had attained a new status in Irish life.

Notes

1. J. Coolahan. *Irish Education: History and Structure* (Dublin: Institute of Public Administration, 1981), p. 8. For a comprehensive history of the Irish language to 1922, see Doyle. *A History of the Irish Language: From the Norman Invasion to Independence* (Oxford: Oxford University Press, 2015).
2. T. Ó Fiaich. 'The Language and Political History'. In B. Ó Cuív (Ed.). *A View of the Irish Language* (Dublin: Stationery Office, 1969), p. 103.
3. This chapter is a precis of the exposition provided by the first-named author in T. A. O'Donoghue. *Bilingual Education in Ireland, 1904–22: The Case of the Bilingual Programme of Instruction* (Perth: The Centre for Irish Studies, Murdoch University, 2000).
4. The following account is based largely on that in T. J. Ó Ceallaigh and Á. Ní Dhonnabháin. 'Reawakening the Irish Language Through the Irish

Education System: Challenges and Priorities', *International Electronic Journal of Elementary Education*, Vol. 8, No. 2, 2015, pp. 179–198.

5. A. Carnie. 'Modern Irish: A Case Study in Language Revival Failure'. In J. D. Bobaljik, R. Pensalfini, and L. Storts (Eds.). *Papers on Language Endangerment and the Maintenance of Linguistic Diversity* (New York: The MIT Working Papers in Linguistics, 1996), p. 101.
6. Ibid.
7. S. Cahill. 'The Politics of the Irish Language Under the English and British'. In *The Proceedings of the Barra Ó Donnabháin Symposium, 2007* (New York: New York University, 2007).
8. A. T. Q. Stewart. *The Narrow Ground: The Roots of Conflict in Ulster* (London: Faber and Faber, 1989).
9. P. Ó Snodaigh. *Hidden Ulster, Protestants and the Irish Language* (Belfast: Lagan Press, 1995).
10. M. Ó Siochrú. *God's Executioner—Oliver Cromwell and the Conquest of Ireland* (London: Faber and Faber, 2008).
11. P. Ó Loingsigh. 'The Decline of the Irish Language in the Nineteenth Century', *Oideas*, Spring, 1975, p. 217.
12. E. O'Flaherty. 'Ecclesiastical Politics and the Dismantling of the Penal Laws in Ireland, 1774–82', *Irish Historical Studies*, Vol. 26, No. 101, pp. 33–50.
13. Quoted in T. Ó Fiaich. 'The Language and Political History'. In B. Ó Cuív (Ed.). *A View of the Irish Language* (Dublin: Stationery Office, 1969), p. 107.
14. D. Mac Giolla Chríost. *The Irish Language in Ireland: From Goídel to Globalisation* (London: Routledge, 2005), pp. 100–101.
15. A. Carnie. 'Modern Irish: A Case Study in Language Revival Failure', p. 103.
16. M. Wall. 'The Decline of the Irish Language'. In B. Ó Cuív (Ed.). *A View of the Irish Language*, p. 82.
17. O. MacDonagh. *O'Connell: The Life of Daniel O'Connell 1775–1847* (London: Weidenfeld and Nicolson, 1991).
18. J. Crowley, W. J. Smyth, and M. Murphy (Eds.). *Atlas of the Great Irish Famine* (Cork: Cork University Press, 2012).
19. B. Ó Cuív. 'Irish Language and Literature, 1845–1921'. In W. E. Vaughan (Ed.). *A New History of Ireland: Ireland Under the Union, 11, 1870–1921* (Oxford: Oxford University Press, 1996), p. 394.
20. G. Fitzgerald. *Estimates for Baronies of the Minimum Level of Irish Speaking Amongst Successive Decennial Cohorts: 1771–1781 to 1861–1871* (Dublin: Royal Irish Academy, 1981), p. 129.
21. V. E. Durkacz. *The Decline of the Celtic Languages*, p. 217.

22. C. Ó Danachair. 'The Gaeltacht'. In B. Ó Cuív (Ed.). *A View of the Irish Language*, p. 120.
23. B. Ó Cuív. 'Irish Language and Literature, 1845–1921'. In W. E. Vaughan (Ed.). *A New History of Ireland: Ireland Under the Union, 11, 1870–1921*, p. 394. This situation was not, of course, unique within the UK. In Scotland and Wales also, in the nineteenth century, the greater economic potential of the English language was quickly recognised. Here, as Baker reminds us, Welsh and Gaelic-speaking parents "were keen for their children to be educated exclusively in English to escape slate quarries and coal mining areas, and the harsh climates and relative material deprivation of remote islands". See C. Baker. 'Bilingual Education in Ireland, Scotland and Wales'. In C. Baker and S. P. Jones (Eds.). *Encyclopedia of Bilingualism and Bilingual Education* (Avon: Multilingual Matters, 1988), p. 128.
24. G. Ó Tuathaigh. *I mBéal an Bháis: The Great Famine and the Language Shift in Nineteenth Century Ireland* (Hamden, CT, USA: Quinnipiac University Press, 2015), p. 39.
25. Ibid., p. 86.
26. Ibid.
27. This account is based on that in R. Foster. *Modern Ireland 1600–1972* (London: Allen Lane, 1988).
28. Ibid.
29. Ibid.
30. S. Dunn. 'Education, Religion and Cultural Change in the Republic of Ireland'. In W. Tulasiewicz and C. Brock (Eds.). *Christianity and Educational Provision in International Perspective* (London: Routledge, 1988), p. 95.
31. T. Ó Fiaich. 'The Language and Political History'. In B. Ó Cuív (Ed.). *A View of the Irish Language* (Dublin: Stationery Office, 1969), p. 103.
32. Ibid.
33. T. Corcoran. *Some Lists of Catholic Lay Teachers and Their Illegal Schools in the Later Penal Times* (Dublin: Gill, 1932), p. 27.
34. Ibid.
35. P. J. Dowling. *The Hedge Schools in Ireland* (Dublin: Talbot Press, 1935), pp. 154–161.
36. M. G. Jones. *The Charity School Movement in the Eighteenth Century* (Cambridge: Cambridge University Press), p. 261.
37. J. Kelly. 'Educational Print and the Emergence of Mass Education in Ireland, c.1650–c.1830'. In J. Kelly and S. Hegarty (Eds.). *Schools and Schooling 1650–2000: New Perspectives in the History of Education* (Dublin: Four Courts Press, 2017), p. 34.

38. C. Anderson. *A Brief Sketch of Various Attempts Which Have Been Made to Diffuse a Knowledge of the Holy Scriptures Through the Medium of the Irish Language* (Dublin: Graisberry and Campbell, 1818), Appendix B, 2.
39. H. J. Monck Mason. *The Life of William Bedell, D.D., Lord Bishop of Kilmore* (London: Seeley, 1843), p. 113.
40. T. W. Jones (Ed.). *A True Relation of the Life and Death of William Bedell, Lord Bishop of Kilmore in Ireland* (London: Camden Society, 1872), pp. 26–44.
41. C. Anderson. *Ireland, but Still Without the Ministry of the Word in Her Own Language* (Edinburgh: Oliver and Boyd, 1835).
42. National Library of Ireland. *Association for Discountenancing Vice, Abstract of the Proceedings of the Association*, p. 5.
43. D. H. Akenson. *The Irish Education Experiment* (London: Routledge and Keegan Paul, 1970), p. 81.
44. Association for Discountenancing Vice. *A Brief View of the Association for Discountenancing Vice and Promoting the Knowledge and Practice of the Christian Religion* (Dublin: Association for Discountenancing Vice, 1801), p. 4.
45. London Hibernian Society. *Summary of the Proceedings of the London Hibernian Society*. 1812, p. 10.
46. V. E. Durkacz. *The Decline of the Celtic Languages*, p. 155.
47. D. E. Jenkins. *The Life of the Reverend Thomas Charles of Bala* (Denbeigh: n.p.), p. 178.
48. C. Withers. 'Education and Anglicization: The Policy of the SSPCK Toward the Education of the Highlander, 1707–1825', p. 42.
49. Quoted in C. Withers. *Gaelic in Scotland, 1698–1981: The Geographical History of a Language* (Edinburgh: John Donald, 1984), p. 137.
50. V. E. Durkacz. *The Decline of the Celtic Languages*, p. 8.
51. Ibid., p. 35.
52. P. Ó Snodaigh. *Hidden Ulster* (Baile Átha Cíath: Clódhanna Teó, 1973), pp. 17–20.
53. C. Anderson. *The Native Irish* (London: n.p., 1816).
54. H. Anderson. *Life and Letters of Christopher Anderson* (Edinburgh: Oliver and Boyd, 1854), p. 136.
55. V. E. Durkacz. *The Decline of the Celtic Languages*, p. 120.
56. A. M. Thompson. *A Brief Account of the Rise and Progress of the Change in Religious Opinion Now Taking Place in Dingle and the West of the County of Kerry* (Dublin: Burnside and Seeley, 1846).
57. J. Coolahan. *Irish Education: History and Structure*, pp. 11–12.
58. Ibid., p. 12.

59. *Copy of the Letter of the Chief Secretary for Ireland to the Duke of Leinster on the Formation of a Board of Commissioners for Education in Ireland*, HCXXIX, 196, 1831–32.
60. J. Coolahan. 'Imperialism and the Irish National School System'. In J. Mangan (Ed.). *Benefits Bestowed? Education and English Imperialism* (Manchester: Manchester University Press, 1998), pp. 77–93. See also P. O'Donovan. *Stanley's Letter: The National School System and Inspectors in Ireland, 1831–1922* (Galway: Galway Education Centre, 2017).
61. T. Ó hAilín. 'Irish Revival Movements'. In B. Ó Cuív (Ed.). *A View of the Irish Language* (Dublin: Stationery Office, 1969), p. 94. Dr. MacHale was professor of dogmatic theology at St. Patrick's College Maynooth from 1820 to 1825, Catholic Bishop of Killala from 1825 to 1834 and Catholic Bishop of Tuam from 1834 to 1881. Both the Diocese of Killala and the Diocese of Tuam contained extensive Irish-speaking districts at the time. Along with his desire that Irish speakers should be educated through the medium of that language, he was also concerned about the need to address the poverty of a great proportion of those within his dioceses. He is remembered for his opposition to the national school system and for his arguments against Papal infallibility at the First Vatican Council (1870).
62. N. Wolf. 'The National-School System and the Irish Language in the Nineteenth Century'. In J. Kelly and S. Hegarty (Eds.). *Schools and Schooling 1650–2000: New Perspectives in the History of Education*, p. 90.
63. D. H. Akenson. *The Irish Education Experiment: The National System of Education in the Nineteenth Century* (London: Routledge and Keegan Paul, 1970).
64. P. Ó Loingsigh. 'The Irish Language in the Nineteenth Century', *Oideas*, p. 6.
65. T. Davis. *Our National Language* (Dublin: Gaelic League, 1945), p. 6.
66. D. Mhic Mhurchú and Phillip Barron. 'Man of Mystery', *Decies: Journal of the Old Waterford Society*, May, 1976, pp. 10–15.
67. *Twenty-Second Report of the C.N.E.I. for 1855* (2142-11), H.C. 1856, XXVII, Pt. 11, Appendix G, p. 76.
68. *Twenty-Third Report of the C.N.E.I. for 1856* (2304), H.C. 1857–58, XX, Appendix, p. 114.
69. N. Atkinson. 'Educational Construction in Malta', *The Irish Journal of Education*, Vol. 3, No. 1, 1969, pp. 32–33.
70. *Twenty-Second Report of the C.N.E.I. for 1855* (2142-11), H.C. 1856, XXVII, Pt. 11, Appendix G, p. 76.
71. *Twenty Fourth Report of the C.N.E.I. for 1857* (2456-11), H.C. 1859, VII, p. 135.
72. Ibid.

73. Ibid.
74. *Twenty-Fifth Report of the C.N.E.I. for 1858* (2593), H.C. 1860, XXV, Appendix, p. 180.
75. *Royal Commission of Inquiry into Primary Education (Ireland)* (Powis Report); Minutes of Evidence, (C. 6-11), H.C. 1870, XXVII, Pt. III, p. 72.
76. Ibid.
77. S. N. Wolf. 'The National-School System and the Irish Language in the Nineteenth Century'. In J. Kelly and S. Hegarty (Eds.). *Schools and Schooling 1650–2000: New Perspectives in the History of Education*, p. 75.
78. M. Mac Gabhann. *Rotha Mór on Tsaoil* (Baile Átha Clíath: Foilseacháin Náisiúnta Teóranta, 1968), p. 27.
79. M. Ní Chinnéide (Ed.). *Peig* (Baile Átha Clíath: Cómhlacht Oideachais na hÉireann, n.d.), p. 22.
80. This quotation is presented in B. Ní Néill. Cúrsaí Oideachais ar an Bhlascaod Mór (Unpublished B.A. Thesis. Thomond College of Education, Limerick, 1984), p. 26.
81. J. Coolahan, 'Imperialism and the Irish National School System', p. 80.
82. Quoted in P. Ó Loingsigh. 'The Irish Language in the Nineteenth Century', p. 14.
83. Ibid., p. 81.
84. Ibid.
85. Ibid.
86. Ibid.
87. T. Ó Fiaich. 'The Great Controversy'. In S. Ó Tuama (Ed.). *The Gaelic League Idea* (Cork: The Mercier Press, 1972), p. 65.

CHAPTER 3

"Saving the Child": The Gaelic League's Campaign for Bilingual Education for Irish-Speaking Districts

Introduction

From its foundation in 1893, the Gaelic League engaged in a wide-scale education programme. Primarily, this involved conducting classes in the Irish language and in Irish history, dancing, music and folklore. It also organised public opinion and used mass meetings, public-letter campaigns, motions in parliament and resolutions from public bodies, to support its efforts. By 1903, it had 600 branches throughout the country and a total membership of 50,000.[1] Further, it won significant concessions in relation to the use of Irish within the education system, and it succeeded in improving the public perception of the language.

In 1904, almost 30 per cent of public examination candidates at secondary school level were studying Irish, and by 1908, half of the secondary schools in the country were offering it as an examination subject.[2] The League could take much credit for these achievements. It also succeeded in its campaign aimed at making Irish a compulsory subject to pass in the matriculation examination when seeking entry to one of the colleges of the National University of Ireland.[3] A most significant achievement was persuading the National Board of Education to sanction the approval of what in 1904 came to be entitled the Bilingual Programme of Instruction (the Bilingual Programme). This programme was for use both in schools in those districts where the Irish language

T. O'Donoghue and T. O'Doherty, *Irish Speakers and Schooling in the Gaeltacht, 1900 to the Present*,
https://doi.org/10.1007/978-3-030-26021-7_3

was the first language generally spoken by the children and in schools in districts where the local population was bilingual in Irish and English.[4]

The remainder of this chapter is concerned with four aspects of the Bilingual Programme. It opens with an account of the Gaelic League's campaign for its design and introduction in Irish-speaking districts. A number of issues that arose during the dissemination of the programme are also considered. Variations on the extent to which local Irish-speaking communities accepted it are then related. The chapter closes with an overview of the role of the Gaelic League's Irish colleges in preparing teachers to teach Irish-speaking children using bilingual teaching methods.

The Beginning of the Gaelic League's Campaign for Bilingual Education

The Gaelic League spent considerable time developing and revisiting its education policy in which it considered the national school system as having a pivotal role to play in the restoration of the Irish language as a spoken language amongst the population of Ireland. Ó hAilín has summarised as follows the eventual policy:

> The educational policy of the League was twofold. Where Irish was the home language, pupils should be taught to read and write Irish and a knowledge of English and other subjects should be imparted through the medium of Irish. Where Irish was not the home language, it should be lawful to teach Irish as a remunerated subject within school hours and at the earliest stage at which children were capable of learning it.[5]

The League's campaign in relation to this policy got underway in earnest when, at a meeting of its Executive Committee on 9 March 1898, it selected delegates to address a conference of national schoolteachers the following month, in Dublin. The brief was to impress upon them the serious problems experienced by Irish-speaking children where English was the language of instruction in schools.[6] Two years later, in 1900, the Executive Council of the League stepped up its campaign by making the following demand of the Commissioners of National Education:

> ...in all places where Irish is the home language pupils shall be taught to read and write Irish from their first entrance into the school, and that a

> knowledge of English and other useful subjects shall be imparted through the medium of Irish.[7]

It also demanded the appointment of Irish-speaking inspectors to the Irish-speaking districts, but in doing so gave hardly any attention to the fact that the vast majority of teachers had no experience of teaching Irish even as a second language, not to mind in using it as a medium of instruction with those who spoke it as a first language.

> The League was adamant it was not opposed to children in Irish-speaking districts learning English. Rather, it sought that provision be made at the earliest possible moment as will enable the system of bilingual instruction to be introduced without delay into our schools, and we ask this in the best and highest interests, both moral and material, of the population of our districts.[8]

It also produced a pamphlet in which it was pointed out that 76,000 of the 816,001 students in the country's national schools were students whose first language was Irish.[9] An outline of these numbers on a barony-by-barony basis for counties Donegal, Mayo, Galway, Clare, Kerry, Cork and Waterford followed. Presenting such detail made stark for readers the reality of the situation in a manner designed to win sympathy for action aimed at the introduction of bilingual education in primary schools.

Support for the League's position in some senior political circles was forthcoming from the late 1890s. In the House of Commons in July 1896, the Chief Secretary for Ireland, Mr. Gerald Balfour, during debates on the estimates for national school education, stated:

> There are districts in Ireland, not very large or populous districts, where Gaelic is the national language of the people, and where this is so, the best way probably would be, in the first instance, to teach the children properly the language they naturally speak.[10]

Through uttering similar statements like the following expressed in East Kerry in 1896, several urban and county councils also lent support:

> We would urgently urge on the electors of East Kerry, to secure that the candidates pledge themselves to obtain for the hundreds of Irish-speaking

> children in the constituency, a national education through the medium of the only language which they speak perfectly.[11]

Four years later, on 20 July 1900, a debate on the value of bilingual education for children in Irish-speaking districts took place in the House of Commons. A large number of Irish members led by Mr. John Redmond, leader of the Irish Parliamentary Party, spoke in favour of it. Mr. O'Malley, MP for Galway, Connemara, opened the debate, arguing it was "monstrous" to have Irish-speaking children handicapped in life by what he called "this stupid unilingual system, which not only leaves the children uneducated, but positively works mental and moral destruction upon them".[12] John Redmond, the leader of the Irish Parliamentary Party, supported him, as did Mr. Herbert Lewis, MP for Flintshire Boroughs, and Mr. Horace Plunkett, MP for Dublin South County and Vice-President of the Board of Agriculture for Ireland.[13] Mr. Arthur Balfour, the Chief Secretary for Ireland, then stated that, for education reasons, schools in Irish-speaking districts should be using a bilingual programme.[14]

Over the next four years, a number of bodies, including the Connaught Committee of Clerical Managers, the Central Executive of the National Teachers' Organisation and the National Teachers' Congress, highlighted the need for bilingual education for Irish-speaking students. In 1900, some MPs who, in 1905, went on to partake in the Liberal administration formed by Mr. Campbell-Bannerman also showed themselves to be favourably disposed towards this view. One of these was Mr. Bryce, who was to become the Chief-Secretary for Ireland, and the other was Mr. Hemphill, who was to become the Attorney-General for Ireland. During the course of a debate in the House of Commons on 31 July 1900, both members supported the use of Irish as a teaching medium in Irish-speaking districts.[15] Such expressed goodwill was helpful in paving the way for the smooth introduction of the Bilingual Programme of Instruction in 1904.

Meanwhile, Mr. Doogan, MP for Tyrone East, was keeping up the campaign in the House of Commons for the implementation of Mr. Balfour's recommendation. In May 1901, he moved a motion proposing the introduction of a bilingual programme for Irish-speaking districts and to equip teachers to teach bilingually. His argument was follows:

> Those children who come from Irish-speaking homes where they may never have heard a word of English in their lives, are set to struggle to acquire English, which to them is a foreign language, through a vocalism to which their tongues have been untrained, their ears are unfamiliar, and they are frequently taught by a teacher who knows not a single word of Irish.[16]

Mr. Thomas O'Donnell, MP for Kerry West, seconded Doogan's motion. In doing so, he quoted from arguments in favour of bilingual education put before the Gaelic League by Professor Alfred Nutt, President of the Folk Law Society; Professor Windisch of the University of Leipzig; Professor Dollin of the University of Rennes; Professor Zimmer of the University of Greifswald; Professor York Powell of Oxford; and Professor Holger Pedersen of Copenhagen.[17] Mr. Wyndham, by now Chief Secretary for Ireland, intimated he favoured the motion. Support for the Gaelic League's campaign also came from within the Irish-speaking districts themselves, where enthusiasm for bilingual education was also growing. One likely reason for this related to the positive experiences associated with the implementation of the regulation of 1883, that gave teachers permission to use Irish as a teaching medium in situations where it was felt it would improve the rate of acquisition of English.[18]

By now, Pádraig Pearse, Irish language teacher, barrister, writer, republican, political activist and revolutionary, who was instrumental in the 1916 Rising, was becoming a major figure in the country-wide language revival movement. On visiting Belgium to study the operation of bilingual education there, he was impressed by the use of the "direct method" of language teaching by teachers of Flemish and the use of visual aids to support pedagogy. He also argued that Irish should be taught in schools in English-speaking areas, as a second language.[19] He opined:

> Where English is the home language, it must of necessity be the 'first language' in the schools, but I would have a compulsory 'second language', satisfied that this second language in five-sixths of the schools would be Irish. And I would see the 'second language' be used as a medium of instruction from the earliest stages. In this way and in no other way that I can imagine can Irish be restored as a vernacular to English-speaking Ireland.[20]

A number of Gaelic League members supported his position and followed his practice of highlighting experiences in relation to bilingual education in a variety of other countries to justify their stance.

Knowledge of developments regarding the use of Welsh in schools in Welsh-speaking districts constituted a specific motivation for Gaelic League members in their activities.[21] Indeed, direct communication between Welsh language enthusiasts and members of the League was established. For example, Douglas Hyde, the first president of the League,[22] in giving evidence to the Palles Commission on Intermediate Education (secondary school education) in Ireland, quoted as follows from a letter he had received from Mr. Owen M. Edwards, a Fellow of Lincoln College, Oxford:

> In our Welsh schools – elementary and secondary – the study of Welsh is taken up with great enthusiasm. The results are most satisfactory. One result is a striking growth in all round excellence in English especially. The study of Welsh arouses the children's mind in a wonderful degree, and the standard of the school rises especially, and in an unmistakable way when the boys and girls are allowed to give some time to their own language.[23]

In 1900, Most Reverend Dr. Walsh, Catholic Archbishop of Dublin and a member of the National Board, built on this position in arguing that the bilingual experience in Welsh-speaking districts in Wales, bore out fully his belief that children in Irish-speaking districts should be taught to read and write in their home language.[24] In similar vein, Eoin MacNeill, a co-founder of the Gaelic League, argued that bilingual education would not be traumatic, as evidenced by the experience of Welsh-speaking pupils in Wales demonstrated.[25]

Dr. Starkie, the Resident Commissioner of National Education in Ireland, was an ally of Dr. Walsh. He regularly argued that the demands of the Gaelic League in the case of the Irish-speaking districts were justifiable on education grounds.[26] In 1900, a small concession was made on the introduction of a revised programme for national schools ("the Revised Programme"). Underpinning this programme was a clause restating, albeit now in more formal tone, the regulation of 1883, that in schools where there were Irish-speaking students, any teacher acquainted with the Irish language could use it as an aid to the elucidation of English. It also stated that inspectors were at liberty to use Irish in conducting their examinations in such schools.

The Revised Programme issued for all national schools in Ireland in April 1900, was in tune with new progressive education ideas on primary schooling circulating internationally at the time.[27] Irish, however, was not amongst the list of obligatory subjects. Rather, as indicated already, it retained its status as an "extra" subject for which additional fees were payable to teachers, with the requirement that a special roll book separate from the ordinary school roll book, be kept to record attendance. Irish could also be taught as an "optional" subject during school hours, again with the stipulation that such teaching should not interfere with the normal school work and that there be no expectation that additional fees be payable for such teaching.

By now, while all of the signs indicated that a bilingual programme of instruction was about to be introduced for Irish-speaking districts, Archbishop Walsh decided to try to hasten the process by offering a prize of 25 pounds for the best example of such a programme to be submitted to him.[28] What he wanted, he declared, were programmes "showing in detail how the whole work of the school is to be carried on, in all the classes, from the infants up to the sixth or highest class". The initiative met with such a favourable response that he was able to select four he considered to be the best entries and then get an inspector of the National Board to adjudicate between them.

The Gaelic League published the four entries so that they would be available to inform initiatives undertaken by school managers and teachers in Irish-speaking districts. It also held that these could be modified, if necessary, to suit the needs of particular localities, or of particular situations prevailing within them. The winning entry was that of a Mr. O'Malley, from the Irish-speaking district of Corr na Móna (Cornamona) in Connemara in County Galway, and it ran to over 5000 words. It recommended the adoption of a minimum set of requirements for all age groups during the early years of implementation and a higher standard once the programme was in operation for about three years.

The Gaelic League now decided to step up its campaign by establishing an education committee, with Rev. Dr. Michael O'Hickey, Professor of Irish at St. Patrick's College, Maynooth, as the chairperson. This committee resolved not only to call upon the National Board to introduce immediately the promised system of bilingual education in the Irish-speaking districts, but also to require that principals and assistant-teachers appointed to schools in such districts have a certificate of competency to conduct their school work on bilingual lines.[29] In March 1904,

Messrs. Lemass and Dilworth, the Secretaries of the National Board, informed the inspectors that a bilingual programme was now being prepared.[30] Mr. Seamus Fenton, a Board inspector who eventually became the inspector in charge of the bilingual schools, later maintained that a Mr. Dalton, who was a senior Board inspector, had been responsible for designing this programme.[31]

The following month the Commissioners approved the Bilingual Programme of Instruction (the programme) for use, during ordinary school hours, in Irish-speaking districts.[32] It contained an outline of targets to be pursued in reading, writing and spelling in both languages over the eight-year grades or "standards" of primary schooling.[33] The use of Irish as the sole medium of instruction for the junior standards or grades, i.e. infant standard, first standard, second standard and third standard, was also permitted, while all other subjects (arithmetic, singing, drawing, drill, needlework, elementary science and object lessons) were to be taught bilingually.

The programme, which was for use with students in schools in Irish-speaking districts and in districts where Irish and English were commonly spoken, was a particular adaptation of the new child-centred Revised Programme. The main emphasis was on the development of students' literacy skills in both languages, while the expectation also was that teachers would teach other subjects bilingually. The Board outlined the same subject-matter content for all classes from infants up to seventh standard.[34] The same reading and spelling, it was stated, should take place in the teaching of English, as was the case for the Revised Programme.

The teaching of literacy in Irish would reduce the time available to be devoted to English, and accordingly, the achievement targets set for reading and spelling in English for all standards, from first to fifth, were limited to one-half of the English content prescribed for children being taught the Revised Programme. However, the achievement targets and subject matter for writing in English for all standards were the same for all pupils, irrespective of whether they were on the Revised Programme or the Bilingual Programme.

The section of the Bilingual Programme dealing with the teaching of Irish was much more specific than the corresponding section on the teaching of English. Set targets in reading, spelling and writing were identified, which all students in each class, from infants up to seventh standard were to meet. These related to reading, spelling and writing for classes from infants up to seventh standard. They also included grammar and composition targets for classes from third standard to seventh standard.

The expectations for the Bilingual Programme were ambitious. Not only were teachers expected to adopt child-centred approaches in their teaching and to teach new subjects, including drill, singing, drawing and manual training, they were also expected to teach bilingually. An appreciation of the enormity of the task they faced becomes clear when one considers that teachers teaching the Revised Programme were themselves experiencing difficulties. For example, Mr. W. Mayhowe Heller, Organiser of Elementary Science, reported as follows in the national newspaper, *The Freeman's Journal*:

> One cannot fail to be struck by the great difficulty one experiences in schools in getting the various classes to respond to the method of treatment which is necessary in science teaching or object lessons. An attitude of mind seems to have been created in the students that makes them almost resent being asked to think out the answer to a question themselves.[35]

In 1908, however, the Commissioners published a revised version of the Bilingual Programme. They also emphasised that it consisted only of suggestions and that managers of schools were free to submit for consideration to the Board alternative programmes to suit the needs of any particular locality.[36] Further, it elaborated on the original statements on developing students' abilities in spoken Irish. While in 1904, for example, those in infants' classes had to be taught how to read, spell and understand words of two and three letters, the language production skill of speaking was the first skill detailed in the revised version. A lengthy outline also stated that teachers should teach these students

> To speak audibly and distinctly. Story telling by the teacher and reproduction by the pupils in their own words of simple incidents in the stories told.
>
> To read off the blackboard, and to understand words of two and three letters, and to read and understand sentences based on these words.
>
> To copy letters off the blackboard.[37]

The Gaelic League welcomed the outline of this new level of detail.[38]

At the same time, there was no major change in the requirements for the teaching of the other subjects on the programme, namely arithmetic, singing, drawing, drill, needlework, elementary science and "object lessons". There was also no advice offered on how to teach these subjects bilingually. Accordingly, criticism along the following lines continued to be forthcoming:

> There is an overcrowded programme in unilingual schools. The bilingual schools have even more to complain of. The following ought to be the maximum for a bilingual school - English, including reading, writing, composition, and grammar. Irish - including reading, writing, composition, grammar, arithmetic, history, and geography, needlework (for girls' and mixed schools), music (optional).[39]

Various bilingual teachers around the country reiterated such criticism, with some suggesting that the programme be introduced on a phased basis.[40] Eventually, by 1910, one-teacher schools were permitted to teach the programme initially to pupils in infant and first standards, and to expand the programme as these pupils progressed through the school.[41]

Issues Associated with the Dissemination of the Bilingual Programme

In 1906, a directive indicated that a school should introduce the Bilingual Programme in schools where Irish was the home language of the majority of the students there, if the teachers could speak Irish fluently, and as long as any exclusively English-speaking students whose parents desired it received instruction through the medium of English. The distribution of schools on a county-by-county basis which met these criteria and which were teaching the Bilingual Programme by 1908 was as follows:

Number of schools teaching the Bilingual Programme in 1908

County	*No of bilingual schools*
Donegal	55
Mayo	8
Galway	18
Clare	1

County	*No of bilingual schools*
Kerry	20
Cork	6
Waterford	2
Total	110

Source Appendix to the Seventy-Fourth Report of the C.N.E.I. for 1907–08, p. 258

The last available similar list of such schools on a county-by-county basis is the following for 1912:

Number of schools teaching the Bilingual Programme in 1912

County	*No of bilingual schools*
Donegal	64
Mayo	19
Galway	47
Clare	3
Kerry	39
Cork	12
Waterford	3
Total	187

Source Appendix to the Eightieth Report of the C.N.E.I. for 1913–14, p. 140

The total number of schools teaching the programme, however, did continue to grow after 1912, with the result that at the time of Independence in 1922, it stood at 239.

The National Board's inspectors played a major role in the dissemination of the programme. To support teachers in Irish-speaking districts to become literate in Irish and English, special organisers were appointed. On these, the Commissioners of the Board of National Education stated:

> Since our last report, we have appointed six organisers of instruction in Irish. In addition to visiting schools and giving model lessons according to the most approved methods of language teaching, these organisers have given Saturday lectures to the teachers of the schools in the neighbourhood in which, for the time being, they are engaged, and have also been of considerable assistance to our inspectors in promoting the study of Irish.[42]

Each organiser was under the direction of an inspector who, in turn, was responsible both for all of the bilingual schools in an allocated district and for the supervision of all teaching of Irish in that district.[43] By 1914, there was consensus in the reports of both the organisers and the inspectors that students were benefitting educationally from bilingual teaching in the Irish-speaking districts.[44]

By the time of Independence in 1922, the National Board deemed that 55 per cent of the total number of schools in the intensely Irish-speaking district were teaching the Bilingual Programme. This figure might have been further increased if the attentions of the League had not been diverted to promoting Irish across other areas within the education sector. To make this point is not to ignore the reality that the status of the League had soared because of its successes in enhancing the position of Irish in the primary, secondary and university sectors. Rather, it is to draw attention to the reality that, despite limited professional development and inadequate payment for the additional work involved, teachers in many parts of the country experienced quite a degree of success in teaching the Bilingual Programme. In particular, it failed to develop appropriate methods for bilingual teaching.

A consequence was that by the time of Independence in 1922, only 49 per cent of the teachers within the schools in the intensely Irish-speaking districts had the specialist qualification entitled "the bilingual certificate".[45] Furthermore, while another 35 per cent had qualifications in the teaching of Irish as a second language, the courses that led to the award both of this qualification and the bilingual certificate were not preparing teachers specifically to teach of the Bilingual Programme. Indeed, the following assessment was offered in 1926:

> I am afraid that the bilingual certificate is largely a certificate which shows that the teacher knows literary Irish fairly well, and that he has a fluent knowledge of Irish in regard to conversation generally in ordinary subjects, but when it comes to technicalities such as are met with in mathematics, I am afraid that the bulk of the teachers holding the bilingual certificate would be weak in teaching that subject through Irish.[46]

At the same time, to highlight this deficiency is not to argue that teachers taught the Bilingual Programme poorly. Rather, it is to draw attention to the reality that they had quite a degree of success in many parts of the country in spite of having had poor preparation provided and also in spite of receiving, in their view, inadequate payment for the additional work involved.

The Responses of Teachers

Patrick Pearse expressed the view of many in the Gaelic League when he argued that the National Board had a duty to provide primary schoolteachers with appropriate preparation to equip them to teach the Bilingual Programme. However, he was also realistic enough to recognise that teachers and school managers would achieve very little unless they approached the programme enthusiastically. "The whole thing", he stated, "is entirely in the hands of the teachers and managers of the Irish-speaking districts....heretofore it was the Board that was on trial; now it is the country".[47]

Many of the teachers in the bilingual schools did embrace the Bilingual Programme enthusiastically. Building on this, Tomás Ó Colmáin, headmaster of An Spidéal (Spiddal) national school in County Galway, proposed in 1908 that "a bilingual teachers' union be established to provide lectures on method, to collect technical terms for bilingual teaching, and to protect the interests of bilingual teachers in the county".[48] This led to the establishment of the Galway Bilingual Teachers' Association, with Most Rev. Dr. Healy, Archbishop of Tuam, being on its list of honorary members. Within less than two years, it had taken under its wing the small number of bilingual teachers in nearby County Clare and had organised various lectures for them aimed at improving their bilingual teaching methods.[49]

In County Donegal[50] and in County Mayo, similar associations were established.[51] An All-Ireland Bilingual Society or Cumann Dhá Theangach na hÉireann was also established, in April 1909.[52] Further, from early 1909, *An Claidheamh Soluis* was reporting on activities undertaken by various regional bilingual associations. A wide range of matters was addressed to do with teaching nature study through Irish,[53] methods of teaching Irish and English in Irish-speaking districts,[54] Irish parsing and analysis,[55] the teaching of Irish history,[56] methods of teaching literacy in Irish to Irish-speaking students,[57] the need to collect local terms in Irish for use in the teaching of singing, drawing and needlework, and the teaching of grammar and arithmetic in Irish-speaking districts.[58]

The National Board's inspectors and organisers, as noted already, supported the work undertaken by the teachers in the bilingual schools. They made it clear they expected thorough planning, to see that literacy in Irish was taught through Irish, and that other subjects were being taught bilingually. They also insisted on such practices as the calling of the school roll in Irish and English on alternate days.[59] Special Gaelic League organisers provided support; a chief organiser and an organiser located in each of the seven counties containing the major Irish-speaking districts had been appointed back in 1902, in anticipation of the introduction of the Bilingual Programme.[60]

The evidence also indicates, however, that the inspectors were struggling to come up with ideas on how to encourage teachers to adopt bilingual teaching methods since they had very few models at their disposal to inform their work. One inspector expressed his frustration on this:

> Teachers taking up the Bilingual Programme must be ready for extra work, especially at first. There are problems of method and organisation in connection with this programme on which problems our standard books of method throw no light....Even native-speaking Irish teachers find it easier to impart instruction in the mode in which they have been trained.[61]

Nevertheless, teachers teaching the programme continued to adopt a positive attitude. In particular, many, after reflecting on their own experiences, regularly publicised various approaches to teaching the different subjects on the Programme. The editors of *Irish School Weekly* and *An Claidheamh Soluis* also published their recommendations in order to try to affirm their efforts.

A particular issue raised in the newspapers from time to time related to the teaching of arithmetic bilingually. The lack of clear guidance on the matter led to various problems, one of which was the lack of availability of suitable mathematical terms in the Irish language. The problem was characterised as follows in the *Claidheamh Soluis*:

> Cuir síos five thousand four hundred and twenty eight; cuir síos faoi sin three thousand seven hundred and ninety six. Anois, subtractáil an dara líne ón gcéad líne.[62]
>
> [Put down five thousand four hundred and twenty eight; underneath that put down three thousand seven hundred and ninety six. Now, subtract the second line from the first line (trans.)].

This illustrates that teachers had to Gaelicise English words to produce such terms as subtractáil for "subtract". The traditional Irish system of notation based upon the score or 20 created a related problem; Irish-speakers reckoned by the score, with trí-scór being equal to 60, ceithre-scór being equal to 80 and so on.

The *Irish School Weekly* gave recognition to the latter problem on 21 November 1908, when it pointed out that the traditional system of notation was very unsuitable for "modern mathematics".[63] Teachers were then introduced to the notion of counting according to deich (10), fiche (20), tríocha (30) and so on, and terms like suim (add), bain (subtract), uimhir (number), figiúr (a figure) and roinn (divide) were outlined. The newspaper went on to offer the following advice:

> It is surprising with what ease the children pick up these new names for the numbers. To assist the children a sheet having the names and numbers written in large type might be suspended near the blackboard. The children can be drilled from this sheet, various methods can be adopted to fix the names in the children's minds.[64]

A number of textbooks for teaching arithmetic bilingually were also written and disseminated amongst schools teaching the Bilingual Programme.[65] The general approach at all times was to use figures rather than words when representing numbers.[66]

There was a failure to address the matter of how to teach English as a second language in schools in Irish-speaking districts in the teacher training colleges and in the Gaelic League's Irish colleges. The general advice given, however, was that the second language should be taught by using the "direct method" when teaching the Bilingual Programme. The argument was that this was as much as could be advised because, as it was put, "our text books on method give us no hints on bilingual method".[67] Many of the teachers in the Irish-speaking areas were familiar with the "direct method", but only in relation to the teaching of Irish to those who did not speak it as a first language.[68]

Teachers of the Bilingual Programme also became active in the Gaelic League through producing bilingual books for teaching Irish to native Irish-speaking students. The Revised Bilingual Programme of 1911 recommended one of these books, *An Chéad Leabhar* (The First Book), as being a suitable text for those in infant standard and first standard. The approach taken was to organise the book into a number of lessons. Each lesson centred on a topic deemed suitable for Irish-speaking students of such a young age. The characters referred to were usually students of their own age or were Irish-speaking parents, while the environment portrayed in the lessons was that of the southern and western seaboard. The major topics for lessons were as follows: An Cuan (The Bay), Bád (A Boat), Éan (A Bird), Súas an Ród (Up the Road), Síle ag Gol (Crying Sheila), Páirceanna (Fields), Pól agus na Ba (Paul and the Cows), Long (A Ship), Geata (A Gate), Bád ar Linn (A Boat on the Ocean), Ag Dul ar Scoil (Going to School) and Ag Tabhairt Bia d'Éanaibh (Giving Food to the Birds). The book also contained one short poem entitled Pól (Paul).

Each chapter consisted of a lesson based on a list of Irish nouns outlined alongside English equivalents. There was an expectation also that teachers would deal with nouns and verbs with the same vowel sounds. For example, a lesson entitled Éan (A Bird) dealt with éad (jealousy), d'éag (died), déan (do), béal (mouth), méar (thumb) and téad (twine). Furthermore, each lesson included a drawing of a scene similar to that described in words. These drawings were included so that teachers could refer to them when seeking to elicit questions and responses using words and sentence constructions from the lesson.[69] *An Dara Leabhar* (The Second Book) and *An Treas Leabhar* (The Third Book) adopted a similar approach.

By the time students reached third standard, the environment horizons dealt with in the text were widened to include such topics as Teacht ón mBaile Mór (Coming Home from the Town), and Ár dTír Dúchais Éire (Ireland, Our Native Land).[70] The "reader" or schoolbook still continued with such topics as scadáin (herrings), uisce (water), gal (steam), salann (salt) and báisteach (rain). The authors also anticipated the notion in psychology that at this age students can internalize ideas of classes and series and can reach the stage of concrete operations.[71] This was reflected in the outlining of such topics as An tEarrach (Spring), An Samhradh (Summer), An Fóghmhar (Autumn) and An Geimhreadh (Winter). An understanding that students of this age are able to explain classes and understand relationships between them, and should be exposed to moral stories, was also reflected in a selection of Aesop's Fables, entitled An Capall agus an Fíadh'(The Horse and the Deer), An Préachán agus an Crúiscín (The Crow and the Jug), An Gadhar agus an Coileach (The Pup and the Cock) and An t-Iolar agus an Cág (The Eagle and the Jackdaw). Those lessons in *An Chéad Leabhar*, *An Dara Leabhar* and *An Treas Leabhar* also catered for the different dialects of Irish in the country. To this end, alternative words appeared in brackets.

Variations in the Acceptance of the Bilingual Programme

The National Board classified a district as being Irish speaking and, consequently, as meriting the introduction of the Bilingual Programme, if 50 per cent or more of its inhabitants spoke Irish. This section of the chapter now considers community responses in the intensely Irish-speaking districts in Counties Donegal, Galway and Kerry, in the less intensely Irish-speaking areas in County Galway and in County Mayo, and in the smaller Irish-speaking districts scattered throughout the south and west of the country.

Responses to the Programme in the Intensely Irish-Speaking Districts in Counties Donegal, Galway and Kerry

Many teachers in Irish-speaking districts in counties Donegal, Galway and Kerry adopted a positive attitude towards the Bilingual Programme. The indications are that many of them had grown up in these districts themselves, had departed to attend secondary school and undergo preparation as teachers and had then returned to their local areas to teach. Thus, some of their enthusiasm for teaching the programme may have arisen out of empathy with their students as they in their own youth are likely to have experienced problems associated with being educated through English only.[72]

Enthusiasm for the programme was deemed to be especially strong amongst teachers in the central third of the County Galway Irish-speaking district, which stretched inland northwards from Galway Bay as far as Tuar Mhic Éadaigh (Tourmakeady) in the southern part of County Mayo, and included the Aran Islands. As one inspector noted in the case of An Cnoc (Knock) National School, which was in this district, they "displayed a keen interest in their business".[73] This disposition also prevailed amongst the teachers in bilingual schools in County Kerry, so much so that Mr. Fitzgerald, the National Board's inspector there, stated as follows as early as the school year 1906–07: "I have been particularly impressed by the alertness and earnestness of these children. They do not suffer from the timidity which characterises the young children of schools in which instruction in English-only is given".[74] The Gaelic

League was also high in its praise of the quality of the bilingual teaching taking place in the bilingual schools in County Kerry.[75]

Another major influence contributing to the successful introduction of the Bilingual Programme in the areas noted so far was the positive attitude adopted towards it by Catholic bishops and priests. Rev. Dr. O'Donnell, Bishop of the Diocese of Raphoe, which included the County Donegal Irish-speaking districts, was particularly supportive,[76] as was Fr. Mac An tSaoir, the inspector of Catholic education in the Diocese from 1914 to 1921. Indeed, on more than one occasion, the latter stated that the teachers throughout the Irish-speaking areas he visited were, in general, fluent native-speakers of Irish and constantly endeavoured to keep the language spoken. He also attested to the positive attitude of the majority of his fellow clerics in the diocese towards the Bilingual Programme when he gave evidence to the Commission on the Gaeltacht in 1925. Furthermore, he stated that the priests always used Irish in sermons and in conversations with the people. He concluded by saying that the Gaelic League classes throughout the Donegal Irish-speaking districts, which were aimed at teaching the adult Irish-speaking population literacy in Irish, were supported by the clergy and the teachers, and that both groups, along with parents, felt that the Bilingual Programme suited the needs of the students.

Members of the clergy were equally supportive in the intensely Irish-speaking district in south-west County Cork, whose core stretched inland from the Beara Peninsula to the Barony of West Muskerry, with tiny pockets at its extremities, including Oileán Cléire (Cape Clear Island), the Cullen District directly north of the core, and the Glandore-Reenascreena district directly south of the core. The Gaelic League regularly praised priests throughout this district in the regional newspapers for their support of the Bilingual Programme, and they agitated to ensure that the primary school in the tiny Cullen district, surrounded by an extensive English-speaking area, offered it.

The support of the Catholic bishops in County Kerry also seems to have contributed to the successful introduction of the Bilingual Programme there. Furthermore, this support increased with the appointment of Bishop Charles O'Sullivan in 1918. He was very committed not only to the maintenance of the language in the Irish-speaking districts in County Kerry, but also to its revival throughout the rest of the county.[77] Amongst one of his first actions following his consecration was to appoint Rev. Tadhg Ua Curnáin, an Irish language scholar, as his diocesan inspector of religious education.

The support of the "regular clergy" in County Kerry for the Bilingual Programme was also very much evident, with some taking steps to ensure that it was not removed from a school when suitably qualified teachers were unavailable. On this, the Cork Examiner reported on a meeting on bilingual education held in Killarney in April 1920:

> The case of the threatened withdrawal of the Bilingual Programme from the Sponkane Boys' National School, at Dromod Parish, near Waterville, was before the meeting and aroused much indignation. The Rev. T. Courtney, F. MacColum and Pádraig O'Shea were appointed to take up the matter with the bishop, the parish priest and the people of the district.[78]

There was, at the same time, occasional opposition from parents in each of the four districts under consideration. For example, in 1911, Úna Ní Fhaircheallaigh, a member of the Gaelic League's National Education Committee, reported that some of the parents of students attending Tráigh Éanach (Templecrone) National School in County Donegal were keeping their children at home because they objected to teaching of the Bilingual Programme. Mr. Morris, the National Board inspector in the district, also noted that the parents of students attending some of the other schools in the county teaching the Bilingual Programme did not allow them to spend their time reading their Irish books when at home. Rather, they got them to concentrate on working with their English books instead.[79] He also noted that, while paying willingly for English books, parents sometimes refused to buy Irish books for their children.

The National Board demonstrated its support for the introduction of the Bilingual Programme in each of the four districts in a number of ways. In particular, it insisted after 1906, that teachers appointed to schools in Irish-speaking districts had to have qualifications to teach in a bilingual fashion. It succeeded also in ensuring that newly appointed teachers who spoke Irish and could read and write it, attended an Irish college and completed a course that led to the award of a bilingual certificate. The schools to which these teachers were appointed were recorded in English as follows: Shallogans National School, Fintown, in County Donegal; Innisbarra National School, Lettermore,[80] Tiernee National School, Carraroe,[81] Killeaney National School, Innishmore,[82]

St. Ronan's National School, Innishmore,[83] and Inisheer National School,[84] all in County Galway; Cromane National School,[85] Ballyguin National School[86] and Kimego National School, all in County Kerry[87]; and Ballycrovane National School, Rossnarown National School and Glengarriff National School, all in County Cork.[88]

The Gaelic League, however, did not help its own cause by adopting a particularly aggressive approach towards teachers appointed prior to 1906 and who, consequently, were not required to teach the Bilingual Programme if they were not at that point in time competent to do so. Dr. Douglas Hyde, the national president of the Gaelic League, issued a statement where he condemned every schoolmaster and schoolmistress in Irish-speaking districts who could not teach the 3Rs in Irish, arguing that they should move to a school in an English-speaking area at once or retire. In February 1912, two County Galway branches of the Irish National Teachers' Organisation (INTO) supported by branches representing teachers in County Mayo objected to Hyde's comments,[89] and in the following month, the Galway INTO branches further condemned an account in *An Claidheamh Soluis*, in which a recently deceased teacher had been castigated for not using Irish during the 25 years he had been teaching in a school in an Irish-speaking district.[90] In the same year, 1912, the Clifden Branch of the INTO describes these types of activities as the "hounding down"[91] of teachers.

Responses to the Programme in County Mayo and in the Less Intensely Irish-Speaking Districts in County Galway

There was much resistance to the Bilingual Programme in the intensely Irish-speaking district in the west of County Mayo. Consequently, no more than about half of those primary schools in the county that warranted its introduction there, hosted it. Parental opposition was particularly strong. The seasonal migration of men in this district as labourers to the east of Ireland, England and Scotland may have contributed to the perception that children required a fluency in English if they were to prosper in life. The general perception amongst the public appears to have been that the programme was designed so that the Irish language could be substituted for English as the sole medium of instruction, and the fact that the rationale for the programme was poorly explained may have impacted on its adoption in schools.[92] The fact that there was very poor explanation provided on the rationale for the programme may also have been significant[93]; overall, the general perception amongst the public appears to have been that the programme was designed so that the Irish language could be substituted for English as the sole medium of instruction.[94]

The continuation of the aggressive action towards teachers in schools in County Mayo, who were not proficient in speaking and teaching Irish, was not helpful. The Belmullet Branch of the Irish National Teachers' Organisation passed a resolution in September 1906, expressing its strong disapproval of Mr. Fitzhenry, Gaelic League organiser, after he had published reports on the schools in the area, in which he criticised particular teachers for paying little attention to teaching Irish and for not using it in instruction on other school subjects.[95] The National Board's inspectors also found it necessary to defend themselves against such action by the League's members. For example, J. S. Cussen, senior inspector for County Mayo, wrote to the Board in 1912, stating that paragraphs have been appearing in the Mayo News saying: "I was antagonistic to Irish, and that measures must be taken to bring me under control".[96]

The introduction of the Bilingual Programme in the eastern and western portions of County Galway, where the Irish-speaking percentage of the population was lower than in the central area, caused disquiet. In this context, by 1908, the Gaelic League was of the view that the Bilingual Programme should be introduced in an effort to reverse the decline in spoken Irish. The League recognised that within these western and eastern sectors in the county, only a minority of the school-going population was by now Irish speaking. There was strong opposition to the League's policy in this region, not only from the National Board, but also from clergy, from teachers and from parents.

The Experience in the Smaller Irish-Speaking Districts

The Bilingual Programme merited introduction in four small but largely Irish-speaking districts. The largest of these was the County Waterford Irish-speaking district, while the smallest was that of Ballymacoda, nearby, but in County Cork. A third area consisted of a number of very small pockets of intensely Irish-speaking districts scattered throughout the western portion of County Clare. Finally, there was a small yet still intensely Irish-speaking district in the east of County Mayo.

Only a small number of schools in the districts under consideration offered the Bilingual Programme. The Ballymacoda district in East County Cork, a strongly anglicised area very much under the influence of the towns of Youghal and Midleton surrounded the district, despite being home to around 1800 Irish-speakers in 1911, did not introduce the Bilingual Programme. Further, there appears to have been no major demand within the district itself for the introduction of the programme, and the Gaelic League and the National Board were not active in trying to initiate a demand.[97]

Although the East County Mayo Irish-speaking district, immediately to the south and east of Lough Conn had around 11,000 Irish speakers in 1911, none of the six schools in the area taught the Bilingual Programme. Neither the Gaelic League nor the National Board were not particularly active here, and Mr. Séamus Fenton, who was an inspector of national schools in eastern Mayo at the time, commented on negative parental attitudes, stating:

> The force against the revival of Irish as a spoken language was amazingly strong - one in almost every household no matter which speech was there. Those of us acquainted with the drama of life in school and home saw that the most powerful forces operating against living Irish were poverty and emigration.[98]

In 1909, the Gaelic League also observed that the people in Attymassy, Bohola and Straide, the major population centres in this district, showed little enthusiasm for continuing to speak Irish.[99]

Eight tiny geographically separated areas with 7800 Irish speakers in total existed in County Clare in 1911. While eight schools in these areas satisfied the criteria to introduce the Bilingual Programme, this only occurred in three, namely Kilbaha Boys' National School, Kilbaha Girls' National School in the Coill Bheathach (Kilbaha) a district at the very tip of the south west of the County, and the National School in Corrbhaile (Corbally) just north of the town of Kilkee. In 1912, the *Clare Journal*, bewailed this low take-up:

> There is a wealth of Irish speech from Kilkee to Loop head. The introduction of the Bilingual Programme into some of the schools and the

> attention paid by the Gaelic League to this stronghold recently has improved matters very much....It is unfortunate, however, that the Bilingual Programme has only found its way into three of them as yet.[100]

The general attitude of the National Board appears to have been that very few students in County Clare needed the Bilingual Programme of Instruction in order to be able to gain benefit from primary school education. Nevertheless, in 1919, Irish-language enthusiasts in the county were encouraged by the following statement delivered by Most Rev. Dr. Michael Fogarty, Bishop of the Diocese of Killaloe, in which the Clare Irish-speaking districts were located:

> Every day it is becoming clearer to us that we shall never be right in this country until we are speaking our own – the Irish language....The more they pursue our native language with the menace of destruction the more careful should we be to learn it, to love it, and to speak it at home, in the market, in the playground, in all the relations of life.[101]

The Bishop concluded by saying that no priest would be ordained for his diocese in future unless he was able to hear the sacrament of confession in Irish and preach sermons in the language.

The intensely Irish-speaking district in County Waterford had over 20,000 Irish-speakers in 1911. Yet, while 12 schools in the district merited the introduction of the Bilingual Programme, it operated in only three of them, namely Maol a' Chóirne (Mulinahorna) National School in Rinn Ua gCúanach (Ring), An Ghráinseach (Grange) National School and Baile Uí Chorráin (Ballycurrane) National School. Again, the poor level of take-up seems to have been associated with a lack of interest on the part both of the National Board and the Gaelic League. Indeed, the only case here on which the League took a major stand related to Maol a' Chóirne National School[102] which, with over 87 per cent of the population (869 individuals) registered as Irish-speakers in 1911, was the most intensely Irish-speaking area within the county. Initially, severe opposition to the Bilingual Programme was mounted by Fr. McCann, the local parish priest, whose hostility to the use of Irish in the schools was commented on angrily as follows a number of years earlier by Rev. Dr. Michael O'Hickey, the Catholic Church's inspector of religion:

> During the year the Catechism in Irish has been abandoned. It is now taught in English. I pass by the want of patriotism which the change involves, but I look upon the change as woefully bad policy, and I have had today ample proof that on the mere ground of practical utility, a huge blunder has been committed....Some who could answer nothing in English and who evidently did not know, or knew imperfectly what I said, could at once answer most accurately and practically when I put the same question (either general questions or questions from the Catechism in Irish).... Does not it seem an outrageous thing that in this school no child should be found able to say the Lord's Prayer in the language he habitually speaks and thinks in.[103]

This was the same Dr. O'Hickey who later became Vice-President of the Gaelic League and Professor of Irish at St. Patrick's College, Maynooth.[104]

The Bilingual Programme, the National Board decreed, was appropriate for the school in Maol a' Chóirne, but Fr. McCann objected in the following terms:

> The people know that the English language and not Irish, is the language they need to learn for the United States and the Colonies. Under these circumstances I do not deem it my duty to force teachers or pupils to adopt the Bilingual Programme which would materially interfere with the teaching of other subjects of comparatively paramount importance.[105]

In 1908, however, the Board issued an order that the programme be introduced and very soon it was apparent that it was being welcomed wholeheartedly by the parents. It was also introduced into the relatively nearby schools at Baile Uí Chorráin and An Ghráinseach, the latter being a school where teaching had already been conducted unofficially along bilingual lines by the headmaster, Déaglán Ó Cuilliú, for quite a number of years.[106] However, no attempt was made to have the programme introduced into the other nine schools in the district (most of which were in the north of the county) which, under the regulations of the National Board, merited its introduction.[107] To some extent this appears to have been due to the fact that the teachers there had been employed prior to 1904 and did not hold bilingual certificates or have sufficient proficiency in speaking and writing language.

The Preparation of Teachers to Teach the Bilingual Programme

Many teachers experienced great difficulty when the Bilingual Programme was first introduced, due to a lack of appropriate training in bilingual teaching methods and the absence of textbooks. The fact that the regular teacher training colleges largely ignored the existence of the programme was also unhelpful.[108] The regular primary school teacher training colleges largely ignoring its existence was also unhelpful. At the time, there were seven such colleges, five of which were for Catholic students, one for Church of Ireland students, and the Dublin-situated Marlborough Street College of the Commissioners which, while open to all denominations, was attended mainly by Presbyterian and Methodist students. In 1900, Irish was one of 14 "additional subjects" taught in these colleges, of which a student was required to take only one. In 1907, Mr. Lehane, the Board's inspector of Irish, made the following recommendation: "In view of the requirement in the last edition of the Board's rules that newly appointed teachers in Irish-speaking districts must know Irish, it would appear desirable that more importance should be attached to this subject during a teacher's course of training".[109] Lehane was being realistic in expecting that his recommendation could be met by the State's Marlborough Street College and the four Catholic colleges because, in 1902, they all, unlike the Church of Ireland College, had a lecturer in Irish. However, while the Gaelic League tried to bring pressure on the colleges to affect the recommendation, it received a very poor response, and by 1916, apart from the De La Salle College for Catholic males, in Waterford, the training colleges neglected the language.[110]

Given the scenario painted so far, it is not surprising that in 1906, the National Board recognised that the best way to prepare teachers for the bilingual schools was through recognising the courses offered by the Irish colleges established by the Gaelic League for the training of teachers of Irish. The following year the Board reported on this as follows:

> The supply of suitably trained teachers who possess the qualifications necessary by us for the teaching of the Irish language is still insufficient to meet the demands of schools situated in Irish-speaking localities. To facilitate the training colleges established for instruction in Irish as much as possible in the work of meeting this deficiency we have now arranged that

> at the end of the courses the professors of the colleges shall examine the teachers who have attended and shall submit the results. The teachers who pass will be recognised as qualified to teach Irish as an ordinary subject, and those who reach what we consider a sufficiently high standard will be regarded as competent to take care of a bilingual school.[111]

The official arrangement was that a college received five pounds for every teacher who had attended a required number of lessons, passed an examination at the end of the course and subsequently taught Irish in a primary school for one year.

The National Board funded the employment of substitute teachers so that the regular teachers could take time-off in lieu of the time they spent at the Irish colleges during the summer vacation.[112] The Commissioners of National Education had to approve records of a teacher's attendance at a college course as well as the timetable of the college, the programme of studies and the lecturers. The colleges were required to provide courses of at least four weeks duration and provide instruction for not less than 80 hours within that time. The number of teachers per lecturer was also not to be greater than 25.

The courses offered in the colleges included instruction in Irish language and literature, in phonetics and in teaching methods. Occasionally, demonstrations were give on the teaching of some school subjects, including mathematics and Latin, in a bilingual fashion. Such activity, however, was more often the exception than the rule.

By 1919–20, all of the Irish colleges outlined in Chapter 1 were recognised by the Board and five pounds was paid to each of them for every teacher who, having attended a required number of lessons there, passed an examination at the end of the course and subsequently taught Irish in a primary school for one year. The "direct method" of instruction, in which the Irish colleges specialised, was, however, inadequate for preparing bilingual teachers since it was primarily a method for teaching students a language other than their vernacular. The situation did not escape the attention of the bilingual teachers; in August 1909, for example, through the newly formed National Bilingual Teachers' Association, they complained that the League's courses in the Irish colleges were inappropriate for bilingual teaching.[113] Nothing, however, eventuated from the expression of such concern. It would, at the same time, be historically anachronistic to suggest that matters could have been otherwise given that the scholarly field we now know as "bilingual education pedagogy" was not even in its infancy internationally at this stage. Indeed, it was to be at least another 50 years before the results of research conducted by psycho-linguistics and socio-linguistics that led to the development of the field began to circulate in academic language and education circles in Ireland.

During the period under consideration, it is clear that the Board of National Education, its inspectors and organisers, were in full support of the introduction of the Bilingual Programme. They relied on the support and advocacy of the Gaelic League to support schools in the adoption of the programme, and in providing much needed professional development for teachers. In general, the clergy in Irish-speaking areas were also very supportive, while the colleges of education seemed to play a more conservative approach to adopting new methods or approaches to promote bilingual teaching in schools. However, public support for the introduction of the Bilingual Programme was not always available, and in many schools and districts which satisfied the criteria for the adoption of the programme, the programme was not taught. Due to many social and economic factors, there was insufficient parental support to introduce a programme which was perceived by many to oust competency in English, which was a fundamental skill for those seeking to emigrate.

Notes

1. B. S. MacAodha. 'Was This a Social Revolution'. In S. Ó Tuama (Ed.). *The Gaelic League Idea* (Cork and Dublin: Mercier Press, 1972), p. 21.
2. Ibid.
3. Ibid.
4. National Library of Ireland. Minutes of the Meetings of the Commissioners of National Education: 1904, p. 100.
5. T. Ó hAilín. 'Irish Revival Movements'. In B. Ó Cuív (Ed.). *A View of the Irish Language* (Dublin: Stationery Office, 1969), pp. 96–97.
6. Conradh na Gaeilge. Minutes of Executive Committee 1897–98, National Library of Ireland, Ms. 9799. Minutes of a meeting of the Executive Committee, held on 9 March, 1898.
7. Rev. M. P. O'Hickey. *Irish in the Schools* (Dublin: The Gaelic League, 1902), p. 2.
8. Ibid.
9. The Gaelic League. *The Case for Bilingual Education in Irish-Speaking Districts* (Dublin: The Gaelic League, 1900), p. 2.

10. National Library of Ireland. Minutes of the Commissioners of National Education in Ireland, 14 May 1901.
11. National Library of Ireland. Conradh na Gaeilge, Ms. 11,706, Minute Book for the Year 1895–96.
12. *Hansard's Parliamentary Debates*, 4th. S., 86, 20., Col. 679.
13. Ibid., Col. 728.
14. Ibid., Col. 707.
15. Ibid., Col. 675.
16. Ibid., Col. 848.
17. Ibid.
18. M. Ó Dómhnaill. *Stair Choláiste na Rinne* (Unpublished typescript, Coláiste na Rinne, Dungarvan, County Waterford); P. Ó hAnnracháin. *Fé Bhrat an Chonnartha*, p. 50; *An Claidheamh Soluis*, 8 October 1904.
19. C. Ó hÁodha. 'An Phíarsach agus múineadh na Gaeilge', *Inniu*, 12 Deireadh Fómhair, 1979, p. 15.
20. Ibid.
21. The Gaelic League. *The Case for Bilingual Education in Irish-Speaking Districts*, p. 6.
22. Hyde was the son of a Church of Ireland clergyman, a graduate of Trinity College Dublin, a president of the National Literary Society and Professor of Irish at University College, Dublin from 1909 to 1932. He was also first President of Ireland, from 1938 to 1945. He was a tireless worker on behalf of the Gaelic League and conducted a highly successful fund-raising campaign on its behalf in America during 1905.
23. Ibid. The Palles Commission was established in 1898 to enquire into the operation of the system established under the Intermediate Education Act and the effects of existing legislation.
24. The Gaelic League. *Bilingual Education* (Dublin: The Gaelic League, 1900), p. 6.
25. Ibid., p. 8.
26. *Daily Independent*, 20 February 1900.
27. R. J. W. Selleck. *The New Education* (London: Pitman, 1968).
28. *Irish Teachers' Journal*, Vol. 34, No. 50, 1900, p. 3.
29. National Library of Ireland. Minutes of the Commissioners of National Education in Ireland, 1902, p. 71.
30. S. Fenton. *It All Happened* (Dublin: M.H. Gill and Son, 1948).
31. Ibid.
32. *Seventy-Third Report of CNEI for 1906–07*, p. 95.
33. *Appendix to the Seventy Third Report of the C.N.E.I. for 1906–07*, Section 2 (H.C. 3 739), 'Rules and Regulations of the CNEI', p. 102.
34. Ibid., pp. 102–103.
35. *Freeman's Journal*, 4 April 1901.

36. *Appendix to the Seventy-Fifth Report of the C.N.E.I. for 1908* (Cd. 4873) H.C. 1909, XX, p. 627.
37. Ibid., p. 627.
38. *An Claidheamh Soluis*, 13 June 1908.
39. Ibid., 13 February 1909.
40. Ibid., 16 October 1909. For example, on 16 October 1909, the teachers in the bilingual schools in County Galway made a request to this effect to the National Board. See National Archives, National School Records. Ed. 9, File 22049.
41. *Report of Vice-Regal Committee of Inquiry into Primary Education (Ireland) 1913–14* (Dill) Third Report (Cd. 7479), p. 242.
42. *Seventy-Fourth Report of the C.N.E.I. for 1907–08* (Cd. 4291) H.C. 1908. XXVII, p. 12.
43. S. Fenton. *It All Happened*, p. 221.
44. See. For example, *Appendix to the Eightieth Report of the C.N.E.I. for 1913–14*, pp. 138–140.
45. Coimisiún na Gaeltachta. *Report* (Dublin: Stationery Office, 1926), n.p.
46. Ibid. See evidence of P. Ó Brolacháin, 17 Aibreán 1925, n.p.
47. *An Claidheamh Soluis*, 7 May 1904.
48. *Irish School Weekly*, 30 May 1908.
49. Ibid., 30 April 1910.
50. *Irish School Weekly*, 31 July 1909, p. 743.
51. Ibid., 25 January 1913.
52. *An Claidheamh Soluis*, 10 April 1909.
53. Ibid., 20 February 1909.
54. Ibid.
55. Ibid., 15 May 1909.
56. Ibid., 14 May 1910.
57. Ibid., 20 November 1909.
58. Ibid., 27 November 1909.
59. National Library of Ireland, National School Records. Ed. 9, File 22275.
60. The following account is based on that outlined by K. R. Doyle in The Irish Language as a Curricular Element in Irish Primary Education in the Period 1831–1935, pp. 72–74.
61. *Appendix to the Seventy-Third Report of the CN.E.I. for 1906–7*, Section 2 (H.C. 3739), 'Rules and Regulations of the C.N.E.I', p. 145.
62. *An Claidheamh Soluis*, 16 May 1908. This was made available to the second-named author by the principal of the school in 1985.
63. *Irish School Weekly*, 21 November 1908.
64. Ibid.

65. A Bilingual Teacher. *Bilingual Arithmetic for Standard III* (Dublin: Educational Company of Ireland., n.d.); Fr. O' Leary, *Eolas ar Áireamh* (Dublin: Irish Book, 1902).
66. P. Ó Laoighre. *Leabhar Núa ar Áireamh* (Baile Átha Clíath: Brún agus Ó Nóláin Teor., n.d.), n.p.
67. *Irish School Weekly*, 17 October 1908, p. 270.
68. Patrick Pearse had dealt with how 'the direct Method' should be used in the teaching of Irish to Irish-speaking students in a bilingual school. See *An Claidheamh Soluis*, 23 December 1905. Here, he argued for the importance of employing teaching stimuli which should be enjoyable if there was to be proper teaching of Irish grammatically and soundly to first-language Irish speakers. He illustrated his argument by describing a lesson he observed in teaching Flemish to Flemish-speaking students in Belgium. In particular, he illustrated how, through the use of fun, sketches, vocabulary could be extended.
69. Conradh na Gaedhilge. *An Chéad Leabhar* (Baile Átha Clíath: Conradh na Gaedhilge, 1911) (2nd ed.).
70. Conradh na Gaedhilge. *An Treas Leabhar* (Baile Átha Clíath: Conradh na Gaedhilge, 1906).
71. R. M. Beard. *An Outline of Piaget's Developmental Psychology* (London: Routledge and Keegan Paul, 1969), pp. 76–97.
72. *An Claidheamh Soluis*, 29 February 1908. See also *Seventy-Seventh Report of the C.N.E.I. for 1910–11* (Cd. 5903) H.C. 1911, XXI, p. 135; B. Fitzpatrick. Bilingualism as a Factor in Education, With Application to the Language Question in Ireland (Unpublished M.A. Thesis, University College, Dublin, 1918), p. 30.
73. Inspectors' Report Book. Scoil an Chnoic, Lettermullen, Co. Galway. For a similar report see Inspectors' Report Book. Rosmuck National School, Co. Galway.
74. *Appendix to the Seventy-Fifth Report of the C.N.E.I. for 1908–09*, p. 205.
75. National Archives, Dublin. National School Records. Ed. 9, File 21885.
76. *Donegal Vindicator*, 2 July 1909.
77. Quoted in P. Cremin. The Irish Language as a Medium of Instruction and as a School Subject, 1800–1921 (Unpublished M.Ed. Thesis, University College, Cork, 1977), p. 337.
78. For example, the *Cork Examiner* reported as follows on a meeting held in Killarney in April 1920 regarding bilingual education in County Kerry: "The case of the threatened withdrawal of the Bilingual Programme from the Sponkane Boys' National School, at Dromod Parish, near Waterville, was before the meeting and aroused much indignation. The Rev. T. Courtney, F. MacColum and Pádraig O'Shea were appointed to take up the matter with the bishop, the parish priest and the people of the district".

79. National Archives, Dublin. National School Records. Ed. 9, File 22179.
80. Ibid., File 22518.
81. Ibid., File 22189.
82. Ibid.
83. Ibid., Ed. 9, File 21428.
84. Ibid., File 21689.
85. Ibid., File 21885.
86. Ibid., File 23557.
87. Ibid.
88. Ibid., File 21811.
89. *Irish School Weekly*, 23 April 1910.
90. Ibid., 24 February 1912.
91. Ibid., 25 May 1912.
92. C. Ó Danachair. 'The Gaeltacht'. In B. Ó Cuív (Ed.). *A View of the Irish Language* (Dublin: The Stationery Office, 1969), p. 120.
93. This generalisation was been arrived at by the present authors after examining the correspondence in the files of all of the national schools in this Irish-speaking district for the period in question.
94. Ibid.
95. *Irish School Weekly*, 15 September 1906, p. 524.
96. National Archives, Dublin. National School Records. Ed. 9. File 24726.
97. The Inspectors' Report Book for Clonpriest National School in this district contains notes dated 20 June 1895 and 26 June 1896, which state that the students in the school had great difficulty in learning to read, write, compose and spell in English as they came from Irish-speaking homes. The report book is now in Gortroe National School, Youghal, County Cork.
98. S. Fenton. *It All Happened*, p. 170.
99. *Connaught Telegraph*, 10 April 1909.
100. *Clare Journal*, 21 March 1912
101. NL, ILB. 300. p. 4, Item 64, M. Fogarty, Bishop of Killaloe, Speech in 1919
102. National Archives, Dublin. National School Records. Ed. 9, File 21846.
103. Ibid.
104. O'Hickey had an unfortunate life following a major disagreement with the Catholic bishops of Ireland following his insistence that satisfactory competence in Irish be a requirement for university matriculation at the National University of Ireland. He appealed his dismissal to the Vatican, but was unsuccessful.
105. Ibid.
106. Coimisiún na Gaeltachta. *Report*, Minutes of evidence taken Dé hAoine, 9ú lá Deireadh Fómhair 1975.

107. These included the national schools officially entitled Modeligo National School, Whitechurch National School, Kilbrien National School, Ballinacourty National School, Tooraneen National School and Coolnasmear National School. Regarding the latter school, the manager was Sir. P. J. Musgrave rather than the local parish priest. An inspector reporting on the school in 1916 recommended that the Bilingual Programme be introduced. Musgrave, however, expressed very strong opposition, arguing that to have any Irish taught in the school would be 'an utter waste of time' and 'an injustice to the children when there are so many subjects that would prove an assistance in later life'. He concluded by stating that he hoped the Board would 'discontinue this wicked waste of time'. The matter seems to have been quietly forgotten after that and the Bilingual Programme was never introduced in the school. See National Archives, Dublin. National School Records. Ed. 9, File 29015.
108. *Seventy-Sixth Report of the C.N.E.I. for 1909–10* (General Report on Irish: Mr. Mangan), pp. 166–167.
109. *Appendix to the Seventy-Third Report of the C.N.E.I. for 1906–07* (Cd. 3961). H.C. 1908, p. 147.
110. National Library of Ireland, Gaelic League, Report of the Árd Fheis 1917, p.21.
111. *Appendix to the Seventy-Third Report of the C.N.E.I. for 1906–07* (Cd. 3961). H.C. 1908, p. 147.
112. Ibid.
113. *An Claidheamh Soluis*, 21 August 1909.

CHAPTER 4

Shifting Concern for "Saving the Child" to Concern About "Saving the Language": 1918–1926

Introduction

The commencement of the Easter Rising on Monday, 24 April 1916, marked a change in the nature of the relationship between the cultural nationalist movement and militant nationalism in Ireland. Following the Sinn Féin successes at the general election of 1918, calls to address the perceived lack of attention given to the Irish language and Gaelic culture in both primary and secondary schools around the country increased, notwithstanding that agitators were aware of the developments noted already in previous chapters. A number of members of the abstentionist parliament of the Irish Republic (Dáil Éireann) made up of the Sinn Féin members who refused to take their seats at Westminster after the election, argued, as Deputy Figgis did, that "the secret of national power lies in the schoolhouses."[1] Others, like Deputy Magenis, noted that education "has been proved everything in the making of a nation".[2] The general notion underpinning such statements was, on attaining political independence, there would be a bolstering of Ireland's distinctiveness as a nation when the majority of the population of the country would come to possess language and cultural characteristics different from those of the majority of the population of the UK.

Professor Michael Tierney of University College, Dublin, reinforced the education ideas of the Gaelic League when he published his *Education in a Free Ireland*. In it, he argued that Irish should be one of

T. O'Donoghue and T. O'Doherty, *Irish Speakers and Schooling in the Gaeltacht, 1900 to the Present*,
https://doi.org/10.1007/978-3-030-26021-7_4

a compulsory core of subjects in any new school programme introduced on the attaining of national independence. He held also that Gaelic traditions and lore should permeate this programme. At the core of his position was that one of the major objectives of Irish education under an independent government should be the promotion of a distinct nationality; "the primary basis of all our teaching", he argued, "must be our own language, our own history, our own music, our own art".[3]

Michael Collins argued along similar lines in his book, *The Path to Freedom*,[4] which was published in the autumn of 1922. Bishop O'Dwyer of Limerick, and Archbishop Mannix after he had left Ireland for Australia, also supported the associated movement. Other clerics equally took up the cause, with young priests such as Fr. Micheál Ó Flanagán, Vice-President of Sinn Féin, becoming very prominent in urging the people to move away from giving political support to the Irish Parliamentary Party. Furthermore, as Catholicism and the national movement became more closely associated after the Easter Rising, some of the "lower clergy" began to argue that Irish was the language most suited to the expression of "the Irish mind".[5] For others, it was seen as being worthy of promotion because it could act as a barrier against Anglicisation.

The association established in the minds of the majority Catholic population between nationalism and the Irish language movement created an expectation in the final years of British rule that was favourably disposed towards promoting debate on the nature of a curriculum based on Gaelic culture to be introduced once national independence would be achieved.[6] At the same time, the original thrust of the Bilingual Programme, considered in the previous chapter, became lost on its original devotees as the Gaelic League now shifted to advocating for an improvement in the position and status of the Irish language throughout all primary schools in the country, regardless of their location and of the language used in students' homes. Given this situation, it is apposite to consider the policies developed on schooling from the time the Sinn Féin leaders took their seats in the First Dáil in 1918, until the publication in 1926, of the report of a State-initiated Coimisiún na Gaeltachta (Commission on the Gaeltacht) in independent Ireland.

The present chapter is concerned with these policies. First, it details early thinking by members of the Dáil on the role they saw for the Irish language within the education system of "a new Ireland". Secondly, an outcome of the deliberations of those who attended a special conference on the matter and that came to be known as the First National Programme Conference is considered. Developments in relation to the place of the Irish language in education, and especially in relation to the changed political scene that prevailed from 1922, the year of national independence, until the publication of the report of the Commission on the Gaeltacht in 1926, are then detailed. The chapter closes with an overview of the main thrust of the proposals of the Commission, including in relation to education

The Dáil, the Irish Language and Education

With many who took their seats in the First Dáil being members of the Gaelic League, it is not surprising that at its sixth session, on 27 October 1918, a Minister (Mr. Seán Ó Ceallaigh and known as "Sceilig") was appointed who had special responsibility for the Irish language. Concurrently, the League proposed that Irish should be taught as a regular subject in all national schools across the country, that at least one hour a day should also be allocated to engaging in spoken Irish, that all subjects should be taught through Irish in Irish-speaking districts, and that if any teachers were unable to teach Irish, the school manager should be obliged to employ an additional and suitably qualified part-time teacher who would be paid by the National Board to do this work. It also requested that the Minister for Irish and the Coiste Gnótha (Executive Committee) of the Dáil should emphasise the importance of their language policy with school managers, state boards, national associations and workers' associations. It also demonstrated its confrontational side in stating that if the National Board did not accept its proposals, parents should not send their children to school.[7]

The League conducted a campaign aimed at harnessing public support for its demands. This action reached a climax when, at a large public meeting in the Mansion House in Dublin in March 1919, a programme for schools in an independent Ireland was presented.[8] The proposed programme set out three separate syllabi for schools: one for purely Irish-speaking districts, one for semi Irish-speaking districts and one for purely English-speaking districts. The broad outlines of the syllabus recommended for those in purely Irish-speaking districts were as follows:

- All school subjects (excepting English and other foreign languages) should be taught through the medium of Irish only.

- Irish history to be taught to all pupils. Even the infants ought to be told stories of our saints and heroes.
- Irish music should be taught in all classes. The words of the old songs ought to be taught as poetry and the music to which they are set ought to be taught in the music class.
- Irish dancing to be permitted as part of the drill lesson and teachers to be encouraged to teach it.

A proposed syllabus for students in semi Irish-speaking districts emphasised the following:

- Irish to be the official school language, i.e. roll call, orders, prayers, etc. to be in Irish.
- A bilingual programme to be in use. After a few years, however, Irish should predominate over English in the higher classes.
- Irish history to be taught to all pupils. Even the infants ought to be told stories of our saints and heroes.
- Irish music should be taught in all classes. The words of the old songs ought to be taught as poetry and the music to which they are set ought to be taught in the music class.
- Irish dancing to be permitted as part of the drill lesson and teachers to be encouraged to teach it.
- Foreign languages—each foreign tongue to be taught through the medium of that tongue or through the medium of the language best understood by the children.

Finally, the broad outlines recommended for the syllabus for students in schools in English-speaking districts were as follows:

- Irish to be the official school language, i.e. roll call, orders, prayers, etc. to be in Irish.
- A bilingual programme to be in use. After a few years, however, Irish should predominate over English in the higher classes.
- Irish history to be taught to all pupils. Even the infants ought to be told stories of our saints and heroes.
- Irish music should be taught in all classes. The words of the old songs ought to be taught as poetry and the music to which they are set ought to be taught in the music class.

- Irish dancing to be permitted as part of the drill lesson and teachers to be encouraged to teach it.
- Foreign languages—each foreign tongue to be taught through the medium of that tongue or through the medium of the language best understood by the children.
- Irish to be taught for vernacular use to each child for at least one hour per day.
- In two years' time, it should be feasible to commence teaching reading, writing, grammar, oral composition, kindergarten, etc. in Irish and English on alternate days in the three lower standards, and all school subjects in the other standards. In five years' time, it should be feasible to have a bilingual programme in all schools, except perhaps in the case of Infants.[9]

All of counties of Waterford, Cork, Kerry, Clare, Galway, Mayo and Donegal were categorised as being populated heavily by Irish-speaking communities, and no attempt was made to identify the particular intensive and semi Irish-speaking areas within each of them.[10]

The Gaelic League now set about encouraging schools to adopt its programme. By its own admittance, however, it had little success.[11] It attributed this to apathy on the part of parents, hostility on the part of the National Board and "an overloaded senseless programme" already in place that would kill "the best efforts of even the most enthusiastic teachers."[12] Regarding the latter, T. J. O'Connell, the General Secretary of the Irish National Teachers' Organisation (INTO) at the time, later recalled as follows:

> Word began to reach the I.N.T.O. Head Office of visits to schools by local enthusiasts who demanded that irrespective of conditions or difficulties, the League's programme should be put into immediate operation. In some areas things were made very unpleasant for teachers who failed to fall in with these demands. Suggestions were made that all teachers in the Irish-speaking districts who were unable to teach the full programme should be dismissed forthwith, and there were school strikes and talks of strikes.[13]

The following resolution was passed at the Annual Congress of the Gaelic League in April 1920, partly in an effort to diffuse the situation:

> That as in our opinion the present school programmes are altogether unsuitable to Irish conditions, we believe that a Committee made up of representatives of the general public, the school managers, the teachers, and such other interests as might reasonably be entitled to representation should be convened to frame a programme, or series of programmes, in accordance with Irish ideals and conditions, due regard being given to local needs and views, the school staff, qualifications and individual tastes of teachers etc.[14]

Two months later, the Central Executive Committee of the INTO decided to establish a working group of its own to come up with a response, and they assembled at what became known as the First National Programme Conference.

The First National Programme Conference

On 6 January 1920, the first meeting of the First National Programme Conference took place.[15] Members decided that parents who might object to having either Irish or English taught as a compulsory subject were to have their wishes respected. They also decided on the obligatory subjects that should constitute a minimum programme for primary schools. These were Irish, English, mathematics, history and geography, needlework for girls in "third and higher standards", singing, drill and a kindergarten curriculum for infants' classes.

The members of the Conference met regularly over the next few months and consulted with teachers around the country, seeking suggestions on the teaching of Irish and on planning programmes for the different subjects. By July 1921, they had produced a draft programme with accompanying notes. The INTO published these in the *Irish School Weekly* the following month, before having them sent to the secretaries of all of its branches throughout the country for discussion at special meetings.[16] The reports from these meetings demonstrate that teachers, in general, were very anxious about the enormous degree of emphasis placed in the programme on the teaching of the Irish language.[17]

The final version of the First National Programme was issued on 28 January 1922. Those in attendance committed to using the curriculum as a vehicle for the revival of the Irish language and they produced a plan that took little account of the expressed anxieties of the rank-and-file members of the teaching force. Instead, they emphasised that they had set out to remedy what they saw as the outstanding defects of the National Board's programme. The first defect identified was that there were too many obligatory subjects and that teachers had very little freedom to choose subjects they felt were appropriate for students from different geographical, social and economic backgrounds. Secondly, it was contended that the Irish language was placed in a subordinate position on the official programme and was out of harmony with the views of those who aspired to it becoming the national and first language of future generations.[18]

The proposal was that the perceived overcrowded curriculum should be dealt with by eliminating drawing, elementary science, cookery, laundry, needlework (in the lower standards), hygiene and nature study, while the prescribed content for history and geography, along with singing and drill, should be reduced. The syllabus for the Irish language related to (a) reading and spelling, (b) writing, (c) composition, and (d) grammar. For the infant standards, it stipulated that teaching was to be entirely in Irish throughout all schools in the country, that junior infants classes were to be taught Irish, drawing, numbers, "kindergarten gifts and occupations", songs and games, while students in senior infants classes were to be taught Irish, arithmetic, singing, drawing, drill, kindergarten gifts and occupations, and object lessons.[19]

English, the home language of the majority of children in Ireland, was to be excluded entirely from the curriculum for "the infant classes". The National Programme also stipulated that instruction in history and geography (which was to commence in "third standard"), and in singing and drill, was to be given through the medium of Irish. In the teaching of singing, all songs taught were to be in the Irish language, while drill was to incorporate Irish step dancing and figure dancing.[20]

The decision that teaching in the infant schools should be undertaken entirely through the medium of Irish was due largely to the influence of Professor Timothy Corcoran S. J., Professor of Education, at University College Dublin. Corcoran had declined an invitation to attend the First National Programme Conference, but he did offer much advice. Specifically regarding the education of children of the early years, he stated:

> There is one educable period at which the habit of using fluent Irish as a vernacular can be acquired… That one period is what may be called the pre-primary or infant period from 3 years to 7 years of age… That essential

> and sufficient habit must be secured in the pre primary or 'infant' Irish language school....The language should be the sole aim of that school... No other work whatever, save the fluent use of the simple spoken language, no grammar, very little reading, no writing should be aimed at....What about English in such a school? It has no place whatever.[21]

Views like this led him to advocate the setting up of separate schools for infants that would offer a three-year programme. These were necessary, he declared, since "it cannot be too much emphasised that at the earlier stage of education, language is the medium of school work; language, first, last and all the time".[22]

Corcoran's ideas were welcomed greatly by the Dáil's Aireacht An Oideachais (Ministry for Irish) since they served to legitimate the emphasis in the First National Programme on totally excluding English from the "infant schools". Overall, this emphasis reflected a desire for a revolutionary approach to the revival of the Irish language through the schools. It was also one that contrasted with the more evolutionary approach advocated by the Gaelic League two years previously.

The Changed Political Scene

By the time the final meeting of the First National Programme Conference had taken place on 28 January 1922, the political situation nationally had changed radically. Following the cessation of hostilities arising out of the national independence physical force movement, and in accord with Article 17 of the Anglo-Irish Treaty that brought to an end the Irish War of Independence, the Parliament of Southern Ireland assembled on 14 January 1922. It approved the Treaty, elected a provisional government chaired by Michael Collins and then dissolved. On 16 January 1922, the Provisional Government went to Dublin Castle, the seat of British rule in Ireland, and a formal transfer of power took place.[23] The new government assumed responsibility for education on 1 February 1922. Two years later, a national Department of Education came into existence. It was responsible for the administration of primary, secondary and technical education along with the National Library, the National Museum, the Metropolitan School of Art and the reformatory and industrial schools.

Following the establishment of the Provisional Government in 1922, and prior to the establishment of the national Department of Education in 1924, the National Board continued for a short time to exercise its functions, but Mr. Fionán Lynch, the Minister for Education, attended all meeting, and all decisions had to have his approval.[24] Then, towards the end of January 1922, Lynch appointed Mr. Pádraig Ó Brolcháin as a special supervisor of the work of the Education Office. One of Ó Brolcháin's first official actions was to inform the members of the National Board that their services would no longer be required as he was taking over all of their responsibilities under the umbrella of the Ministry of Education of the Provisional Government.

Mr. Ó Brolcháin, in his capacity as the new Chief Executive Officer of National Education in Ireland, now proceeded to clarify the policy for education in the new Ireland:

> In the administration of Irish education it is the intention of the new Government to work with all its might for the strengthening of the national fibre by giving the language, history, music and tradition of Ireland their natural place in the life of Irish schools.[25]

The Minister for Education of the Provisional Government followed up by decreeing that from 17 March 1922, Irish had to be "taught or used as a medium of instruction for at least one hour a day in every school where there is a teacher competent to give the instruction".[26] Concurrently, the new Irish Government accepted the report of the First National Education Conference. Then, on 1 April 1922, the recommended programme, considered in this chapter already, came into operation.[27]

The new programme presented the primary school teachers in independent Ireland with an enormous challenge. For one thing, a great number of them had no proficiency in the Irish language. This is not surprising given the perilous state of the language nationally and also given that prior to 1922, Irish, as will be recalled, had been offered only as an optional subject in the teacher training colleges and only a small proportion of student–teachers opted to study it each year. Furthermore, of those who chose to be examined in Irish in the training colleges, only a small percentage attained the pass standard necessary to obtain the National Board's "Certificate of Competency" in Irish.

It is true that between 1904 and 1922 a sizeable number of practising primary school teachers who did not have competence in spoken and written Irish benefited from attendance at Irish language colleges.

Nevertheless, official figures show that at the time of the launching of the First National Programme in April 1922, the great majority of primary school teachers in the new State still had no qualification whatsoever for teaching the language.[28] The government, being acutely aware of the shortfall in the number of qualified teachers, immediately set about addressing the problem. In May 1922, courses were developed for teachers who were not qualified to teach the new programme in primary schools. The objective was to upskill teachers to enable them to teach the language, initially to the junior classes, as well as laying a foundation whereon they could build a good knowledge of the language.[29]

In May 1922, it outlined details of courses for primary school teachers whose knowledge of Irish did not qualify them to teach the new programme in primary schools. It was hoped that during the conduct of them, teachers would obtain a knowledge of Irish sufficient to enable them to teach it, and especially to the junior classes, as well as laying a foundation for subsequently acquiring a good knowledge of the language. The courses were held in the Irish colleges and other designated centres. Attendance was obligatory for every teacher under the age of 45 who did not hold a "Certificates of Competency" in the teaching of Irish. Under special circumstances, teachers 45 years of age or older could also attend. The colleges held the first course between 4 July and 25 August 1922. Each course ran for four hours per weekday and for two hours on Saturdays. On completion, teachers sat an examination and those who passed were awarded a certificate of competence to teach through the medium of Irish.[30]

The 19 Irish colleges in operation around the country, along with 100 other centres, hosted the summer courses.[31] They continued to operate for this purpose up to and including 1928.[32] Attendance resulted in the award of one of three different types of certificates: the Ordinary Certificate, the Bilingual Certificate and the Higher Certificate. In 1922, students received an Ordinary Certificate or the Bilingual Certificate, depending on the level of their results on the same examination paper. In later years, the colleges awarded the Bilingual Certificate or the Higher Certificate to a large number of teachers who had already obtained the Ordinary Certificate.[33]

Teachers who initially supported the process were outraged when in November 1923, the Department of Education decreed that all teachers' salaries were to be reduced by 10 per cent to pay for course attendance.[34] Teachers expressed anger at the fact that, not only were they obliged to devote a considerable portion of their summer holidays to learning Irish, they also had to foot the bill. A subsequent shift on the part of the government, decreeing that from 1924 onwards attendance at courses would be optional, went some way towards assuaging the concerns of teachers. Nevertheless, they still had plenty of associated deficiencies to contend with, not least of which was a lack of resources for language teaching.[35]

In 1925, the government promised to address the long-term need for primary schoolteachers with competence in speaking Irish and in using it as a teaching medium, by establishing special new secondary schools called preparatory colleges, to supply well-educated Irish-speakers for the primary school teacher training colleges.[36] The plan was to recruit approx. 150 students per year into training colleges from these special preparatory colleges, while the remainder would come from secondary schools. The next chapter considers the scheme under which the colleges were established.

In the interest of maintaining a sense of the overall context of education developments at the time, it is also important to keep in mind that from the school year 1927–28, all secondary schools recognised by the State had to offer Irish as a school subject, and from 1932, all students attending a secondary school had to study the language.[37] Furthermore, from 1928 onwards, Irish became a subject one had to pass in order to obtain an Intermediate Certificate overall (for those who had completed three-to-four years of secondary schooling). A similar regulation was introduced in 1934, in relation to the Leaving Certificate examination, which one usually took after completing five-to-six years of secondary schooling.

The Department of Education recognised that the developments it had set in train, if they were to bear fruit, necessitated "that the work should be in the hands of efficient teachers who are masters of the subject they propose to teach as well as being fluent speakers of Irish".[38] Thus, just as for primary school teachers, it conducted summer courses to help secondary school teachers achieve competence in the language. Furthermore, from 1926, secondary school teachers were required to pass an oral Irish examination to satisfy the requirements of registration.

The Department of Education also encouraged the authorities of secondary schools to use Irish as the medium of instruction. To this end, it categorised secondary schools into three types: Grade A, Grade B and Grade C schools. In the first category, namely Grade A schools, Irish was the sole medium of instruction. In Grade B schools, Irish was the medium of instruction for some subjects. Finally, in Grade C schools, Irish was a school subject only. An extra grant of 25 per cent, based on the number of students attending, was paid to Grade A schools. Grade B schools also received special financial incentives, the amount varying in proportion to the extent of the teaching through the medium of Irish that took place.

In 1926, the government also responded to criticisms made by primary school teachers that the First National Programme was too exacting by establishing the Second National Programme Conference. On 5 March, a report by the Irish National Teachers' Organisation was published that was drawn up after consultation with members.[39] It recommended that Irish, English, mathematics, history, geography, needlework (girls), and music, or rural science, or nature study be taught as obligatory subjects, and that drawing, physical training, manual instruction (boys) and cookery (girls) or laundry (girls) or domestic economy (girls) be offered only as optional subjects.[40] It was held that the teaching of those subjects through the medium of Irish in infants' classes had caused great difficulty for teachers. Nevertheless, the notions regarding the education of this age group that underpinned the First National Programme Conference programme of 1922 were still upheld and were elaborated upon as follows:

> It was argued with much weight that a "direct" method of teaching Irish, continued during the length of an ordinary school day for a few years between the ages of 4 and 8, would be quite sufficient - given trained and fluent teachers – to impart to children a vernacular power over the language; while in the case of older children, it was shown that such a result would be more difficult of attainment. The members of the Conference were, therefore at one in holding that the one and only method of establishing Irish as a vernacular is the, effective teaching of it to the Infants.[41]

While the commitment to maintaining an immersion experience of the language persisted, as required by the 1922 syllabus, the second programme contained the concession that "the work in the infants' classes between the hours of 10.30 a.m. and 2 p.m., be conducted entirely in Irish where the teachers are sufficiently qualified". This meant that classes before 10.30 a.m. could be conducted through the medium of English if desired.[42] Teachers unable to use Irish as a medium of instruction for the various subjects on the curriculum were required to teach the language for at least one hour per day and to use it as much as possible during daily work in the school.

For classes above the infants group, the Second National Programme specified a higher course and a lower course in both Irish and English. Where the circumstances suited, the higher course in Irish was to be studied in conjunction with the lower course in English, and where the standard of Irish was low, then the lower course was to be taken in Irish and the higher course in English. The notion was that as competence in Irish improved amongst the population of the nation, the amount of Irish taught could be increased and the amount of English taught could, correspondingly, be decreased.

In both courses, there was also to be more emphasis on engagement in conversation in Irish than had been the case under the 1922 programme. Furthermore, the rigid regulation of 1922, requiring that history, geography, music and drill be taught through the medium of Irish, was modified. Although the official position was still to encourage the teaching of "ordinary" school subjects through the medium of the language, allowance was to be made for teachers not sufficiently competent to do so.[43]

Professor J. M. O'Sullivan, Minister for Education, presented the report of the Second National Programme Conference to the Dáil on 7 May 1926 and announced that it was now the official programme for national schools.[44] In taking this action, he was heralding that there would be no turning back from using the primary schools as the principal instrument in moving the population of the nation away from one vernacular and towards another. The irony of this situation is that the very institution identified for so long by the great majority of language revivalists as being responsible for the decline in the Irish language during the nineteenth century was now to be used by the Irish government to redress the situation. Furthermore, in committing to this approach, the plan of the Gaelic League in 1920, proposing that separate that differentiated programmes should be produced for Irish-speaking districts, partly Irish-speaking districts and English-speaking districts, was abandoned. Finally, the Bilingual Programme of Instruction introduced in 1904 was given no place in the new scheme of things. Within a few decades, bilingual education was neglected and successive governments concentrated their energies on the restoration of the language throughout the whole country rather than specifically on its maintenance in the Irish-speaking districts.[45]

Report of Coimisiún na Gaeltachta 1926

The Commission on the Gaeltacht, officially entitled Coimisiún na Gaeltachta, was appointed by the Executive Council of the government of the Irish Free State in January 1925.[46] Chaired by Deputy Richard Mulcahy of the governing Cumann na nGaedheal Party, the Commission was charged with defining geographically the Gaeltacht regions, making recommendations for the improvement of the economic and education opportunities for Irish speakers in these regions and recommending ways of carrying out the administration of the Gaeltacht through Irish. Amongst its 12 members were Dáil deputies and representatives of the universities, the inspectors of schools, schoolteachers and the civil service. It quickly set about interviewing representatives of government departments, of the Garda Siochána (the national police force) and of the inspectors of primary and secondary schools, along with others deemed to be relevant expert witnesses. Using the most recent Census of Population (2011) to identify the counties where the highest density of Irish-speakers lived, a general enumeration of the population of Irish speakers was conducted.

The Commission recommended that where 80 per cent or more of the population of a district was Irish speaking, it could be regarded as being "Irish speaking", regardless of the extent to which English was in daily use. In 1925, these districts, known as the Fíor-Ghaeltacht, had a total population of 164,774 of whom 146,821 (89.1 per cent) were speakers of Irish. Districts, where more than 25 per cent and less than 80 per cent of the population were Irish speaking, were deemed to be "partly Irish-speaking districts", known as the Breac-Ghaeltacht. The Breac-Ghaeltacht had a total population of 294,890 of whom 110,585 Irish-speakers (37.5 per cent). While the figures indicated an alarming decrease of 31 per cent in Irish-speakers between 1911 and 1926, they also indicated the existence of Irish-speaking communities in 12 of the new State's 26 counties.

The accuracy of the census carried out by the Gaeltacht Commission was criticised later on a number of grounds. The Garda Síochána had conducted the survey, despite the fact that as few as 3.4 per cent of the force were native Irish speakers, and hence, the majority of the Garda were poorly equipped to assess the Irish competence of the population.[47] This resulted in an exaggeration of the strength of Irish where the language was already quite strong. Further, much of the huge area deemed to be Breac-Ghaeltacht was already English speaking at the community level, with most of the Irish speakers being in the older age group. Indeed, the same was also true even in the case of some of the Fíor-Ghaeltacht regions. The Commission also chose to ignore the level of geographical fragmentation in terms of Irish language use in the Fíor-Ghaeltacht and the Breac-Ghaeltacht districts, portraying the overall situation as being more homogeneous than it actually was. This, Betts has argued, was a conscious decision, the rationale being that by including areas where Irish was fading or had already disappeared, opportunities might arise to enable the "creep back" of the language.[48]

Regarding administrative and economic matters, the report argued that Irish speakers should be able to interact with state agencies through the medium of Irish, and that linguistically competent public servants should receive financial incentives to attract them to work in the Gaeltacht. The State, however, did not act on this suggestion, and even though competence in Irish was an entry requirement for admission to the public service, Dáil deputies representing Gaeltacht regions complained repeatedly that public servants, such as local pension officers, lacked fluency in Irish.

The Gaeltacht Commission clearly identified the concurrence of poverty with the capacity to speak Irish, and that the Irish speakers were the poorest inhabitants of these geographical regions. On this, it stated that

> Even in poor districts, it will be generally found that the persons on the poorest holdings are the Irish speakers. The outstanding fact is that the Irish speaking population is insecurely rooted in the land-the only stable basis of livelihood possessed by this population.[49]

The overall conclusion arrived at was that there would be no improvement of the economic condition of the Gaeltacht until the people living there possessed more viable land holdings. It drew special attention to this matter in relation to what it termed "special areas" in Gaeltacht districts in counties Donegal Galway, stating:

> The problem which exists in these areas is, from the point of view of congestion, very serious-so serious in fact that, hitherto, every responsible authority has hesitated to approach it. From the point of view of the language it is vital. The largest homogenous populations of Irish speakers in the country are involved in this problem, in the counties of Donegal and

> Galway. These populations have been almost entirely excluded, in the past, from the operation of economic land resettlement and migration.[50]

It was recommended that the State should acquire some large farms in eastern counties which could be divided into smaller, viable holdings, on which Irish-speaking families could be settled. Again, however, the government refused to act on this proposal, arguing that it would be neither practicable nor equitable to differentiate between Irish-speaking and non-Irish-speaking families in the resettlement of land. In decreeing along these lines, consideration of the inequitable situation that existed in the first place for Gaeltacht families was not forthcoming, although as later chapters indicate, a later government undertook some developments along the proposed lines.

It was of the view, however, that the establishment of new manufacturing industries or tourism would diminish the prominence of Irish, as workers coming into the Gaeltacht would not have the language, and the English-based terminology of the workplace would prevail. The conservative fiscal policy of the government of the day, overseen by Ernest Blythe, the Minister for Finance and an Irish language enthusiast, assured there would be no major financial investment of any major type in the Gaeltacht. Indeed, it was not until 1952, with the passing of the *Undeveloped Areas Act*,[51] that the State initiated regional economic policies to address the spatial variations in economic development.

In the sphere of education, the Commission criticised the inadequacy of primary school education in the medium of Irish across the country and the general lack of secondary school education in either English or Irish. Members drew attention to the great need at all levels of the education system for teachers who were qualified to teach through the medium of Irish. To address the shortage of teachers competent in the language, it recommended, as noted already, the establishment of seven special secondary-schools, entitled preparatory colleges, where native Irish language speakers could be enrolled and encouraged to become primary school teachers.

The government, in its White Paper on the report of the Commission, baulked at a proposal that teachers be relocated to positions outside of the Gaeltacht if, within three years, they did not learn the Irish language and become skilled in using it in the teaching of all subjects on the curriculum. It is reasonable to assume it adopted this position out of fear of opposition from the Catholic bishops and the local clergy who, in most cases, were the school managers. They, it was, who appointed the teachers, and they took a dim view of any attempt to encroach on their power.

Specifically in relation to secondary school education, the Commission on the Gaeltacht recommended that the State make provision at this level in each of the Gaeltacht regions. Again, however, the government held back. In its "white paper", it stated:

> The fact that the majority of the parents in the Irish-speaking districts consider it necessary that their children should earn their livelihood and supplement the family income from the age of 12 years onwards has been one of the difficulties that has had to be surmounted in compelling them to send their children to the primary schools up to the age of 14 years. The proportion of such parents who would be willing to allow their children over primary age to attend any type of school which does not produce immediate wage-earning results, would, therefore, be so small that the establishment of Day Secondary Schools would not produce results commensurate with the cost.[52]

One can again assume that this statement reflected, to some extent, the new State's unwillingness to draw the ire of the Catholic bishops, the regular clergy and the religious orders, who jealously guarded their right to provide secondary education. While on the one hand they insisted they had the right to receive State financial assistance in this provision, they also sought to restrict access to education lest they might generate graduates interested in more than realising the Church's aim of providing future religious and a loyal middle class. Thus, it was easier for the State to lay the blame for the under provision of secondary schooling in the Gaeltacht with the parents, rather than adopt a view that it had a major role to play itself in ensuring educational opportunity for all. To a certain extent, this was also the case in relation to large sections of English-speaking Ireland, even though it was not expressed as explicitly. It was to take until the mid-to-late 1960s, for State policy to change radically and for the provision of free second-level education for all throughout the nation to follow shortly afterwards.

Following the establishment of the Irish Free State, the philosophical underpinnings of the Gaelic League which had promoted bilingualism and the regeneration of Irish in the Gaeltacht were quickly forgotten. The prize of creating an Irish-speaking country, where the national identity of the people would be bound up in their language and traditions, and all things English were diminished, proved too alluring. The reality that English was the dominant language of the people, and that the usage of Irish even in the Gaeltacht and Breac-Ghaeltacht regions was declining, failed to be appreciated. The new state initiated an aggressive policy of compulsory immersion Irish education in all schools across the nation, despite the fact that insufficient numbers of teachers were competent in the language, and fewer still were qualified to teach through the medium of Irish. While teachers undertook intensive language courses, at their own cost and during their holiday periods, their demands for a more staggered approach to the implementation of the policy in schools had little impact on the government. The absolute belief that schools that they believed had been the dominant tool in killing the language in the nineteenth century could now single-handedly revitalise the language, permeated the thinking within the government. Consumed with the move to gaelicise all national schools, little attention was paid to the Irish-speaking districts. The poverty of the Gaeltacht regions, and the necessity of the young people to emigrate to find employment, contributed to the continuing decline in Irish speakers in these areas. The romantic view of these remote and barren areas where the people were to be the preservers of the language, where there was little access to secondary education or any form of employment other than labouring on the land, persisted and there was no attempt to bring much-needed investment to these regions.

Notes

1. *Irish School Weekly*, 16 December 1922, Vol. 81, p. 1169.
2. *Dáil Éireann* Debates, Vol. IX, Col. 632 (5 March 1923).
3. M. Tierney. *Education in a Free Ireland* (Dublin: Martin Lester, 1919), p. 245.
4. M. Collins. *The Path to Freedom* (Dublin: Talbot Press, 1922).
5. R. Fullerton. 'The Place of Irish in Ireland's Education', *Irish Educational Review*, V, 1911–12, pp. 456–466; D. Chenevix French. *What Is the Use of Reviving Irish* (Dublin: Maunsel, 1909), p. 26; Rev. P. E. Kavanagh. 'The History of Ireland', *Catholic Bulletin*, Vol. I, February 1911, p. 72.
6. D. H. Akenson. *A Mirror to Kathleen's Face* (Montreal: McGill Oueen's University Press, 1975), pp. 36–37.
7. Cúntas na hÁrd Fheise, 1918, Gaelic League, pp. 5–6 (Translated from Irish).

8. Cúntas na hÁrd Fheise, 1919, Gaelic League, pp. 12–13 (Translated from Irish).
9. *Irish School Weekly*, Vol. 69, No. 1, 14 August 1920, p. 2.
10. *Irish School Weekly*, Vol. 69, No. 5, 11 September 1920, p. 94.
11. In August 1920, it reported that the only place where progress was being made was in Cork City. See Árd Fheis Conradh na Gaeilge, 1920, pp. 15–16.
12. *Irish School Weekly*, Vol. LXIX, No. 3, 28 August 1920, p. 46.
13. T. J. O'Connell. *One Hundred Years of Progress* (Dublin: Irish National Teachers' Organisation, 1966), p. 342.
14. *Irish School Weekly*, Vol. 68, No. 37, 24 April 1920, p. 884.
15. The following representatives attended: Pronsías Ó Fathaigh, Aireacht An Oideachais (Department of Education); Einrí Ó Fríghil, General Council of County Councils; Máire Ní Chinnéide, Seán Ó Muirthile, Gaelic League; Thomas Farren, National Labour Executive; Tomás de Búrc, Association of Secondary Teachers; John Harbison, D. C. Maher, Cormac Breathnach, Eamonn Mansfield and T. J. O'Connell, I. N. T. O. Máire Ní Chinnéide was elected chairman and T. J. O'Connell honorary secretary of the Conference.
16. T. J. O'Connell. *One Hundred Years of Progress*, p. 346.
17. *Irish School Weekly*, Vol. LXXI, No. I, 7 January 1922, pp. 2–4.
18. National Programme Conference. *National Programme of Primary Instruction* (Dublin: Browne and Nolan, 1922).
19. Under the heading of Language for Junior Infants, the students were "to be taught to speak audibly and distinctly by means of conversation, object and picture lessons, story telling and recitation". The Senior Infants requirement was as follows: "To be taught to speak audibly and distinctly and to express themselves clearly by means of conversation, picture and nature lessons, and to read from blackboard short sentences formed by the pupils in the course of such lessons, story telling and recitation". Language here refers to the Irish language.
20. No specification was set out in the Programme about the allotment of time to the various subjects.
21. T. J. Corcoran. 'How the Irish Language Can Be Revived', *The Irish Monthly*, June 1923, pp. 26–27.
22. Ibid., pp. 29–30.
23. Since the Provisional Government was not recognised by those opposed to the Treaty, a pro-Treaty *Dáil Éireann* was maintained. Fionán Lynch was Minister for Education for the Provisional Government and Michael Hayes was the *Dáil*'s Minister for Education. See J. Coolahan. *The ASTI and Post-Primary Education in Ireland 1909–1984* (Dublin: Cumann na Meanmhúinteóiri, 1984), p. 405, n. 20. Here, it is stated that both

ministers reached a working agreement. Lynch had responsibility for national education and Hayes had responsibility for secondary education. However, this arrangement ended when the Civil War broke out after the June election. In September 1922, when the Provisional Government elected in June met for the first time, Eoin MacNeill was appointed Minister for Education.

24. *Irish School Weekly*, Vol. 71, No. 9, 4 March 1922, p. 194.
25. Ibid.
26. Ibid., Vol. 71, No. 9, 4 March 1922, p. 204.
27. T. J. O'Connell. *One Hundred Years of Progress*, p. 352.
28. Department of Education. *Report of the Department of Education for the School Year 1924–25* (Dublin: Stationery Office, 1926), p. 34.
29. Ibid.
30. *Irish School Weekly*, Vol. 71, No. 19, 13 May 1922, p. 453.
31. *Irish School Weekly*, Vol. 71, Nos. 27/28, 8 & 15 July 1922, p. 635.
32. Ibid., Vol. 71, No. 33, 26 August 1922, p. 779.
33. The pass rate was generally in the region of 25 per cent.
34. Ibid., Vol. 74, No. 50, 15 December 1923, p. 131.
35. Ibid., Vol. 74, No. 33, 18 August 1923, p. 792.
36. *Dáil Éireann* Debates. Vol. 12, Col. 815 (11 June 1925). This account is a shorter version of that which I have provided in Tom. A. O'Donoghue. *The Catholic Church and the Secondary School Curriculum in Ireland, 1922–62* (New York: Peter Lang, 1999), pp. 71–72.
37. J. Coolahan. *Irish Education—History and Structure*, p. 76.
38. Department of Education. *Report of the Department of Education for the School Year 1925–26–27*, pp. 189–190.
39. National Programme Conference. *Report and Programme* (Dublin: Stationery Office, 1926), p. 27.
40. Ibid.
41. Ibid., p. 11.
42. Ibid., p. 22.
43. Also, the lightening of requirements in mathematics, history and geography, and rural science was permissible for certain sizes of schools as a compulsory subject.
44. This is discussed in T. J. O'Connell. *One Hundred Years of Progress*, p. 361.
45. For a detailed account of the activities of the Cumann na nGaedheal government of 1922–32 aimed at promoting the notion of 'a Gaelic Ireland' see J. Knirck. *Afterimage of the Revolution: Cumann na nGaedheal and Irish Politics, 1922–1932* (Madison: University of Wisconsin Press, 2014).
46. For a full exposition on the Commission, see J. Walsh. *Díchoimisiúnú Teanga: Coimisiún na Gaeltachta 1926* (Dublin: Cois Life, 2002).

47. R. Hindley. *The Death of the Irish Language: A Qualified Obituary* (London: Routledge, 1990)
48. C. Betts. 'Irish: Scarce Better Off the Under the British'. In C. Betts (Ed.). *Culture in Crisis: The Future of the Welsh Language* (Upton Wirral: Ffynnon Press, 1957), pp. 226–235.
49. Coimisiún na Gaeltachta. *Coimisiún na Gaeltachta Report* (Dublin: The Stationery Office, 1925).
50. Ibid.
51. R. W. G. Carter, B. Carter, and A. J. Parker (Eds.). *Ireland: Contemporary Perspectives on a Land and Its People* (Oxford: Routledge, 1989).
52. Government of Ireland (1928). *Statement of Government Policy on Recommendations of the Gaeltacht Commission* (Dublin: The Stationery Office, 1925), n.p.

CHAPTER 5

Schooling of Students from the Gaeltacht and the National Policy of "Saving the Language" Through All Primary Schools, 1922–1965

Introduction

As already pointed out in Chapter 3, the Department of Education in the Irish Free State came into existence on 8 June 1924.[1] This chapter is concerned primarily with schooling in the Gaeltacht between then and 1965. Each of the three main types of schooling that existed in Ireland over the period, namely primary schools, secondary schools, and vocational schools, is detailed, both in relation to the situation in the country as a whole and also specifically in relation to the Gaeltacht. Further, within the account on secondary schooling, two particular types of secondary schools are given special consideration. The first of these types is what were known as "preparatory colleges"; these were established in order to provide at least half of the intake of about 150 students per year to the primary school teacher training colleges, with the other half to be filled by open competition. The second type of school belonged to a group termed "lay secondary schools".

In reading the chapter, it is helpful to keep in mind that the vast majority of schools were Catholic; in 1965, of the 4848 primary schools in the State, 4400 were Catholic schools and 444 were Protestant schools. Furthermore, of the 4848 Catholic primary schools, 3789 were under the management of local parish priests, and the remaining 615 were under the management of religious orders of nuns and brothers.[2] Within the 615 religious-order-managed schools, 2948 of the teachers

T. O'Donoghue and T. O'Doherty, *Irish Speakers and Schooling in the Gaeltacht, 1900 to the Present*,
https://doi.org/10.1007/978-3-030-26021-7_5

employed were brothers and nuns, and 1990 were laypeople. However, as the great majority of religious taught in the cities and towns, their presence in schools in the Gaeltacht, other than in the case of those Catholic preparatory colleges located there, was almost, though not totally, non-existent.

Primary Schooling

The new programme prescribed in the early 1920s for primary schools throughout the Irish Free State differed greatly from the child-centred programme in operation during the last two decades of British rule.[3] As indicated in the previous chapter, the range of subjects was restricted to Irish, English, mathematics, history, geography, singing, drill and needlework (for girls), and the content and focus were very Ireland-centred. Furthermore, all were to be taught Irish for one hour per day and it was compulsory to use the language as the medium of instruction in infant classes.

In 1926, some changes, as also noted in previous chapters, were made to the new programme. These included the introduction of higher and lower course in the Irish and English languages, with the particular course for a school depending on the language ability of the teachers and students. Some teaching of English in infant classes could also take place from now onwards. Furthermore, from 1934, all schools had to adopt the higher course in Irish, and the lower course in English was for all students outside of infant classes. In addition, English was no longer to be taught in infant classes in schools where there was a teacher competent to both teach through Irish and use the language as a medium of instruction. Overall also, for all students, from infants' level to sixth class, the general view was that they needed to be filled with knowledge and moulded by strict discipline and the amassing of vast quantities of facts.[4]

The Irish language gained a new status in the 1937 Irish Constitution, with Article 8.1 declaring it to be the first official language.[5] Nevertheless, by now the nature and extent of the emphasis on promoting the language was leading to a backlash by many, with primary school teachers in particular resenting the way in which it was imposed in a top-down manner. In 1941, this became apparent on the publication of the results of research on teaching through the medium of Irish conducted by the INTO which,[6] it will be recalled, represented primary school teachers. Against a background of challenging economic circumstances nationally, teachers were also experiencing low morale generally, following a cut in primary school teachers' salaries by 10 per cent in 1923, the introduction of a "marriage ban" on female teachers in 1934 and the introduction of enforced early retirement for female teachers in 1938. In 1946, discontent amongst primary school teachers reached a new height when dissatisfaction with salary levels led to a strike by INTO members.[7]

Primary Schooling for Students in the Gaeltacht

The annual reports of the Department of Education for the period under consideration indicate that, at any one time, only about half of the schools in the Gaeltacht were offering instruction through the medium of Irish, with the exception of the subject entitled "English", that in all schools was taught through the medium of English. In 1927–28, the Department noted that only in the Donegal Gaeltacht was Irish the sole teaching medium in all Gaeltacht schools.[8] Relating to here also, it was further noted that the great majority of students left school on reaching 14 years of age. The Department posed economic reasons for this situation, drawing particular attention to the matter of students being required for service at home. Equally, it was pointed out there were hardly any "wage-earning occupations for boys and girls"[9] available locally that could have acted to encourage them to stay on longer at school if it had been possible to do so in order to acquire work-related qualifications.

An extensive report was published the following year (1928–29), on what was termed "most of the Connaught Gaeltacht",[10] a district that included those portions of the Gaeltacht in County Galway and in County Mayo. This report stated that while a number of teachers had "been working earnestly at Irish, and their efforts have been successful", there were "many others of whom this could not be said".[11] It went on as follows:

> Some good work was accomplished during the early years, but since 1926 there has been a perceptible weakening. In schools where the teachers knew no Irish one could not expect to find the children speaking Irish at present, but in the schools where the teachers were able to speak Irish, and teach it, the pupils should certainly be Irish-speaking by now. Instead of such being the case, however, English and Irish have an equal footing in

> the majority of our schools. The lower classes are weakest in this respect, particularly the Infants' standards.[12]

The following year, a similar report appeared, stating

> The progress so far in the use of Irish as a teaching medium in the Galltacht [English vernacular] schools has been slow. Conditions are, of course, much better in the Gaeltacht, but even there a considerable proportion of the pupils, up to 50% in some areas, are still being taught either wholly or partly through English in the standards above the Infant Classes. In the Gaeltacht area, as defined in the Gaeltacht Commission Report, only 41% of the schools (175 out of 422) are doing all their work through Irish, and in the Breac-Ghaeltacht, as defined in the Commission Report, in which there are 756 schools, only 8 schools are doing all their work through Irish. The position with regard to the use of Irish as a teaching medium is therefore no better in the Breac-Ghaeltacht than in the purely English speaking areas, in which, in 45 schools out of 4,200, all the work is being done through Irish.[13]

Regarding the distribution of schools, it was noted that of the 5378 national schools in the State in 1929–30, 422 were in the Fíor-Ghaeltacht as defined by the Gaeltacht Commission Report of 1925, yet only in 175 of them was all of the work being conducted through Irish.[14] Further, in only eight of the 756 schools in the Breac-Ghaeltacht were teachers conducting their teaching through Irish. Of the remaining 4200 schools outside of the Gaeltacht, only 45 schools conducted their work through Irish.

A sense of urgency appeared in the tone of other sections of the reports mentioned above. This was evident again in the Department of Education's report for the school year 1932–33. Here, it was stated that "the position generally in the Irish-speaking district is unsatisfactory", and that "the language is still receding as a living language in the vast majority of the areas in the Fíor-Ghaeltacht and in all the districts of the Breac-Ghaeltacht".[15] It was also stated that in over two-thirds of the Gaeltacht, Irish "is dying as the home language, owing to the fact that though the older people know Irish they cannot see any economic value in speaking it to the children, whereas the economic value of English is self-evident".[16]

The report of the Department of Education for the school year 1932–33, following the election of a Fíanna Fáil government, also highlighted a view that it was important to do something “to change the attitude of the people so that they would be keen to speak Irish to the children”.[17] “Propaganda”, it went on, “had been tried for over 30 years and failed”. Something therefore was needed, it was argued, that would bring home to every household in the Gaeltacht that

> ... there is a money value in talking Irish to the children, and after full consideration of all the circumstances, it was felt that there was no way in which this could be done except by the payment of a small annual bonus to the parent (or guardian) for each school-going child in the Gaeltacht or Breac-Ghaeltacht who clearly came to school from an Irish-speaking home, and who as a result was able to speak Irish fluently and naturally.[18]

This led to the issuing of a circular early in 1934, to schools in the Gaeltacht that read as follows:

> A bonus of £2 per annum may be paid to the parent or guardian of each child in attendance at a primary school in the Gaeltacht or Breac-Ghaeltacht between the ages of six and fourteen years, where the Department is satisfied that Irish is the language of the child’s home and that the child, in consequence, speaks Irish naturally and fluently. This bonus will be payable in respect of the school year ending 30th June, and regular attendance and satisfactory progress at school throughout the school year will be essential conditions for the award. Subject to the fulfilment of these conditions, the first payment will be in respect of the school year in which the pupil reaches the age of seven years, and the final payment in respect of the school year in which the pupil reaches the age of fourteen years. The bonuses will be paid on the basis of special reports furnished by the Department’s Inspectors, and the first payments will be in respect of the school year ended 30th June, 1934.[19]

Because publishing of reports on the teaching of Irish in the Gaeltacht became rare from now onwards, it is difficult to gauge the success or otherwise of this scheme. At the same time, the few reports issued indicated a slightly more optimistic tone amongst the schools’ inspectors, with the report for 1941–42, stating that while “not all the schools in the Gaeltacht are doing all subjects through Irish, all are doing some”.[20]

Other schemes for primary school students in the Fíor-Ghaeltacht were also introduced. These included the *School Meals (Gaeltacht) Act*, 1930,[21] that resulted in grants being made to Boards of Health, under regulations of the Minister for Local Government and Public Health, for the supply of food to students attending national schools in the Gaeltacht districts in the County Health Districts of Cork, Donegal, Galway, Kerry and Mayo. Another scheme provided transport for some Gaeltacht students to attend primary schools. This was a continuation of a scheme introduced by the pre-Independence administration and in operation since 1908. It provided grants towards the cost of van services for the conveyance of students to primary schools in cases where no such schools were available within a reasonable walking distance of their homes. A similar grant was available for the provision of boat services for the conveyance to schools on the mainland and other islands of children residing on islands where no education facility existed.

The total number of services at various intervals under the schemes noted above which applied primarily though not exclusively to children from the Gaeltacht[22] for various years was, on a county-by county-basis, as follows:

1928–29:
Vans: Cork - 5, Donegal - 2, Kerry - 1, Mayo - 4,
Boats: Donegal - 2, Galway - 4, Mayo - 5.

1942–43:
Vans: Cork - 1, Donegal - 2, Galway - 1, Mayo - 7
Boats: Galway - 4, Mayo – 2.

1952–53:
Vans: Cork- 4, Donegal - 4, Galway - 9, Kerry - 12, Mayo - 12, Waterford - 1
Boats: Donegal - 1, Galway - 3, Mayo – 1.

1962–63:
Vans: Cork - 7, Donegal - 7, Galway - 23, Kerry - 8, Mayo - 18, Waterford - 1
Boats: Galway - 2

Grants were also awarded to cover the cost of boarding fees at schools on the mainland for island children attending school there. In 1933, 14 students were in receipt of these grants.

Scholarships for attendance at secondary school became equally available for students from the Fíor-Ghaeltacht. The annual report of the

Department of Education for 1930–31 gave the following detail on these:

> Scholarships for students from the Fíor-Ghaeltacht ... were initiated in September 1931. These scholarships are open only to children who have been reared in districts where Irish is the home language of the majority of, the people of the area, in whose homes Irish is the language of ordinary use, and who have received their education through the medium of Irish. Particulars of the schemes of Scholarships have been widely published, but their principal features may be summarised as follows: Scholarships in Secondary Schools. Eighteen Scholarships tenable for four, or, where necessary, five years, in an approved secondary school will be awarded annually for candidates from the Fíor-Ghaeltacht. Of these 18 Scholarships, not less than 9 will be awarded to girls and, subject to this restriction, a specified number of the scholarships will be reserved for candidates from each of the principal areas forming the Fíor-Ghaeltacht. In this way, it is intended to overcome the difficulties which children from some of the areas concerned might experience in securing a share of the scholarships, because of the part played by the economic conditions of the area in their earlier education. The competition for the award of the Scholarships will be held at the same time as the Examination for Entrance to the Preparatory Colleges, and the subjects and programme will be the same as for that examination. During the tenure of the Scholarships, the school fees will be paid by the Department, and so that no student may be debarred by his home circumstances from availing of a scholarship, a grant in aid of outfit and travelling expenses will be paid in three portions each year to the candidate, through the conductors of the school. Provision is also made for a grant in aid of expenses of attendance at the examination for each candidate whose answering shows promise, and for a gratuity to the teacher of the school for each successful candidate.[23]

By 1933, 24 students were in receipt of scholarships.[24] Usually, successful candidates were free to choose their school from the Department of Education's approved list of secondary schools, although in the case of girls scholarships were tenable only at schools at which Irish was the dominant medium of instruction and instruction took place in domestic economy and science.

The number of scholarships awarded annually from then onwards to students from the Gaeltacht to attend secondary school continued to be small. For example, in 1942–43, the total number holding them was 64 males and 53 females.[25] By 1952–53, the former number had dropped to 50 and the latter to 38. Indeed, it was not until the beginning of the 1960s that the overall number increased significantly; in 1962–63, the number was 229, 80 scholarships having been offered the previous year and another 80 in that year.

Each year, some students from the Gaeltacht also won scholarships available to all students nationally. At the same time, the number of such students was very small, given how few scholarships were available anyway. Again, it was not until 1962, that there was a considerable increase in the number and value of these nationally available scholarships.[26] This resulted in 5622 students sitting for the examination, compared to the 322 who sat for it in 1961. Furthermore, the total number of scholarships awarded in 1962 was 139, compared to 620 in 1961. During 1962 also, the Department of Education made arrangements for the establishment of a special scheme of post-primary scholarships for students attending island national schools and it awarded 20 such scholarships the following year. These were tenable for five years and were valued at £130 for boys and £120 for girls in the first year and £120 for boys and £110 for girls thereafter.

Secondary Schooling

The new programme for Irish secondary schools introduced in 1924 can be traced back to a Dáil Commission on Secondary Education set up in 1921, to investigate the kind of secondary school education deemed to be desirable for an independent Ireland.[27] This new programme stated that one of the conditions for the recognition of a secondary school was that it should offer instruction in an approved programme in stipulated subjects. For the school year 1924–25, these subjects were Irish or English, a language other than that offered already, and science, or Latin, or Greek, or commerce. Irish became an essential subject from 1927 to 1928 onwards.[28] Over the next 40 years, the curriculum also had to include provision for singing, physical training or games for all, as well as domestic science for girls. The Department of Education introduced two new examinations, the Intermediate Certificate examination (usually taken at 16 years of age) and the Leaving Certificate examination (usually taken at 18 years of age).[29] Examination preparation was dictated by the Department of Education's requirement of a pass in five subjects in order to pass the Intermediate and Leaving Certificate examinations overall. A pass in Irish was compulsory if students were to pass both examinations overall, to pass in the matriculation examination for entry to a college of the National University of Ireland and to pass the examinations for entry to the civil service.

The Catholic bishops were happy to cooperate with the State in using the schools as the prime instrument for restoring Irish as the national language of the country in accordance with the initiatives taken in the 1920s and 1930s. At the same time, they mounted immediate resistance in 1937 to government proposals aimed to intensify the language revival process through the redistribution of portions of time devoted to the teaching of English and the classics in secondary schools to the further teaching of Irish.[30] This resistance, influenced by fear that the proposed change might lead to a reduction in the high level of proficiency in English deemed essential to the missionary role of future priests, religious brothers and nuns, and also to reduced proficiency in Latin, an essential subject for seminarians, was successful.

Data relating to the number of religious teachers in the system at the time are revelatory: there were 2384 religious teachers in secondary schools in the State in 1965.[31] The religious consisted of 1347 nuns, 519 brothers and 518 priests, while amongst the lay teachers, 889 were men and 837 were women. All of these figures relate only to teachers paid by the Department of Education as full-time teachers; the religious orders had many members not trained as teachers, also teaching in their schools in an unpaid capacity, while they employed a small number of untrained laypeople as teachers alongside them, though on low salaries.

Secondary Schooling for Students in the Gaeltacht

As was the case in relation to the primary school curriculum, there was no difference between the secondary school curriculum prescribed for students from the Gaeltacht and that prescribed for those in the rest of the country. Furthermore, the report for the school year 1925–26–27 noted that at that stage there was only one school in "the Gaeltacht proper"[32] (Daingean Uí Chúis [Dingle] Christian Brothers' School), that only one teacher there was able to speak Irish, and no instruction was being given there through Irish. The report went on:

> There has been an improvement [in the situation in the school] this year, and at present a fair amount of the instruction is being given through Irish. It concluded by saying that of the 29 Secondary Schools in the

> semi-Gaeltacht, four used as Irish as the language of instruction for all subjects apart from English, three taught about half of their subjects through Irish, and seven taught a small number of subjects in this manner.[33]

The reference to secondary schools in what was termed "the semi-Gaeltacht" is most likely to have related to those located within reasonable travelling distance from the homes of any Gaeltacht students willing and able to attend. These included Caherciveen Christian Brothers School in County Kerry, Dungarvan Christian Brothers School in County Kerry Waterford and Macroom Convent of Mercy Secondary School in County Cork, along with the secondary schools in Galway City. Later establishments were Béal a' Mhuirid Convent of Mercy Secondary School in County Mayo, which was functioning in 1950. In the same year, An Spidéal Convent of Mercy Secondary School was operating in the County Galway Gaeltacht and in 1959 by the Convent of Mercy Secondary School opened in An Cheathrú Rua, in the same district.

The report for the school year 1925-26-27 also stated that a scheme to aid the publishing of books written in Irish for use in secondary schools was underway, that a special committee had met for the first time on the 7 May 1926, and that since then it had held 18 meetings.[34] By this stage, the Department of Education had published eight books and 11 more were with the printers. Amongst this 11 were seven novels, two works of drama, an anthology of poetry and an arithmetic book.

Some despair regarding the promotion of Irish in the secondary schools close to Gaeltacht districts is evident in the report of the Department of Education for 1927–28:

> There is only one secondary school in the Gaeltacht...and the amount of the instruction given in it through the medium of Irish is not considerable. In regard to schools situated in the semi-Gaeltacht, while great advances have been made by the Connacht schools, both in the teaching of the language itself and in the use of Irish as a medium of instruction, the same cannot be said of Munster.[35]

Two years later, during the school year 1930–31, the State introduced a scholarship scheme to enable some secondary school graduates from the Fíor-Ghaeltacht to attend university.[36] These were tenable only at University College Galway (which had a special responsibility for promoting Irish), unless course the student wished to take was not offered there. When first introduced, their value was £110 per annum.

In September 1931, five scholarships were awarded under the latter scheme, with the Ulster, Munster and Connacht Gaeltacht areas being represented amongst the successful candidates. In 1932–33, 13 such scholarships were awarded—9 to males and 4 to females. By 1942–43, the total number held was 20, and by 1952–53, it had increased only to 22.[37] In 1961, the number jumped to 98. This brought the total held to 170. In any one year also, a relatively even breakdown existed between the number of males and the number of females holding scholarships.

The Preparatory Colleges

The scheme drawn up to guide the development of the preparatory colleges stated that they would enable the State to recruit students with a very good proficiency in the Irish language, including students from the Gaeltacht, and give them a secondary school education in which Irish would be the language of instruction.[38] The graduates of the colleges would then go on to train as primary school teachers. The hope was that the standard of spoken and written Irish in the primary schools would improve. It was also envisaged that the teaching staff members of the colleges would be fluent speakers of Irish and also would be competent to teach the secondary school programme up to Leaving Certificate standard through the medium of Irish.

In the Dáil, various objections were raised to the establishment of the colleges. Most prominent amongst these was an expression of fear that primary school pupils would not achieve an appropriate standard of English because of the recruitment of the new type of teacher envisaged. Deputy Gorey of the Farmers' Party was one Dáil deputy who expressed great reservations along such lines. He was sympathetic to the movement aimed at the maintenance and teaching of Irish, but feared that the nature of the newly proposed policy could result in English, "being driven out of Ireland". On this, he went on to state that "the English language means bread and butter to the people of this country and will mean that for future generations in this country ... I do not believe in splendid isolation or in the doctrine of fanatics".[39]

In his agitation, Deputy Gorey, like a number of other Dáil deputies, was giving expression to a common view that because English was the language of business, Irish would come to represent isolationism if given primacy over English in teaching and in the school curriculum. What he favoured was the development of a population that would be equally proficient in both Irish and English.[40] Professor Thrift from Trinity College Dublin, argued along similar lines when speaking out against the establishment of the preparatory colleges. What he sought, he said, was that primary school teachers, like secondary school teachers, would receive a university education of such a nature that they would acquire a broad outlook on life. As with Deputy Gorey, he also held that what was required was the adoption of a bilingual education policy so that proficiency in English would be high and would be equal to that in Irish. An outcome of following such a policy, he argued, was that Ireland would not end up being at the periphery of the world of commerce internationally.[41]

Another very strong advocate of the latter position was Deputy T. J. O'Connell of the Labour Party. His particular concern was that 13 years of age were too young to be making a decision that would bind one to a teaching career. He stated:

> It is proposed to take boys and girls of approximately fourteen and fifteen and put them into institutions or preparatory colleges with a view to training them as teachers. Such a scheme has its advantages of course, but I am not clear that there is not a disadvantage in segregating boys and girls at that age and having them specialise … I think that the lessons and lectures that these boys and girls will get right from the age of fourteen will be in one particular groove, and I do not think that that will tend to the broadening of their views on other matters.[42]

O'Connell then went on to propose an alternative scheme, namely, selecting regular Leaving Certificate graduates to undertake a university-based preparation that would lead to a qualification to teach in primary schools.[43]

The various arguments mounted by opponents, however, did not deter the government. Deputy Mulcahy of the ruling Cumann na nGaedheal party was amongst the most enthusiastic of the voices holding forth that the colleges were important not just because of their role in the language revival movement, but also because of the opportunities they provided for students from the Gaeltacht to become teachers. The experiences he had while conducting work as a member of the Commission on the Gaeltacht had greatly coloured his view. In particular, his observations in the Gaeltacht districts gave him an acute awareness of the economic, social and education deprivation of their populations and he became committed to examining ways to make access to secondary school education available for Gaeltacht children.[44]

From the outset, Professor O'Sullivan, the Minister for Education, made it clear that, upon acceptance of a place in a preparatory college, all students had to give a pledge "that they were going to take up teaching as a career".[45] The State paid for the building and maintenance of the colleges. Those established were as follows: Coláiste Móibhi (Dublin), a co-educational college for Protestant students under Church of Ireland management; Coláiste Mhuire (Galway), a single-sex college for Catholic boys under the management of the Catholic Church; Coláiste Chaoímhín (Dublin), a single-sex college for Catholic boys under the management of the Catholic Church; Coláiste na Múmhan (Co. Cork), a single-sex college for Catholic boys under the management of the Catholic Church and later moved to Coláiste Íosagáin (Co. Cork); Coláiste Íde (Co. Kerry), a single-sex college for Catholic girls under the management of the Catholic Church; Coláiste Éinne (Co. Donegal), a single-sex college for Catholic girls under the management of the Catholic Church; and Coláiste Bhríghde (Co. Donegal), a single-sex college for Catholic girls, also under the management of the Catholic Church. Parents, who could afford to do so, were required to pay a yearly fee of 40 pounds. Students in the colleges all studied religion, following syllabi set by the authorities of the Catholic Church for all Catholic schools in the country and by the Protestant churches for the schools managed by the Church of Ireland.

Places in the colleges were open to those between 13 and 15 years of age. The programme of study for the entrance examination was that laid down for seventh class in the primary schools. Students were examined in Irish, English, arithmetic, history, geography, drawing, nature study, music and needlework (for girls). Applicants had to present themselves for oral and written examinations. Half of the vacancies were reserved for those who obtained 85 per cent or more in the oral Irish entrance examination, and half of those places, in turn, were reserved for native speakers of Irish who also fulfilled the other conditions for entrance.[46]

A college course was of four years' duration, with students spending the first two years studying for the Intermediate Certificate examination and the next two for the Leaving Certificate examination. In June 1930, the first group of students in the colleges sat the Leaving Certificate examination. The academic programme they had pursued had been restricted to Irish, English, mathematics, history, geography and science. Justifying this narrow emphasis, Deputy Ernest Blythe, Minister for Finance and a great supporter of the colleges, stated as follows in the Dáil in 1932:

> The work of giving a full secondary course through Irish was an experimental matter when the preparatory colleges were set up. It was necessary to have a minimum curriculum in the beginning because of the difficulties involved.[47]

Nevertheless, within a year the curriculum was extended to include rural science, drawing and music for all, while domestic science was also introduced for girls and manual instruction was introduced for boys. Furthermore, while Latin was an optional subject in the colleges, most male students studied it. The female colleges introduced art at a later stage.

The importance of paying attention to the health and welfare of all students was emphasised,[48] with each college having a doctor attached to it. He or she paid a weekly visit and sent a general report to the Department of Education on the state of health of the students. Physical education and sport were also encouraged. Furthermore, students' minds were regularly orientated towards teaching throughout their stay in the colleges and all had to engage in practice teaching in the second term of the third year of their course. This took place in the junior classes of the preparatory colleges and in selected primary schools.

There was also an expectation that the strong emphasis on the Irish language in the colleges would be accompanied by practices aimed at ensuring that a Gaelic ethos would prevail in them.[49] Professor O'Sullivan, the Minister for Education, gave public expression to this view when opening Coláiste Chaoímhín in Dublin, the college entrusted to the Irish Christian Brothers. In his speech, which was reported in the national newspapers, he stated that the students "would live in an Irish atmosphere" and that "everything outside would be as Irish as everything inside the classroom".[50]

A study of those who entered the primary school teacher training colleges from two of the preparatory colleges between 1925 and 1955, namely the De La Salle Training College in Waterford and St. Patrick's Training College in Drumcondra in Dublin,[51] demonstrated an increase in the number of students from the Gaeltacht both in the late 1930s and early 1940s. This was followed by a decline in the 1950s.[52] Specifically regarding the De La Salle College, in 1925, of the 115 students enrolled there, the majority came from the south of the country, and particularly from counties Kerry, Cork, Waterford and Kilkenny. Amongst these were a few students from Gaeltacht areas in County Cork, County Kerry and County Donegal, but they did not constitute a significant concentration. By 1935, however, the influence of the preparatory colleges was recognisable. On this, of the 74 students admitted to the training college that year, a substantial number were from Gaeltacht districts,[53] and that 25 of them had attended Coláiste Chaoímhín and 10 had attended Coláiste Éinne.

St. Patrick's Training College recruited 97 students in 1925. They were drawn from a variety of areas throughout the country, with some partial concentration from counties Clare, Donegal, Mayo and Kerry. In 1930, the majority of the students came through the preparatory college system, and especially from Coláiste Chaoímhín. The situation five years later was as follows:

> ... the intake of preparatory college students continued, with over 60 per cent of the students having attended Coláiste Chaoímhín or Coláiste Éinne. The total enrolment in St. Patrick's that year was 59. The spatial distribution of training college students illustrates a concentration of students from the Donegal Gaeltacht, East Mayo and East Galway There were few students from Munster entering the college in 1935 – the majority of them were entering the De La Salle College.[54]

In 1940, the number of students admitted to St. Patrick's College was only 47. This was due to the government of the day deeming there was a surplus of primary school teachers in the country. Of the 47 involved, however, 46 were from Coláiste Chaoímhín, Coláiste Éinne and Coláiste na Múmhan. Furthermore, 15 of the 46 came from the Gaeltacht districts along the Dingle Peninsula, others from the Connemara Gaeltacht west of Galway city, and others yet again from Gaeltacht districts in County Donegal. This situation "marked for St. Patrick's the greatest concentration of students from the Gaeltacht heartland, and amply reveals the success of the Gaelicisation at its height".

By the early 1950s, demand for primary school teachers across the country rose again following a post-Second World War-war baby boom in Ireland. St. Patrick's College was now required to increase its student intake. Of the 80 students admitted there in 1950, 41 came from the preparatory colleges and an open competition determined who the remainder of the entrants were. Again, the geographical spread of new students revealed an over-representation of students from the western seaboard, including from Gaeltacht districts. On the other hand, while 131 new students were recruited in 1955, only 37 of this number were entering from the preparatory colleges.

Taking stock of the situation specifically in relation to the overall proportion of students from the Gaeltacht districts who had entered the preparatory colleges from 1926 to the mid-1950s, Johnson concluded as follows:

> Young boys and girls from the Gaeltacht grasped at the economic and educational opportunity the policy of language revival provided. This is not surprising given the limited possibilities for many Gaeltacht dwellers. The opportunity eliminated for a few the inevitability of the emigrant ship and instead made them part of the cultural policy of the state. Notwithstanding that, this was overall a small contribution by the state to tackling the socio-economic problems of the Gaeltacht. By giving priority to educational policy over regional socio-economic objectives, the government, ironically, pursued a national cultural vision at the expense of an effective socio-economic policy that might have ensured the preservation and extension of the Gaeltacht as a viable cultural region.[55]

The education arguments against the scheme also continued to mount. Back in 1944, even General Mulcahy, the Dáil member who probably more than any other had supported the foundation of the preparatory colleges in 1926, was finding fault with what he characterised as their discriminatory nature of recruitment because of the preference given to applicants from the Gaeltacht.[56] Other members of the Dáil supported him. Consequently, in 1958, the system of recruitment for the teacher training colleges was changed.

Henceforth, the colleges were to use results in the Leaving Certificate examination to shortlist potential students, regardless of whether one had attended a preparatory college or a "regular" secondary school. In order of merit, eligible candidates then had to sit for an oral examination in Irish and English, as well as an interview to seek to determine their suitability for teaching.[57] As a result, the preparatory colleges lost the level of influence they had held in relation to entrance to the teacher training colleges.

In 1960, the government decided to close the colleges. The argument put forward by Dr. Patrick Hillery, the Minister for Education, was that requiring a student to take a pledge to take up teaching at such a young age was unfair on parents, who had to pay back the costs involved in sending his or her child to a college if one decided not to become a teacher.[58] He also declared that students were not old enough on selection. The following year the government ordered the closure of the six Catholic colleges. Colaiste Móibhí, the Protestant college, remained open as a preparatory college until 1968, in order to continue to assist the Church of Ireland primary school teacher training college in recruiting students with a proficiency in Irish of a standard required for teacher preparation.[59]

The Lay Secondary Schools in the Gaeltacht

The majority of secondary schools in Ireland over the last 200 years have been Catholic schools run by religious orders and by diocesan priests. Laypeople, however, established small clusters of secondary schools in various parts of Ireland from the early 1900s. Some authorities consider them to have been a revival both of the earlier tradition of the hedge schools and of the classical or "superior" schools that came into existence at the time of the Penal Laws (1700–1829).[60] The hedge schools had decreased in number following the foundation of the national schools in 1831. Nevertheless, some continued to exist up to the passing of the Intermediate Education Act of 1878, and even for a while afterwards.[61] Developments set in train under the Act of 1878 led to a surge in the growth and management of religious-run Catholic secondary schools such that, by the time of national independence in 1922, only a very limited number of lay-managed hedge schools and "superior schools" survived. Yet, within 13 years, a number of new small lay secondary schools existed. While the initial impetus was slow, a momentum developed gradually, albeit in a piecemeal rather than in a planned fashion, that led to the development of more of them.

While all of the lay secondary schools in the State in 1922 were officially classified as being non-denominational, amongst them were a few small schools that had been established by people associated with one or other of the Protestant denominations in the country, but which were not officially connected to any of them. The great majority of the lay schools, however, were, de facto, Catholic schools.[62] This was because their lay founders were "conventional" Catholics who were committed to transmitting the religious culture in which they themselves had grown up. To this end, their schools were, in the main, infused with a religious ethos, with Catholic religious emblems displayed on the classroom walls, Catholic doctrine taught during religious education classes and prayers said at various times throughout the school day. At the same time, parents of a small number of students from other religious denominations occasionally enrolled their children in some of the lay secondary schools, and ministers of their own religion provided religious instruction either there or out of school.

Overall, growth up to 1962 was as follows: there were 17 lay secondary schools in 1939–40; by 1955–56, the number had reached 48; and by 1961–62, it had reached 57.[63] The national Department of Education gave official recognition to these schools for payment of the same capitation grants for each pupil enrolled as were paid to the authorities of all secondary schools in the nation. Equally, qualified teachers were eligible for the payment of an incremental salary. No secondary schools, however, whether run by the churches or by laypeople, were in receipt of State finances for buying premises, for building works or for maintenance. Accordingly, while those who established the lay schools were able to provide for themselves, they were, by-and-large, not engaged in a very profitable venture.

The permission of the Department of Education was required for the establishment of lay schools, just as it was for the establishment of all other publically funded schools. Suitable premises with proper equipment, lighting and heating had to be available, staff had to possess officially prescribed academic and teacher preparation qualifications, and in the first year of a school's existence, it had to have a minimum of 12 pupils. Furthermore, one had to make a convincing case that there was a distinct need for a school in the district in which it was to be located.

The foundation of the lay secondary schools was not driven by a homogenous group of people who shared a set of common aims. Rather, their founders constituted a diverse group, some of whom were committed to teaching as a vocation, having been inspired by parents who were, or had been, dedicated schoolteachers. Awareness that establishing a school might provide them with the opportunity to invest their small savings, inheritances or financial support provided by their families, in an enterprise that had the possibility of providing them with a steady income, was a motivating force for others. Making such an investment was a particularly attractive venture for experienced teachers who had gained employment for a number of years, often only on a year-by-year basis, in religious-run schools and, even then, only by moving around the country from school to school.

In a small number of cases, another motivating force yet again was a desire to be involved centrally in the nationalist project of the early decades of independent Ireland. Some came to believe they could play a particularly prominent role in helping to revive the Irish language if they ran a school of their own. Amongst them were members of the Gaelic League, while others were active in the Gaelic Athletic Organisation.

In the decades following independence, individuals and groups established five lay secondary schools in Gaeltacht districts: two were in County Mayo, one in County Waterford, one in County Kerry and one in County Cork. The first of the schools established was Scoil Damhnait, which opened in Achill Sound in County Mayo in 1948.[64] It was located in the disused and abandoned terminal building of the Achill railway line, with locally cut turf used as fuel to provide heating. Further, an old courthouse across the road was a classroom for those enrolled in their final year.

One of Mac Suibhne's first initiatives was to purchase a minibus to collect girls and boys every morning from various parts of Achill Island and nearby. Initially, as principal and manager of the school, he found it difficult to retain teachers because of the geographical isolation of Achill. To address the problem, he paid those he employed a sum of money greater than the regular annual school salary.

Mac Suibhne and his teachers taught all subjects through Irish and placed particular emphasis on using the distinctive Achill dialect spoken by the pupils. Eventually, he had a teaching staff of three working alongside himself. After some time, his wife joined them. Initially, she taught singing and established choirs in the school. Later on, she commenced studies for a BA degree and a secondary school teaching qualification through attending lectures at night at University College Galway. Following graduation, she took up a position as a regular secondary school teacher in the school.

The other lay secondary school established in a Gaeltacht district in County Mayo was Scoil Naomh Chomáin in the north-west of the county.[65] This was a sparsely populated and very economically deprived area. A general view amongst the local population was that most young people growing up there would emigrate. The nearest secondary school was in Béal a' Mhuirid, 16 miles away, while the prospect of becoming a boarding school student in the further-distant all-boys' St Muredach's Diocesan College, in Ballina, and in Crossmolina girls convent, was not a realistic option for consideration by most parents in the area, given their limited financial resources.

Irish language activists were, by 1954, drawing attention to government neglect of the physical, economic and social infrastructure of the district. This included the dilapidated road network that served the district in which Scoil Náomh Chomáin came to be established. Associated agitation, it has been argued, created a new consciousness amongst the local community; "Tuigeadh go raibh atmaisféar cruthaithe ina mbéadh bá agus tacaíocht an phobail ar fáil d'aon bheart chun tairbhe nó chun forbartha a bheartófaí do phobal Gaeltachta Ros Dumhach/Ceathrú Thaidhg".[66] ("People sensed that an auspicious atmosphere had been created in which the support and sympathy of the community would be in favour of any action that would benefit the Gaeltacht community of Ros Dumhach and Ceathrú Thaidhg".) Soon, parents were seeking the establishment of a secondary school. On this, they had the support of a Fr. Diamond, the parish priest in the local Corrán Buí parish.

Gael Linn was established in Dublin in 1953, with an aim of fostering and promoting the Irish language as a living language throughout Ireland, and as an expression of identity, both within the Gaeltacht districts and across the nation more widely. In 1959, Mr. Dónal Ó Móráin, chairman of the organisation, and Roibeárd Mac Góráin, the secretary, visited the Ros Dumhach and Ceathrú Thaidhg area to seek the support of both Fr. Diamond and the local Catholic bishop of Killala, Dr. O'Boyle, for the establishment of a secondary school.[67] The eventual agreement was that Fr. Diamond would also be a member of the school organising committee and would teach religion to the students through the medium of Irish. A problem arose, however, because the Bishop, while supporting the school, was not prepared to declare his official approval for its establishment.[68] As a result, the Department of Education would not give it official recognition. Nevertheless, the officers of Gael Linn advertised for a principal teacher to take charge, having inspected the premises proposed as accommodation by the local committee. This was a former Garda Síochána barracks that required some repair work.

A Mr. Bearnárd Ó Dubhthaigh became the first principal of the school. It was co-educational and opened its doors on 6 October

1959, with 40 pupils in attendance. Fr. Diamond continued to give his wholehearted support to the venture, including through raising funds to provide transport for pupils to the school. Gael Linn provided the necessary monies for the payment of teachers and the running of the school, drawing on the funds it was generating nationally through a lottery-type scheme, the aim of which was to raise finance to promote local enterprises that would boost the economy of Gaeltacht areas and create employment for Irish speakers so that they could be encouraged to remain on their landholdings rather than emigrate. This approach to the preservation and promotion of the language was one that contrasted greatly with the more literary attitude to it adopted by other Irish language organisations at the time.

The teachers in Scoil Náomh Chomáin were not in receipt of an incremental salary by the Department of Education, as they were not officially registered. Rather, they had to depend for their livelihood on the fees paid by the pupils, complemented by subsidies from Gael Linn. Dónal Ó Móráin has stated that its funds kept the school going in spite of a lack of support from the local bishop; "Níor ghéill sé dár n-iarratas ar a bheannacht ach bhí sparán Gael-Linn láidir...". (He [Bishop of Killala] did not grant us his blessing [approval] but Gael-Linn had ample funds literally, "a strong purse".)[69]

A number of Gael Linn activists also taught in the school on a temporary basis in order to ensure its survival. One of these, Micheál Ó Séighin, who was a graduate of University College Galway, expressed as follows an awareness he had at the time of what he saw as the problems facing the school: "Dúirt mé go dtiocfainn dhá bhliain. Thairg mé teacht dhá bhliain le cineál 'stability'"[70]; ("I said that I would come for two years. I offered to come for two years to provide some stability".) The eventual outcome of Ó Seighin's arrival at the school to teach for two years was that he became a permanent member of the staff and went on to spend 40 years teaching there, retiring only in 2001.

In his early years at Scoil Náomh Chomáin, Ó Dubhthaigh taught Irish, commerce, mathematics and Latin, all through the medium of Irish. Gael Linn arranged with a Mr. Seán Ó Maoilchaoin, who had a degree in agricultural science, and who worked nearby at Glenamoy agricultural research station, to teach agricultural science to the boys. Chaitlín Bean Uí Ír, whose husband also worked in Glenamoy, taught domestic science to the girls.

Ó Dubhthaigh insisted on using Irish as the language of Scoil Náomh Chomáin and encouraged his pupils to enter for Irish language writing competitions run by magazines and newspapers. Regarding this work, he stated:

> Spreag mé na daltaí le suim a chur i bhfoilsiú na Gaeilge: cuireadh ábhar i gcló uathu in irisí ar nós Inniu, An tUltach, Ar Aghaidh agus An Gael Óg. I 1965, bhain duine dena daltaí an chéad áit amach i gcomórtas scríbhneoireachta Inniu agus ghnóthaigh duine eile craobh na hÉireann i gcomórtas díospóireachta Ghael-Linn.[71]
>
> (I encouraged the pupils to have their writing published: their work was published in magazines such as Inniu, An tUltach, Ar Aghaidh, and An Gael Óg. In 1965 one of the pupils won first prize in the competition in Inniu and another pupil won first prize in the Gael-Linn debating competition.)

He departed the school in 1965 on his appointment as an inspector of technical and vocational school education within the national Department of Education and Máire Ní Dhonnchadha from a Gaeltacht district in Donegal replaced him. Pupil numbers continued to increase, and they reached a peak of 57 in 1968, the year after the introduction of the "free education" scheme nationally.

Those who established a lay secondary school in the Gaeltacht districts of Rinn Ua gCuanach and An Sean-Phobal, in County Waterford, in 1959, were motivated by a desire on the part of some local people in the area, where spoken Irish was still prominent amongst a sizeable proportion of the population, to preserve Irish as the spoken language of the area.[72] Over previous decades, it had gradually disappeared in other parts of the county where once it had been strong, including by the coast at Ardmore, and inland in the Tooranena and Modeligo regions, as well as just over the county boundaries in Slieve Rua, County Kilkenny; in Ballymacoda, County Cork; and in Newcastle, County Tipperary. A fear was that if young people in Ring and Old Parish who sought a secondary school education continued to travel to schools in the relatively nearby towns of Dungarvan and Youghal, Irish as a living language amongst the community might die out. To address the situation, Méanscoil San Niocláis opened its doors on 15 August 1959.

The school project was spearheaded by the influential An Fear Mór or Séamus Mac Eochaidh, who for many years had been manager of

Ring Irish College, and by an tAthair Piaras de Hinderberg, a nationally renowned linguist with a particular interest in the local dialect of Irish. Because of the absence of suitable textbooks in the Irish language to teach such subjects as geography, agricultural science and accountancy, Nioclás Mac Craith, the first principal of the school, and other staff members, wrote and produced their own during after-school hours. The school's authorities also arranged with County Waterford Vocational Education Committee for the supply of teachers who could teach domestic science through the medium of Irish.

Local taxis transported small numbers of pupils from outlying areas, including Ardmore, which was 12 miles distant; Clashmore, which was 15 miles distant; and Aglish, which was 20 miles distant. The hope was that by drawing pupils from such outlying regions the "Ring and Old Parish Gaeltacht" district could be extended to reincorporate areas where spoken Irish had survived up to the late 1940s. Mac Craith and colleagues were also realistic in their approach. They encouraged pupils who did not have fluency in Irish to achieve competence in the language in the early months of their school enrolment through the adoption of a bilingual approach to teaching. On this, they held a view that they should not expect the same level of fluency from students who had not grown up in Rinn Ua gCuanach and An Sean-Phobal and who had not attended the all-Irish medium Gaeltacht primary schools there.

In 1961, Mrs. Síle Mulcahy and her husband, Áidán, established a lay secondary school in Castlegregory in County Kerry.[73] They were both very conscious of the precarious state of the Irish language in the nearby Cloghán district, designated as a Breac-Ghaeltacht at the time. They sought to reverse the state of decline in the spoken language there. They rented Pearse Hall in Castlegregory, for £16 per annum, but had to put up decorations and pictures on the walls each weekend so that it could operate as a dancehall. They struggled with broken floors, broken doors and draughty windows. The problem and the expense associated with acquiring suitable school furniture, however, were solved very early on; the managers of a school in Tipperary Town, which was closing down, gave them their school furniture for free. The local Castlegregory Gaelic Athletic Association also allowed them to use their football pitch.

A minibus transported students to and from school each day, the charge being 2 shillings and 6 pence per week per person to cover costs. They became active participants in such national Gaelic cultural events such as Slógadh and Fleadh Cheól na hÉireann, as well as in regional

Gaelic football and camogie competitions. A school band was established, and céilithe were organised in the nearby and unoccupied Ballyduff National School. When a priest, An tAthair Ó Laochdha, was appointed as a curate to An Clochán, he supplemented the work of the school by conducting an Irish language revival campaign in the community. So persuasive was the effort that the Fine Gael-Labour Party coalition government of the time (1973–77) granted the area recognition as a Ghaeltacht district.

The final lay secondary school to be considered is Meánscoil Mhuire, founded in the Béal Átha'n Ghaorthaidh Gaeltacht in County Cork, in 1959, by Mr. Fionnbarra Ó Murchú.[74] He arranged for minibuses to bring students to school every day from surrounding districts, with the service being subsidised by the Department of the Gaeltacht. One bus transported students from Cill na Martra (Kilnamartyra) and Cúil Aodha (Coolea), while a second bus collected students from areas to the south of Béal Átha'n Ghaorthaidh. Ó Murchú also transported students in his own car from areas close to Bantry.

At this time, the Cork Vocational Education Committee had two vocational schools nearby, one in Béal Átha'n Ghaorthaidh and another close-by in the Baile Mhúirne Gaeltacht district, but because attendance at both was particularly low, their existence did not threaten the viability of Meánscoil Mhuire. Secondary school education through the medium of Irish was also available for boys in Coláiste Íosagáin in Baile Mhúirne. This, however, was a preparatory college and a boarding school. Accordingly, attending it was not possible for most of those of secondary school-going age in the district.

By 1968, Meanscoil Mhuire had a total enrolment of 126 students. They participated in extra-curricular activities, including taking part in Irish language plays written and directed by their teachers. Other cultural activities included entering for, and winning awards in the annual Glór na nGael competitions for the communities and villages promoting the use of the Irish language.

Vocational Education

A separate vocational education system was established in 1924, when the Department of Education took over a variety of technical instruction schemes that up until then had been managed by local statutory committees. State grant-in-aid was given to the 65 technical schools involved, mainly for the provision of evening instruction in the domestic economy, manual instruction, home spinning, lace-sprigging, knitting, commerce and Irish. In the larger towns, there were also trades preparatory schools.

In 1927, the government published a report of a commission on technical education it had established as part of its policy aimed at investigating ways to improve productivity in the Irish economy.[75] This commission included members from Sweden, Switzerland and South Africa. The major recommendation was the improvement of the existing greatly underdeveloped technical education system through the establishment of both "continuation schools" and classes for both full-time and part-time education for students aged 14–16 years. The continuation schools envisaged would be secondary schools with a strong practical bias. This, and a recommendation that they be under the control of local statutory committees, raised the concern of the Catholic Church. A particular fear of the bishops was that the schools might not offer religious instruction. They also feared that some amongst the relatively small number of those likely to attend secondary schools might be enticed to attend technical schools instead.

The passing of the Vocational Education Bill in 1930, provided for the establishment of a system of continuation and technical education, grouped together under the title "vocational education". New vocational education committees (VECs) were empowered to establish and maintain continuation schools,[76] but not before the Minister of Education allayed concerns of the Catholic bishops, by assuring them that the new schools would not be in competition with secondary schools.[77] In accordance with this commitment, permission to sit for the Intermediate and Leaving Certificate examinations was withheld from students enrolled in continuation schools.

When the Minister for Education, Prof. John Marcus O'Sullivan, was discussing the Vocational Education Bill in the Dáil, he announced that the curriculum of the continuation schools would have "a distinctly practical bias".[78] He also made clear that rural science, rural arithmetic, domestic economy, handwork and metalwork would play a very definite part in the schools' programmes. By implication, the post-primary vocational education curriculum was to be clearly different from the curriculum of the secondary schools.

The VECs were also empowered to establish and maintain technical schools and contribute to the expenses of persons seeking a technical education, which was defined as "pertaining to trades, manufactures, commerce, and other industrial pursuits".[79] Further, in 1942, the Catholic Church succeeded in having a statement inserted in new curriculum directives that resulted in religion being a compulsory school subject in continuation schools.[80] The Church was also able to police developments in these schools since it was commonplace for VECs not only to co-opt a priest as a member, but also to elect him as committee chairperson.

Vocational Schooling for Students from the Gaeltacht

In the early years following independence in 1922, no vocational education of any significance was taking place within the Gaeltacht districts around the country. Soon after the establishment of the vocational education system, however, a number of students in County Donegal were being prepared for examinations conducted by the technical education branch of the Department of Education. In the school year 1933–34, they sat for them at Coláiste Bríde in Falcarragh and the McDavitt Institute in Glenties,[81] both of which were in the Gaeltacht.

The number of vocational school buildings erected in a number of Gaeltacht districts expanded steadily over the next three decades. As with vocational schools in small towns and rural areas, they were usually 2–4 teacher schools, with some additional teachers being employed on a part-time basis; those in schools large towns and the cities had significantly larger teaching teams. The various schools and the years of opening were recorded as follows, in nearly all cases under the English form of their names:

1933–34:
Carraroe, Co. Galway
Rosmuc, Co. Galway
Cashel (Achill), Co Mayo
Dingle, Co. Kerry

1934–35:
Annagry, Co. Donegal
Murreagh, Co. Kerry
Dingle, Co. Kerry

1938–39:
Ballingeary, Co. Cork

1935–36:
Loughanure, Co. Donegal

1949–50:
Ballyvourney, Co. Cork

1951–52:
Dungloe, Co. Donegal

1953–54:
Kilronan, Inis Mór, Co. Galway

1954–55:
Cnoc na hAille, Indreabhán, Co. Galway

1955–56:
Eachleim, Co. Mayo

1959–60:
Gortahork, Co. Donegal

1963–64:
Gweesaila, Co. Donegal
Gorumna Island, Co. Galway

By the school year 1945–46, there were also schools for students in the Gaeltacht in schools recoded under the titles of Carndonagh, County Donegal; Carrigaholt, County Clare; Loch an Inbhir, County Galway; and Magheraroarty, County Donegal.

By 1967, a vocational school was operating in Baile Ghib, one of the small villages in County Meath that obtained Gaeltacht status in that same year. There were also vocational schools in a number of towns with Gaeltacht hinterlands. These towns included Dungarvan, County Waterford (1934), Béal a' Mhuirid, County Mayo (1933), Kilrush, County Clare (1934), and Waterville, County Kerry (1934).

The vocational education section of the national Department of Education focused from the early years of the new state on what in its report for 1925-26-27 was termed the "problem of training instructors competent to give instruction through the medium of Irish to meet the requirements of the Gaeltacht".[82] Over the next few years, attention was given to addressing this matter. In 1931, for example, special courses of instruction were established at Waterford Technical Institute in Waterford City, to train competent manual instructors to carry out their duties through the medium of Irish (the term "instructor" was preferred over that of "teacher".) Each of the 23 teachers who passed the final examinations of the course gained employment almost immediately in vocational education schemes. The course was run again in

October 1932, as more employment for instructors was available than had been anticipated. At the same time, it was recognised that, overall, there was still a lack of instructors with an appropriate knowledge of the Irish language. The argument made was that because skill in a trade or craft formed a very important factor in the selection of candidates, Irish speakers "resident for the most part in areas in which a high degree of craftsmanship could not be obtained in the ordinary way".[83] A decision then taken was to modify the conditions of admission to training and develop a new course that would "provide a sufficiency of instructors for the Gaeltacht".[84]

The Department also set about "improving the general standard of instruction in Irish at the Irish Training School of Domestic Economy"[85] located at Kilmacud, Stillorgan, Co. Dublin. This school was under its direct control, and one-third of the places for new entrants were reserved for candidates with a good oral knowledge of Irish. In 1933, of the 11 successful candidates who gained admission to the College's three-year residential diploma course, three were from the Gaeltacht, and most of those who graduated were qualified to teach through the medium of Irish as well as English.[86]

In the Department of Education's report for 1935–36, developments at the Killarney School of Housewifery were outlined as follows:

> The object of this School is to provide a systematic training in cookery, housemaids' and parlourmaids' work, needlework and laundry- work, such as to fit the students for domestic service or the care of a home. Certificates of a satisfactory standard of attainment are issued on the completion of the full course of training, which occupies twelve months. There is accommodation for twenty-one students. Admission is now confined to girls who are fluent speakers of Irish (the majority of the places being filled by girls from the Gaeltacht). Seventeen students are at present following the course. Instruction is given through the medium of Irish, and those who satisfactorily complete the course of training are placed as far as possible in Irish-speaking households, principally in Dublin.[87]

A similar development, commenced in 1936, resulted in the Department of Education offering 10 scholarships to girls from the Gaeltacht to enable them to train as children's nurses. To be eligible to apply for them, native speakers of Irish had to be between the ages of 18 and 25; success was determined on the basis of one's results in a written and oral test in Irish based on the sixth standard programme for the national schools.

In the first year of the scheme, 10 scholarships were awarded, four going to girls from County Galway, two to girls from County Donegal, two to girls from County Kerry and one each to girls from County Mayo and County Cork.[88] These scholarships entitled the holders to free accommodation and education while enrolled in the 18 months course at St. Patrick's Infant Hospital and Nursery College, Temple Hill, Blackrock, County Dublin. They also received a grant of £20 towards the costs of outfits and travelling. The expectation was that they, and girls who would graduate in subsequent years, would eventually go on to take up appointments in the Gaeltacht and in other parts of the country, where they could be influential in spreading the language.

In 1931, the Department of Education issued an explanatory memorandum on continuation education to the VECs located around the country, indicating they should develop a system of education suited to the particular needs of their constituent areas. Instruction given was to be of a general vocational nature, along with some preparation for occupations available to young people living locally. Eleven years later, in 1940, a document entitled Memorandum V.40,[89] endorsed this conception of a continuation school. A common first-year course was prescribed. This consisted of a mix of general literary, business, practical and religious education during a 28-hour school week. The Department of Education also recommended that county borough, urban and rural areas offer separate courses suited to local circumstances. The notion was that each such course would help one to develop manual skill and develop an interest in rural life. Rural science and gardening were also to be taught, to develop pupils' intelligence along with their manual skills. Further, teachers were to teach domestic economy in a manner such that the concern was not just to be with utilitarian considerations. In other words, continuation courses were to have more of an education, as opposed to a purely training, value.

The reports of the Department of Education from the mid-1930s, and through the 1940s, also indicated that quite an amount of detail on various bespoke courses were offered during block teaching periods and in evening classes. These were for both young and older students in the Gaeltacht. In 1935–36, the Department observed a "healthy development of classes in connection with home spinning and dyeing"[90] in technical schools. It went on:

> In Galway, instruction was given entirely in Irish in the Gaeltacht areas, and included instruction in the dyeing and carding of wool and the spinning and knitting of the wool thus dyed. Vegetable dyes only were used and the girls were taught to collect and prepare the raw material from which the dyes were obtained.[91]

The centres at which this took place were Béal a' Mhuirid in the County Mayo Gaeltacht, and at Ros Muc and Ros a' Mhíl in the County Galway Gaeltacht, and the articles made for home-use included socks and gloves. The activity took on some urgency during the Second World War due to a shortage of imported clothing. The VECs in counties Clare, Galway, Leitrim and Roscommon responded by giving instruction in the home crafts of spinning and dyeing. The County Galway Vocational Education Committee went a stage further, purchasing 150 spinning wheels and distributing them in the Connemara Gaeltacht in County Galway, where it set about establishing a hand spinning industry, commencing with 40 students.

A report of the Department of Education published in 1935–36 stated that the County Donegal Vocational Education Committee was taking a very active part in establishing the artificial silk industry into the Donegal Gaeltacht. It also stated that

> A Dublin firm engaged in the trade decided to open a branch factory at Crolly with the assistance of a loan secured under the Trades Loans Act. Employees were required and the Donegal Vocational Education Committee readily made the necessary arrangements for providing the preliminary training necessary to fit young people for the type of factory work required. As a first stage a course was conducted by the committee's engineering instructor to give a group of selected students a training in the use of tools, to enable them to carry out simple repairs and adjustments, and to impart a manual dexterity which would afterwards help them to adapt themselves more readily to the working of actual machines. This course was followed by forty-two students who were divided into two groups. At the termination, three of the best pupils were selected by the factory authorities and sent to England to receive specific training in the manipulation of machines to be used in the factory.[92]

The Donegal Vocational Education Committee agreed to make a grant of 400 pounds available towards the cost of the salary of two key personnel in the factory for one year and towards the cost of class materials for demonstration purposes. The two individuals employed were engaged in training those students who had already followed the short course in engineering in the general techniques of the industry mentioned above. It was made clear also that the intention was "to employ in the factory only those who are native speakers".[93]

A related development took place in County Mayo in 1935–36.[94] This arose out of a decision to establish a toy-making factory under a Gaeltacht scheme conducted by the Department of Lands, in a disused coastguard station at Elly Bay near Béal a' Mhuirid. The County Mayo Vocational Education Committee agreed to cooperate by giving preliminary training to those selected for work in the industry. They employed a teacher competent to give instruction through the medium of Irish and installed the necessary machinery-lathes, band saws, circular saws and carving tools at Béal a' Mhuirid in a newly erected technical school. Very soon, training was taking place with 32 male teenagers drawn from the Elly Bay and Béal a' Mhuirid districts on the manufacture of wooden toys, while they also received an education in general continuation school subjects. County Mayo Vocational Education Committee drew up associated plans to provide training for 32 girls in the manufacture of soft toys.[95]

Two decades later, the authorities at An Cheathrú Rua Vocational School in the County Galway Gaeltacht initiated a similar development. This followed the establishment in 1957, of Gaeltarra Éireann, the Irish state industrial development agency set up specifically for the Gaeltacht. Each year, the school provided training for 12 young women in office work and administration, primarily preparing them for positions in factories around the country. The course was of 2 years duration, entry being by competitive examination, and young women from all Gaeltacht areas attended. Young men from all Gaeltacht areas also took part in an apprenticeship course at Gairmscoil Cholmcille, which was relatively nearby in Na hAile, Indreabhán, and they went on to get positions mostly in design and textile factories.

The Department of Education expressed great satisfaction in observations made by its inspectors and noted in its reports for the school year 1935–36, and on through the 1940s, that in many instances day and evening classes were now taking place exclusively through the medium of Irish in Gaeltacht areas. It drew particular attention to full-time day courses and evening classes at An Cheathrú Rua and Ros Muc in County Galway, at An Árd Mhór in County Waterford and at Charraig a Chabaltaigh in County Clare. Specifically in relation to the latter district, it noted that "a rural day continuation course embracing woodwork, drawing, mathematics, rural science, Irish and organised games was followed successfully throughout the session by sixteen boys", whilst "seventeen girls received a whole-time course in domestic economy, including cookery, laundry, needlework, housewifery, first aid, household accounts, Irish and organised games".[96]

Throughout all of the Gaeltacht districts, and in other areas where there was interest shown by the local population, VECs also put a lot of effort during evening classes into instruction on the production of Irish plays, on promoting debates in Irish and on the preparation of individuals to compete in county feiseanna or national cultural festivals. Such activity took off in earnest following the preparation in 1938–39, of a report by the Technical Branch of the Department of Education on ways to assist the revival of the Irish language through the promotion of associated extra-curricular activities.[97] It was proposed that every vocational education committee in the State should appoint a county director of Irish and that specialist teachers similar to the Gaelic League's timirí taistil, or itinerant teachers, of the pre-independence era, be employed and be given special training in teaching Irish songs, dancing, drama and local history. The proposal was that people be brought together in an environment in which they would use the Irish language in regular conversation. The hope expressed was that this might help in bridge the gap that existed between the learning of Irish in the schools and the use of the language more widely. An outcome of the report was the establishment, in 1941, of the first of several courses to train the timirí, or local organisers, for the task.

The timirí gave encouragement to communities to produce and stage plays in Irish. There was a view that this was helpful in stimulating language usage. Indeed, such work was valued to such an extent that, from 28 June to 22 July 1949, the Department of Education conducted a course in the production of Irish drama, at An Taibhdhearc, the national Irish language theatre of Ireland in Galway, for 19 teachers of Irish employed by VECs. The stated purpose was "to enable teachers, particularly those working in the Gaeltacht or Breac-Ghaeltacht, to foster local interest in Irish drama"[98] and the instruction given was very much of a practical nature. VECs also provided a number of scholarships for students to take part in a month-long course in the

Gaeltacht during the summer months. In 1936, for example, they awarded around 500 such scholarships.[99]

Notes

1. See J. A. Murphy. *Ireland in the Twentieth Century* (Dublin: Gill and Macmillan, 1975).
2. This account is based on that in P. Duffy. *The Lay Teacher* (Dublin: Fallon, 1967).
3. The following account is based on that in Walsh, T. 'Conceptions of Childhood in Ireland in the Twentieth Century: A View from the Primary School Curriculum 1900–1999', *Child Care in Practice*, Vol. 11, No. 2, 2005, pp. 253–269.
4. T. O'Donoghue, J. Harford, and T. O'Doherty. *Teacher Preparation in Ireland: History, Policy and Future Directions* (Bingley, UK: Emerald Publishing, 2017).
5. Article 8.2 The English language is recognised as a second official language. Under Article 8.3, however, provision may be made by law for the exclusive use of either of the said languages for any one or more official purposes, either throughout the State or in any part thereof.
6. Irish National Teachers' Association. *Report of the Committee of Inquiry into Irish as a Teaching Medium* (Dublin: Irish National Teachers' Association, 1941).
7. See T. O'Donoghue, J. Harford, and T. O'Doherty. *Teacher Preparation in Ireland: History, Policy and Future Directions.*
8. Department of Education. *Report of the Department of Education for the School Year 1927–28* (Dublin: The Stationery Office, 1928).
9. Ibid., p. 23.
10. Department of Education. *Report of the Department of Education for the School Year 1928–29* (Dublin: The Stationery Office, 1929), p. 232.
11. Ibid.
12. Ibid.
13. Department of Education. *Report of the Department of Education for the School Year 1929–30* (Dublin: The Stationery Office, 1930), p. 26.
14. Ibid.
15. Department of Education. *Report of the Department of Education for the School Year 1932–33* (Dublin: The Stationery Office, 1933), pp. 35–38.
16. Ibid., p. 37.
17. Department of Education. *Report of the Department of Education for the School Year 1929–30* (Dublin: The Stationery Office, 1930).
18. Ibid.

19. Department of Education. *Report of the Department of Education for the School Year 1934–35* (Dublin: The Stationery Office, 1935), p. 2.
20. Department of Education. *Report of the Department of Education for the School Year 1941–42* (Dublin: The Stationery Office, 1942), p. 83.
21. See http://www.irishstatutebook.ie/eli/1930/act/23/enacted/en/html.
22. The figures outlined below are taken from the annual reports of the Department of Education for the years in question.
23. Department of Education. *Report of the Department of Education for the School Year 1930–31* (Dublin: The Stationery Office, 1931), pp. 39–40.
24. Department of Education. *Report of the Department of Education for the School Year 1933–34* (Dublin: The Stationery Office, 1934), p. 26.
25. Department of Education. *Report of the Department of Education for the School Year 1942–43* (Dublin: The Stationery Office, 1943), p. 19.
26. Department of Education. *Report of the Department of Education for the School Year 1962–63* (Dublin: The Stationery Office, 1963), p. 61.
27. *Irish School Weekly*, 1 October 1921, p. 104. See also *The Times Educational Supplement*, 1 October 1921, p. 434.
28. See Department of Education. *Report of the Council of Education: The Curriculum of the Secondary School* (Dublin: The Stationery Office, 1962).
29. See T. O'Donoghue. *The Catholic Church and the Secondary School Curriculum in Ireland, 1922–1962* (New York: Peter Lang, 1999).
30. Ibid.
31. See P. Duffy. *The Lay Teacher.*
32. Department of Education. *Report of the Department of Education for the School Year 1925–26–27* (Dublin: The Stationery Office, 1927), p. 191.
33. Ibid.
34. Ibid., p. 140.
35. Department of Education. *Report of the Department of Education for the School Year 1927–28* (Dublin: The Stationery Office, 1928), p. 182.
36. Department of Education. *Report of the Department of Education for the School Year 1930–31* (Dublin: The Stationery Office, 1931), pp. 39–40.
37. See Department of Education. *Report of the Department of Education for the School Year 1942–43* (Dublin: The Stationery Office, 1943), p. 40; Department of Education. *Report of the Department of Education for the School Year 1952–53* (Dublin: The Stationery Office, 1953), p. 22.
38. See N. C. Johnson. 'Nation-Building, Language and Education: The Geography of Teacher Recruitment in Ireland, 1925–55', *Political Geography*, Vol. 11, No. 2, 1992, p. 179.
39. *Dáil Éireann Debates.* 1926: 981.
40. Ibid.
41. *Dáil Éireann Debates.* 1926: 989–990.
42. *Dáil Éireann Debates.* 1926: 974–979.

43. Ibid., p. 989.
44. *Dáil Éireann Debates*. 1926: 995.
45. *Dáil Éireann Debates*. 1926: 1003.
46. Department of Education. *Report of the Council of Education on (i) The Function of the Primary School and (ii) The Curriculum of the Primary School* (Dublin: The Stationery Office, 1954), p. 70.
47. *Dáil Éireann Debates*. 1932: 756.
48. A detailed account of life in this college is provided in T. O'Donoghue and J. Harford. *Secondary School Education in Ireland: History, Memories and Life Stories, 1922–1967* (London and New York: Palgrave Macmillan, 2016), pp. 217–221.
49. Ibid.
50. The Christian Brothers. *The Educational Record* (Dublin: The Christian Brothers, 1927), p. 284.
51. N. C. Johnson. 'Nation-Building, Language and Education: The Geography of Teacher Recruitment in Ireland, 1925–55', *Political Geography*, Vol. 11, No. 2, 1992, p. 179.
52. Ibid.
53. Ibid., p. 183.
54. Ibid., p. 184.
55. Ibid., p. 188.
56. *Dáil Éireann Debates*. 1958: 640–641.
57. *Dáil Éireann Debates*. 1944: 272.
58. *Dáil Éireann Debates*. 1960. Cols. 72–73.
59. See V. *Jones. A Gaelic Experiment—The Preparatory System 1926–61 and Coláiste Moibhí* (Dublin: The Woodfield Press, 2006).
60. See T. O'Donoghue and J. Harford. 'Church-State Relations in Irish Education', *Comparative Education Review*, Vol. 55, No. 3, 2011, pp. 316–341.
61. See T. Fahey. 'Catholicism and Industrial Society in Ireland'. In J. H. Goldthorpe and C. T. Whelan (Eds.). *The Development of Industrial Society in Ireland* (Oxford: Oxford University Press, 1994).
62. See J. O'Malley. 'An Account of the Growth of the Lay Schools in Ireland, 1922–70, the Motives of the Lay founders, the Demise of the Lay Schools, and the Impact of Lay Education During That Period'. Paper presented at the History of Education Society Conference, Trinity College Dublin, Dublin, November 2004.
63. See the annual reports of the Department of Education for the years in question.
64. K. Waldron. *Out of the Shadows: Emerging Secondary Schools in the Archdiocese of Tuam* (Barnaderg, Tuam, Co. Galway, 2002), p. 75

65. See J. O'Malley. The Catholic Lay Secondary Schools of Rural Ireland, 1922–75 (Unpublished Ph.D. Thesis, University College Cork, 2011), p. iii.
66. Gael Linn Archive, Dublin. *Aide memoire* written by Roibeárd Mac Góráin (National Secretary of Gael Linn in the early 1950s).
67. Gael Linn archive. Minutes of a meeting of Gael Linn trustees, 12 September 1959, p. 1: 'Bhí curtha in iúl ag an Easpag go raibh sé sásta go rachadh an scoil ar aghaidh ach bhí luaite aige ins an litir go dtí an tAth. Ó Díomáin go bhféadfadh sé fanúint ar an gcoiste scoile agus an bhainisteoireacht a ghlacadh. Ní bheadh an socrú sin sásúil dúinn.' ("The Bishop had informed us that he was happy that the school should go ahead but he had mentioned in his letter to Fr Diamond that he could remain on the school committee and take responsibility for the management. That decision would not have been to our liking".)
68. See S. O'Connor. *A Troubled Sky: Reflections on the Irish Educational Scene 1957–68* (Drumcondra, Dublin: Educational Research Centre, 1968), p. 21. O Connor, in reference to the 'unwritten rule commented "that for many years any lay person seeking to open a secondary school for Catholic students was required to submit evidence that the Catholic bishop of the diocese did not oppose the venture." He also commented that the opening of Canon's school, Sandymount High School in 1947 and the opening of the Gael Linn school 'against the wishes of the bishop of the diocese' ended the monopoly of the Catholic hierarchy. The evidence in the Gael Linn material is that a compromise was reached but that the issue of who controlled the management of the school was not resolved at the time of opening of the school.
69. Quoted in J. O'Malley. 'The Catholic Lay Secondary Schools of Rural Ireland, 1922–75,' p. 229.
70. Ibid., p. 240
71. Ibid.
72. Ibid., p. 241.
73. Ibid., p. 248.
74. Ibid., p. 338.
75. Sáorstát Éireann. *Report of the Commission on Technical Education* (Dublin: Stationery Office, 1927).
76. *Vocational Education Act 1930*. Part 1, Section 4.
77. See S. Ó Buachalla. *Education Policy in Twentieth Century Ireland* (Dublin: Wolfhound Press, 1988).
78. *Dáil Éireann* Debates. Vol. 34, Col. 1743 (14 May 1930).
79. *Vocational Education Act 1930*. Part I, Section 4.
80. Sáorstát Éireann. *Memorandum V.40, 1942. Organisation of Whole-Time Continuation Courses in Borough Urban and County Areas* (Dublin: Department of Education).

81. Department of Education. *Report of the Department of Education for the School Year 1933–34* (Dublin: The Stationery Office, 1934), p. 8.
82. Department of Education. *Report of the Department of Education for the School Year 1925-26-27*, p. 71.
83. Department of Education. *Report of the Department of Education for the School Year 1932–33* (Dublin: The Stationery Office, 1933), p. 71.
84. Ibid.
85. Ibid., p. 84.
86. Ibid.
87. Department of Education. *Report of the Department of Education for the School Year 1935–36* (Dublin: The Stationery Office, 1936), p. 107.
88. Department of Education. *Report of the Department of Education for the School Year 1936–37* (Dublin: The Stationery Office, 1937), p. 95.
89. Sáorstát Éireann. *Memorandum V.40, 1942. Organisation of Whole Time Continuation Courses in Borough Urban and County Areas* (Dublin: Department of Education).
90. Department of Education. *Report of the Department of Education for the School Year 1935–36*, p. 73.
91. Ibid.
92. Ibid., p. 80.
93. Ibid., p. 89.
94. Department of Education. *Report of the Department of Education for the School Year 1935–36*, p. 86.
95. Ibid.
96. Ibid., p. 90.
97. See M. O'Riordan. 'Technical-vocational Education, 1922–52: The Cultural Emphasis', in The Proceedings of the Education Conference held in University College Cork, 24–26 March, 1977, pp. 194–199.
98. Department of Education. *Report of the Department of Education for the School Year 1948–49*, p. 44.
99. Department of Education. *Report of the Department of Education for the School Year 1936*, p. 95.

CHAPTER 6

Marginalised Amongst the Marginalised: An Overview of Schooling in the Gaeltacht Up to the Mid-1960s

Introduction

The previous two chapters detail the developments in relation to schooling in the Gaeltacht from the advent of national independence in 1922, until the middle of the 1960s. These developments are now analysed. To this end, the first section of the chapter considers the provision of schooling in the Gaeltacht in comparison with the provision of schooling nationally. Discussion then turns to a major effort in 1935, to relocate Gaeltacht families to rich farming land outside of the Gaeltacht, and to developments in relation to the education of their children. The chapter closes with an overview of the developments that took place aimed at reviving Irish beyond the Gaeltacht over the period, and particularly in relation to the State harnessing the education system to that end.

The Provision of Schooling in the Gaeltacht in Relation to the Provision of Schooling Throughout the Nation as a Whole

In its consideration of the proposals of the Commission on the Gaeltacht issued in 1926, the State disassociated its deliberations on the survival of the Irish language from the economic conditions prevailing in the Gaeltacht. In other words, while the *Gaeltacht Commission Report* suggested some solutions for the Gaeltacht's economic problems,

T. O'Donoghue and T. O'Doherty, *Irish Speakers and Schooling in the Gaeltacht, 1900 to the Present*,
https://doi.org/10.1007/978-3-030-26021-7_6

the government's "white paper" responses reflected a position that, on the one hand, eulogised the Gaeltacht as the cultural core of the nation, yet, on the other hand, separated considerations on its survival from the economic circumstances prevailing there. Three critical issues, in particular, were not addressed. First, in the 1920s, the State, apart from taking action in the case of one small project, declined to alter landholding arrangements that would specifically favour families from the Gaeltacht by refusing to redistribute land to create viable-sized holdings for them. Secondly, it did not immediately order to provide people in the Gaeltacht with the incentive and confidence to continue using Irish. Thirdly, it refused to take a lead in providing adequate second-level education through Irish in the Gaeltacht. It is to the latter of these issues that the rest of this section of the chapter now turns.

The provision of primary schooling and the nature of the curriculum taught in the primary schools throughout the Gaeltacht during the first four decades following the advent of national independence reflected the situation in relation to primary schooling throughout the country as a whole. There is also no reason to believe that the managers of the primary schools in the Gaeltacht did not follow the general pattern established throughout all of the period under consideration of establishing "secondary tops". The latter were primary schools in which students usually studied a maximum of six core secondary school subjects for a year or two before leaving, although some did proceed to sit for the Intermediate Certificate examination. Throughout most of the period under consideration, the number of "secondary tops" increased and was attended much more by girls than by boys.[1] For example, in 1939–40, the number of secondary tops in the State was 61, with 3627 girls and 259 boys in attendance. By 1956–57, there were 87 secondary tops with 5570 girls and 511 boys in attendance. This development was encouraged by the State as it provided a relatively cheap way of extending the provision of secondary school education without the State becoming directly involved in the building of new secondary schools and having to meet the associated capital expense.

The situation regarding secondary schooling "proper" was very different. While the new independent State glorified the Gaeltacht districts and romanticised about the unbroken cultural linkage between their populations and the Gaelic past, it took very few positive steps to provide education opportunities there at second level in order to bring the situation into line with much of the rest of the country. On this, the Report of the Commission on the Gaeltacht recommended that the State should take the initiative by establishing day secondary schools at 25 centres throughout the Gaeltacht. The only aspect of this implemented, however, was the establishment of some of the preparatory colleges in the Gaeltacht (which only enrolled small numbers, many of whom were not from the Gaeltacht). The Department of Education, seeking not to enter into a domain the churches saw as being their own preserve, preferred to leave the provision of secondary school education to private initiative for reasons of economy and convenience.[2]

The result nationally of the latter policy was that by 1933–34, there were only 32,384 pupils in secondary schools, as opposed to 420,494 pupils attending primary schools. The number of pupils in secondary schools by the school year 1955–56 had only reached 59,306.[3] The situation in 1961–62, which was six years later, was summarised by Coolahan as follows:

> When the [number of] pupils in secondary tops are added to those in secondary schools the grand total amounted to 87,041. The census of 1961, recorded a total of 233,832 in the age range 15 to 19. Taking 52,000 as a rough guide to the age cohort at the time, there would have been a total of 333,000 between the age of 13 and 18 in 1961. Thus, while the numbers obtaining secondary education increased significantly in the 1950s, the great majority of the age range was still unaffected by it. About 30,000 pupils were in full-time attendance at vocational schools in 1961.[4]

In general, apart from a small minority of students, secondary schooling was not available to those in the poorer sectors of Irish society; as late as 1961, the children of professionals, managers and employers heavily outnumbered those from lower-status occupations in the secondary schools, yet their parents constituted only 13 per cent of the workforce.[5] Children of unskilled and semi-skilled manual workers are benefited least from secondary school education. Students from the lower classes also were the least likely to obtain a university education and the most likely to drop out of secondary school at an early age.[6]

The situation as portrayed above applied to the Gaeltacht as much as it did to elsewhere. The number of scholarships made available to children from the Gaeltacht to attend a secondary school was, as with the provision of scholarships for the potential secondary-school-going population throughout the nation, also inadequate as an aid and as an incentive for a substantial number to pursue a secondary school education. Furthermore, secondary schools were not distributed evenly throughout the State was not even, with some areas being particularly disadvantaged. The north-west and south-west of the nation, which had large stretches of poor land and very heavy emigration, and which included the greatest number of Gaeltacht districts in the country, stood out in this regard. For example, in 1939–40, the following towns in the north-west did not have a secondary school: Gaoth Dobhair (Gweedore), An Clochán Liath (Dunglow), Na Gleannta (Glenties), Killybegs, Donegal Town, Bangor-Erris, Boyle, Castlerea, Claremorris, Clifden, An Spidéal (Spiddal), and Oughterard. Neither did the towns of Sneem, Kenmare and Bantry in the south-west, which at the time were on the fringes of Gaeltacht regions.

Given the situation portrayed above, the neglect by the State of the provision of secondary schooling within the Gaeltacht has to be seen as part of its neglect of the north-west, west and south-west of the country overall. In the early years of the new state, assistance went little beyond trying to address economic distress, that in certain western districts was, in the words of An Taoiseach, W. T. Cosgrave, "approaching famine".[7] There continued to be report on dire levels of distress over the next few years, and particularly in relation to Connemara.[8] Very little over the next four decades, however, was undertaken to try to address poverty and isolation, to provide support for the growth of a fishing industry, and to improve travel and communications. While some grants and loans were made available for housing, land reclamation and kelp production, these "did not stabilise the west, which was ravaged by emigration in the 1950s, a decade when half a million left Ireland".[9] Further, as Ferriter has argued, many of the nation's politicians who had spent time in the Gaeltacht "in pursuit of cultural and linguistic purity" and who extolled the areas in question "as containing the essence of an ancient, distinctive Irish civilisation worth nurturing and championing"[10] were not very successful in matching the rhetoric with practical help.

Previous chapters have indicated how, specifically in relation to secondary school education, the State blamed parents in the Gaeltacht for under provision of schooling in this sphere, rather than adopting a view that it had a major provision role to play itself in the interest of promoting equality of educational opportunity. This approach reflected its position in relation to provision throughout the rest of the country. To legitimate it, a common view promoted was that there was opposition in parts of rural Ireland to sending children to either a vocational or a secondary school after they had reached 14 years of age.[11] Joseph O'Neill, Secretary of the Department of Education, gave expression to this view in the 1940s, when he stated that a secondary school education was not greatly sought after, being perceived to be an education only for those "intended for the Church, the professions [and] the civil service" and that it was known that "these callings were only for a limited few".[12]

The population of the Gaeltacht received particular mention in the latter regard. As early as 1931, the inspectors of the Department of Education carried out an investigation to determine why children from the Fíor-Ghaeltacht areas of County Galway, County Mayo and County Donegal were not availing of secondary school education by taking up more places in the preparatory colleges. One reason put forward was that six years acted "as a great deterrent to the Gaeltacht parents who are anxious to supplement their meagre incomes by their children's earnings at the earliest possible date".[13] Furthermore, change to the general outlook on this matter, inspectors claimed, could not easily be promoted. Later, in 1954, a similar investigation in relation to the Gaeltacht area around An Cheathru Rúa in the west of County Galway, led to the issuing of a report stating that the people did not desire secondary school education, but rather preferred to continue the custom of sending their children to work at 16 years of age.[14]

The portrayal of people living in equally poor English-speaking areas was along similar lines. Yet, the statistics outlined already on attendance at secondary tops nationally suggest that a much greater number would have attended a secondary school if there had been one for them to attend. Equally, the statistics on attendance at secondary schools nationally indicate that a greater number would have stayed on there for longer periods if they had been in a position financially to do so.[15] On this, a pattern emerged throughout all of the period under consideration of a certain proportion of those attending secondary schools commencing for a year or two and then dropping out.[16]

A view was also promoted that where parents in the Gaeltacht did give consideration to the possibility of their children obtaining some post-primary schooling, they were unable to see benefit in an education where both the experiences to which pupils were exposed and the skills being taught could not be related directly to the world of work. Guided by such thinking, a cabinet committee in the early 1930s[17] concluded that if the State developed some form of secondary schooling in the Gaeltacht, the curriculum would have to be work-oriented. Yet, even on this, there was a reluctance by the State to engage in an extension of the vocational education system's continuation education schools beyond the sparse provision noted in Chapter 5. Rather, the Department of Education proposed a cheaper option following the advent of the Fianna Fáil Party to power in 1932. "Central post-primary tops", it was argued, should be developed to offer a new type of programme that would extend over a four-year period, beginning at 12 years of age.[18] A considerable portion of school time for these proposed institutions was to be devoted to teaching manual instruction to boys and rural science to girls. The teaching of history, geography and arithmetic, it was proposed, should focus on agricultural life, while the "purely literary subjects" were to be oriented towards "the pleasures that surround a rural community".[19] To this was added a statement on the importance of generating interest in academic subjects through the establishment of school plots, practical gardening, simple biological work, bee-keeping, experiments with farm crops, and dairying and poultry keeping.

The nature of the proposals outlined above was consistent with the governing Fianna Fáil Party's policy on the development of a native Irish culture and on making the country a self-contained economic unit. It also, however, clearly indicated a view that the State should try to maintain the people of the Gaeltacht in a perceived state of innocence, while simultaneously eulogising them. There was certainly no desire that students should have their critical faculties nurtured through receiving an education similar to that provided by the existing secondary schools. The latter, while definitely not organised to try to produce transformative individuals, could, if provided, possibly have opened up social consciousness more than the education available at a continuation school, or at one of the proposed "central post-primary tops" could have done if they had been established.

The Department of Education stalled, judging that the problems that the Catholic bishops would raise would be insurmountable if it tried to progress with its proposals. As a result, it dropped them rather than consult with various interest groups to discuss the issues involved. Mr. De Valera, it will be recalled, also became acutely aware of the extent to which the Church guarded its interest in both providing second-level schooling in areas where it wished to do so, and in ensuring that such schooling was not provided widely, following his experience of being hindered in 1937, in trying to accelerate his "Gaelicisation" project. The outcome was that he was not prepared to address this matter head-on.

Nevertheless, in 1939, Joseph O'Neill, Secretary of the Department of Education, in his evidence to the Commission on Vocational Organisation,[20] made the case once again for the establishment of "central post-primary tops". By now, there seems to have been some pricking of consciences within the walls of the Department of Education that so little was taking place aimed at promoting post-primary schooling both in the Gaeltacht and in equally poor English-speaking regions, while at the same time holding that there should be no interference with the prevailing system of secondary school education.[21] Furthermore, O'Neill argued that a proposal that there be an extension of the vocational school system, with an objective of having one vocational school for every five primary schools, would be too expensive. Instead, he reiterated the earlier proposals, adding that existing primary schools should be extended through the addition of "post primary tops" that would be staffed by primary school teachers who would receive special additional training in agricultural and craft subjects. Between now and 1947, these proposals were also put forward in various fora, and it was indicated each time by the Department of Education that it wanted to proceed with them, but sufficient political support could not be harnessed.

Those teaching in the continuation schools erected across the country more widely found it difficult to make an impact on farm life as most of the students from rural areas who attended them did so with the intention of being educated for non-agricultural occupations; only about 30 per cent of boys returned to farming.[22] On this, Joseph O'Neill commented as follows:

> Young people look to the vocational schools as a means of obtaining jobs for the children in the towns and cities, rather than as a means of bettering life and work on the land, and that the young people tend on their account to neglect the rural science classes for attendance at classes in other subjects.[23]

It is likely he was accurate in this view, since life in much of rural Ireland at the time was harsh, agriculture could not support all of those born into farming families,[24] emigration was running at over 24,000 per annum, and there was a movement off the land and into Dublin and other urban areas. The problem was particularly acute in the West of

Ireland; while the population decline in the State was 5.2 per cent between 1926 and 1951, the loss in the western counties of Clare, Kerry, Galway, Mayo, Leitrim, Sligo and Donegal over the same period was 24 per cent or 226,000 people.[25]

By the middle of the 1950s, the character of the continuation schools throughout much of the country had taken on a definite shape. The general picture was one of a two-year course that was essentially practical, was oriented towards the world of work and was suitable for early school leavers. In the public mind, this meant that what the schools were offering was an education that prepared pupils for a wide range of limited occupations. This had an effect of ensuring that middle-class parents more or less ignored them, preferring instead to send their children to secondary schools. Another outcome was the development of a culture in areas where a secondary school already existed and a new continuation school appeared, of clerics and their loyal middle-class allies, regularly speaking disparagingly about the new school in dismissive tone.[26]

At the same time, it is likely that the relatively small number of schools associated with the vocational school system built in the Gaeltacht regions by local VECs had a greater impact there than did those provided in parts of the country where secondary schools were also available. Accordingly, while certainly not sufficient in number to ensure universal provision, those established were, in the main, welcomed with open arms. Particularly valued were the local "timirí" of the VECs who offered night classes to youths and adults alike in the continuation schools already noted.[27] By the school year 1944–45, there were 2600 students enrolled in classes at 75 centres in County Cork alone.

The Movement of Gaeltacht Families to County Meath

The work of the Congested Districts Board in the West of Ireland in the pre-Independence era has already been noted in Chapter 1. The Board remained active until 1923. The Land Commission, which, under the *Land Act of 1923* and the *Land Act of 1933*, had the power in certain circumstances to purchase large farms for division and for redistribution to the landless and those living on very small land-holdings, then replaced it. During the first decade following Independence, a small-scale resettlement programme resulted in the allocation of 17 farms ranging in sizes between 100 acres and 200 acres, in County Meath, to migrant families from the west of Ireland.[28] These families met resentment from some local people, who felt it was they who should have been the first to have been considered for the allocation of any available land within the county.

Following the advent of Fianna Fáil to power in 1932, there was an acceleration of the process set in train. By now, individuals had established several Gaeltacht pressure groups to demand action to save the Gaeltacht from decline and to make the farms of Gaeltacht farmers more viable. These organisations included the Gaeltacht Defence League and Cumann na Gaeltacht.[29] The most radical of them was a left-wing group named Muintir na Gaeltacht, led by the Gaeltacht intellectual and social advocate, Máirtin Ó Cadhain. Members of this group set out on bicycles from Connemara to Dublin on 29 March 1933, to confront the government on the issues facing the Gaeltacht regions. In a petition, they sought land acquisition outside of the recognised Gaeltacht areas for Gaeltacht families.[30]

The following year, 1934, land near the village of Athboy, in County Meath, was identified for the purpose of resettling a group of families from the Gaeltacht in the townland of Rathcarron (now known as Ráth Chairn) and a plan was also drawn up for further groups to be settled in the nearby townlands of Gibbstown (now know as Baile Ghib) and Kilbride.[31] The new plots were to be, on average, 22 acres each. While these were much smaller than the holdings set aside under the previous government, the policy was in line with the Fianna Fáil vision of a self-sufficient Ireland with as many families as possible farming the land.

Following the migrations, opposition in County Meath came from a number of local Fine Gael TDs, including Capt. Patrick Giles, who reported what he claimed was disgraceful happenings, claiming that some of the recent arrivals were vagrants. He called for more patrols by the Garda Síochána (the national police force) in the vicinity to protect the lives of local residents. On 2 November 1936, The Irish Press also reported that Giles had characterised the newcomers as being "fish out of water" and stated that they were to be found at the labour exchange every day queuing up to receive unemployment benefits.[32]

Another vocal opponent of the project was Patrick Belton, TD. He accused the Minister for Land of presiding over a "shocking waste of public money" in "simply trying to find homes for imbeciles on the land".[33] He also accused the migrant population of being adverse to honest work, not arising out of bed until 1.00 p.m., and making poteen (illicit spirits) the rest of their time.[34] Such vocal opposition gave encouragement to a small but active section of the local County Meath people who, on several occasions, engaged in acts of intimidation towards the migrant community. Some of the houses due to be occupied were attacked, with shots being fired into several of them, while one was broken into and items were stolen. Inscriptions that included "no more migrants wanted here" and "this land is not for Connemara people – it is for Meath men"[35] appeared on the houses built for the newcomers. Further, there was an attempt to burn down a house built for migrants in the Baile Ghib district[36] and migrant women were hassled by "gangs" and instructed to "quit talking that gibberish [Irish] here".[37]

The overall point made by locals involved in intimidation was that many of them had found themselves unemployed following the taking over by the Land Commission of their former employers' lands. Further, they indicated that while the Commission did eventually allocate land to some local landless men, it only did so after the migrant families received theirs. These locals, whose newly acquired plots were the same size as those of their migrant neighbours, also complained that they were given less favourable treatment by the Land Commission since, unlike them, they did not receive equipment and stock.

Matters settled a little following the organisation in July 1938, of an event aimed at breaking down the barriers between the communities. An Taoiseach Éamon De Valera and Tómás Derrig, the Minister for Education, attended. The Meath Chronicle, which from the beginning was generally supportive of the project, stated that "barriers were broken down and a new spirit pervaded".[38] The Drogheda Independent, however, took a very different stance and continued to do so for at least a decade. On 31 August 1946, for example, under the headline "Reign of terror in part of Meath",[39] it compared the migrants to "Corsican bandits and red Indians" who had descended on peaceful people and disrupted their lives.

A number of the migrant families also felt insufficiently supported by the Land Commission. While part of their resettlement package entitled them to the communal use of equipment and livestock, there were complaints that farm machinery required to work the land arrived too late in their first year of residence to be of value. As a result, some soon found themselves in financial difficulty and ended up appearing in court for failing to pay rates; one such case that came before Meath District Court in 1936 was based on an argument that the defendants had been waiting for 14 months for the arrival of some vital farming equipment.[40] Rates in

County Meath were also much higher than promised and they found it difficult, as a result, to make ends meet.

In 1939, the Fianna Fáil government decided to halt the project, claiming that costs were spiralling out of control. About 660 people by now had moved to the Ráth Chairn and Baile Ghib areas from Gaeltacht regions in the west of Ireland. The Land Commission report for the period 1 April 1938 to 31 March 1939 stated it had created 99 holdings in all. It went on to state:

> We are satisfied that the experiment, though somewhat costly, has been justified by the results obtained. The migrants generally have now definitely made good in their new holdings and are able to maintain themselves and their families at a higher standard of living than heretofore.[41]

The Commission also declared that for every family that moved east under the scheme, quite a number of previously uneconomic holdings in the West of Ireland had been improved. Overall, between 1935 and 1940, 63 families moved from Connemara to the townland of Ráth Chairn. Later, 18 families from County Mayo, 21 from County Kerry, 18 from County Donegal and two from County Cork arrived to settle in the nearby townlands of Killbride, Allenstown and Clongill.

Over 70 years after the first Fianna Fáil-sponsored migrations, the fact that there is still a Gaeltacht region in County Meath, with an estimated population of 1591, is a vindication for the Land Commission's statement outlined above. Some have attributed the situation partly to the fact that a primary school established in Ráth Chairn by the Office of Public Works when the migrants first arrived has always conducted all teaching apart from the teaching of English, through the medium of the Irish language. Regarding the first 13 years of the school's existence, Pegley has stated as follows.

> The roll book of Ráth Chairn National School showed that the first students, seventy in total, enrolled together on 1 July 1936. Their ages ranged from five to fifteen; on average aged seven and a half. In the years covered in this study the classes only went to fifth class, the exception being 1937 when there was one boy, aged sixteen, in sixth class who was the oldest pupil seen between 1936 and 1949. The students in 1936 were all from Ráth Cairn but in 1937 when the Kilbride colony was established there was an influx of thirty children with one other child from An

> Clochán. This remained the picture until 1943 when other townlands in the immediate area begin to be represented.[42]

Since 1967, following official recognition being given to what has come to be known as the County Meath Gaeltacht, this school, along with the primary school in nearby Baile Ghib, has been an all-Irish school. There is now also an all-Irish second-level school in the area and, since 1968, Irish language summer course for students aged 10–18 years of age have been run there at Coláiste na bhFiann.

Developments in Relation to the Revival of Irish Beyond the Gaeltacht, Including Through the Education System

By the late 1930s, the continuing shrinkage of the Gaeltacht resulted in an awareness developing amongst those concerned about the maintenance and revival of Irish that hopes that teaching it would enlarge the Breac-Ghaeltacht and strengthen the Fíor-Ghaeltacht were not being realised. There was also a serious questioning of the State's gaelicisation project through the schools serving the majority English-speaking population. Overshadowing all such concerns, as indicated already in this chapter, however, is the fact that emigration from all parts of the country, Gaeltacht or otherwise, was rife. There were both push and pull factors operating. On the one hand, there was a lack of employment. On the other hand, the lure of the urban world led to a certain rejection of rural life, and parents of children in the primary schools in particular were demanding an education that would fit their children for life in English-speaking countries. Thus, a notion of earlier decades that as the people would become more proficient in speaking the Irish language, morale would rise and economic development would follow, was being disproved as thousands continued to leave every year. "Their going", as de Paor has put it, "made nonsense of the official ideology of the twenty-six county State of what was taught in the schools and preached from pulpits and platforms".[43]

The manner in which the nation mobilised itself during the Second World War, according to Browne, weakened the enthusiasm of the general public for the revival of Irish as it demonstrated it was possible for the 26 counties that made up the Irish Free State to be a nation state without the distinguishing marks of language and Gaelic culture.[44]

In particular, he held, the State had become an entity in a new way in those years, one that its citizens had been mobilised to defend in arms. Concurrently, the emphasis on promoting the Irish language through the primary schools outside of the Gaeltacht was resented by many students, teachers and parents.

Certain efforts made at government level to try to initiate developments to try to improve the use of Irish in the schools also came largely to nothing, a matter that added to the demoralisation of teachers. For example, an inter-department committee on the film industry established in 1938, and which presented its report to the cabinet in 1942, concluded that the Irish language and Gaelic culture could be promoted by the establishment of a "national film and cinema board" that would cater for "the exhibition of suitable educational, cultural and propaganda films".[45] To achieve this end, it proposed the use of portable projectors in urban centres and self-contained "travelling cinema units" in rural areas. The Department of Education investigated this matter further and, in a six-page report, recommended that a National Film Institute of Ireland be established and that it be empowered to acquire films, to subtitle them in Irish, and that it organise for them to be shown in schools.

The Institute was established and it received money annually through the national State budget estimates. There were very few efforts, however, to promote the use of film as an education aid in schools and out of schools for the teaching of Irish and other subjects.[46] Progress with a project for the preparation of local histories written in Irish, while initially holding out much promise, was also largely uneventful. In seeking permission from the government of the day to establish the project, the Minister for Education argued as follows:

> Apart from the importance of the subject itself, it is feared that the policy of the Department in regard to the Irishisation (sic) of Irish education cannot be satisfactorily developed and extended unless local history and historical geography become much more important features in the work of the schools.[47]

The work got underway in July 1932, when the Department of Finance approved a pilot scheme on County Roscommon and County Monaghan, overseen by Fr. Micheál Ó Flanagáin, a prominent member of the Gaelic League.

Progress with the project was slow, although the Department of Education had produced books on counties Roscommon, Monaghan, Kerry and Carlow by 1942. Despite the fact that An Taoíseach, Mr. De Valera, was anxious to facilitate the production of further histories, the Department of Finance sought the discontinuance of the project following Fr. Ó Flanagáin's death, as it deemed the cost of production to be too high. Through the intervention of De Valera, however, the government offered grants to interested and suitably qualified individuals to produce works at a set rate of payment.

The results of the intervention disappointed officers in the Department of Education. They pointed to a "barrage of criticism from the Department of Finance", even though much work was underway.[48] They also reported that translations of works into Irish on counties Sligo, Cork and Wexford were with the printers and one on County Donegal was nearly completed. The feeling expressed was that these and further books were needed "to reinforce, strengthen and make more interesting and effective the teaching of both history and Irish".[49] Of the books produced, each was about 350 pages long and contained over 100 short chapters devoted mainly to folklore and legends. Maps, diagrams, sketches and photographs were included throughout. Thus, they could have been very useful for enlightened teachers who, in their teaching, were not restricted by the demands of the State examinations. It was not possible to produce them in sufficient quantities, however, to make them readily available. The whole project also received little public exposure and nobody made much of an effort to advertise the availability of those works that did appear. It is likely that the lack of enthusiasm for the project was due also to the fact that there was no assessment of pupils' knowledge of local history in any of the State's secondary school examinations.

Of the small number of projects pursued in the interest of fostering a love of the Irish language, that run jointly by the Irish Folklore Commission and the Department of Education, with the co-operation of the national school teachers around the country, was by far the most successful. It commenced in 1937 and aimed at the preservation of the folklore of the country. The Department of Education published a handbook *Irish Folklore and Traditions* that was sent to all primary schools to guide teachers in instructing pupils on the type of material meriting collection and on the recording of it.

One can glean a sense of the importance the Department of Education attached to the project from the opening paragraph in the "Foreword" to the handbook:

> The collection of the oral traditions of the Irish people is a work of national importance. It is but fitting that in our primary schools the senior pupils should be invited to participate in the task of rescuing from oblivion the traditions which, in spite of the vicissitudes of the historic Irish nation, have, century in, century out, been preserved with loving care by their ancestors. The task is an urgent one for in our time most of this important national oral heritage will have passed away for ever.[50]

The subjects identified for research ranged over a wide area, from hidden treasure stories, funny stories, riddles and local heroes, to weather lore, herbal cures, customs associated with all of the principle events in the human life cycle, and descriptions of local craft. Seán Ó Súilleabháin, one of the major folklorists involved in the scheme, stated that engagement in this work, including by children in the Gaeltacht who collected folklore in the Irish language, was highly successful. This success, he said, was not just in terms of being a valuable academic exercise, but also as an educational activity, as it brought together young students and senior citizens to discuss the way of life and folklore which was prevalent throughout the country in previous decades.[51]

For much of the period under consideration, there was also a steady increase in the number of all-Irish secondary schools located around the country. For example, the number of "A schools" (schools where the language of instruction for all subjects apart from English was Irish) increased from 24 in 1930–31, to 97 in 1937–38, and to 102 in 1947–48.[52] However, it had dipped back down to 81 by 1957–58. The difficulty of obtaining suitable textbooks in Irish contributed partly to the decline. While an Irish state company entitled An Gúm had the task of producing literature and education material in the Irish language, it was not sufficiently funded to respond to the demand for books that could be used for teaching at secondary school level. In 1954, the Irish Christian Brothers conducted a national survey and discovered that there was a serious shortage of textbooks for Latin, French, chemistry and physics.[53]

It was not until six years later, in 1960, that oral examinations were introduced in Irish, and then only for Leaving Certificate students, even though their importance had been stressed for decades. Furthermore, the general attitude of the universities towards the language was not helpful. For example, when An Bráthair Ó Coileáin of the Irish Christian Brothers approached the authorities of University College Dublin in 1949 and asked them to set entrance scholarship examinations in Irish as well as in English; he was told that "no good purpose would be served by it" and that "the work of scholarship demands a precision of language which at present does not exist in Irish".[54]

Nevertheless, the Irish Christian Brothers, who conducted a large number of boys' primary schools and the largest number of boys' secondary schools in the country, did continue to promote the Irish language with enthusiasm through their schools throughout most of the period in question. They also produced two dozen textbooks written in Irish, while Cumann Gaelach na mBráithre promoted the language amongst members of the order. Furthermore, in 1946, the Brothers established Ógra Éireann, a youth organisation with school branches which promoted Irish through debates, concerts, céilí dancing and games, and which published two magazines—*An Réiltín* and *Réiltín na nÓg*—to coordinate activities. A central committee of the Brothers also organised summer courses in the Gaeltacht for students from 1952. Even this group of devotees, however, was, by the early 1960s, beginning to question the wisdom of its efforts in view of the fact that the State was not, in its opinion, equally serious about the matter. Equally, what was required, as the brothers were coming to realise, was a positive attitude towards Irish in the general society.

At the same time, certain individuals and group were displaying a positive attitude, as they began to take responsibility for the revival of Irish into their own hands. There had been active promotion of Irish traditional music since the 1930s. In 1935, An Cumann le Béaloideas Éireann (the Society for Irish Folklore) became the Irish Folklore Commission and received State finance for the collection of folktales throughout the country, and the Irish Manuscripts Commission, founded in 1928, began to publish facsimiles of manuscripts and republish out-of-print historical studies. Various reviews of plays, exhibitions and concerts expressed the theme of Irish tradition. This contributed, as Browne has put it, to the prevailing republican ethos that "the ancient Gaelic Irish nation had finally thrown off the thrall of the foreign subjugation" and that her destiny now "lay in cultivating her national distinctiveness as assiduously as possible".[55]

In 1939, the Gaelic League revived the annual Gaelic festival, An tOireachtas, and in 1943, the Irish-language journal, *Comhar*, and the Irish-language newspaper, *Inniu*, were founded. In the same year, Comhdháil Náisiúnta na Gaeilge, an umbrella body for the various Irish language organisations that existed, was formed, and it began to investigate ways in which the Irish language might be promoted through the non-State sector. There were also indications by the late 1940s and early 1950s that the State might be about to take a leading role in planning for language development as it sought to promote national economic and social development more broadly through adopting a policy of state capital investment. This commenced with the introduction of a land rehabilitation scheme, the setting up of the Industrial Development Authority and An Córas Tráchtála (The Trade Board), progress in housing construction, and an intensive and successful drive to eradicate tuberculosis. Furthermore, as indicated in earlier chapters, Gael Linn, a non-State organisation, was engaged in activities aimed at trying to improve the economic and social conditions in the Gaeltacht.

In 1956, the State began to step up its own role in relation to life in the Gaeltacht with the establishment of Roinn na Gaeltacht (Department of the Gaeltacht). The aim of this new body was to stem the population drain in the Gaeltacht by providing employment opportunities and essential amenities in order to try to improve living conditions there. In the same year, the Gaeltacht districts were, for the first time, defined precisely, with the boundaries being broadly similar to the existing Fíor-Ghaeltacht areas. This meant that official Gaeltacht districts were now located only in counties Donegal, Galway, Mayo, Kerry, Cork, Meath and Waterford.

In 1958, Roinn na Gaeltacht established a statutory board, Gaeltarra Éireann, to act as its principal instrument for industrial development in the Gaeltacht. The original responsibility of Gaeltarra was to assist, in a modest manner, those involved in the operation of the few existing traditional industries, and this it did during the first seven years after its establishment. Then, in 1965, its powers were augmented dramatically when Roinn na Gaeltacht granted it the liberty to develop new industries and to enter into development schemes with non-government organisations and firms. Later chapters deal with how matters fared from then onwards.

Notes

1. The following statistics are taken from the annual reports of the Department of Education for the school years 1939–40 and 1956–57.
2. T. O'Donoghue. *The Catholic Church and the Secondary School Curriculum in Ireland, 1922–62* (New York: Peter Lang, 1999).
3. The following statistics are taken from the annual reports of the Department of Education for the school years 1933–34 and 1955–56.
4. J. Coolahan. *The ASTI and Post-primary Education in Ireland, 1909–1984* (Dublin: The ASTI, 1984), p. 184.
5. Government of Ireland. *Investment in Education: Report of the Survey Team Appointed by the Minister of Education in October 1962* (Dublin: The Stationery Office, 1962).
6. T. A. O'Donoghue. 'Patterns of Attendance at Irish Secondary Schools from the Establishment of the Independent Irish State to the Introduction of the "Free Education" Scheme in 1967'. In Judith Harford (Ed.). *Reflecting on Fifty Years Since the Advent of 'Free Post-Primary Education'* (London: Peter Lang, 2017).
7. *Dáil Éireann Debates*, Vol. 5, No. 12, 18 May 1922.
8. D. Ferriter. *On The Edge: Ireland's Off-shore Islands: A Modern History* (London: Profile Books, 2018).
9. Ibid., p. 112.
10. Ibid., p. 2.
11. M. Brennan. 'Agriculture and Our School System, Irish Ecclesiastical Record', Vol. 60, 1942, pp. 6–8.
12. NLI. Minutes of Evidence of the Commission on Vocational Organisation. Ms. 928, p. 2290.
13. Archives Dept, UCD. Blythe Papers. File P24/302. Memo entitled 'Memo on Preparatory Colleges' dated 1931.
14. Mulcahy Papers. P7/C/154.
15. The Limerick Rural Survey 1958–64, p. 13: found that while there was an increase in the number of pupils from the farm-working classes in East Limerick taking up places in secondary schools by the middle of the 1950s, most of them had to leave after a year or two as their parents could not meet the associated costs…..and some had to withdraw their children as they decided to emigrate.
16. The following statistics are from the annual reports of the Department of Education for the school years in question: Of the 4527 boys who entered the first year of secondary school in 1932–33, 21 per cent had dropped out by 1934–35. This rate of drop out increased in the 1940s and 1950s; of the 5244 boys who entered the first year of secondary school in 1943–44, 25 per cent had dropped out by 1945–46, and of the

6971 boys who entered first year in 1953–54, 27 per cent had dropped out by 1955–56.

17. SPO Dublin. Cabinet Files., File S7.450 'Gaeltacht Secondary and Vocational Education', 23 June–24 August 1933.
18. SPO Dublin. Cabinet Files. File SI. 969, "Secondary Education in the Gaeltacht", and File S. 2512, "Higher Primary Schools in the Gaeltacht".
19. Ibid.
20. NLI. Minutes of Evidence of the Commission on Vocational Organisation. Mss. 922-41, Vol. 929, p. 2544.
21. Ibid.
22. P. K. O'Leary. The Development of Post-primary Education in Ireland since 1922, with Special Reference to Vocational Education (Unpublished Ph.D. Thesis, QUB, 1962), p. 98.
23. See Minutes of Evidence of the Commission on Vocational Organisation. Ms. 929, p. 3.
24. Saorstát Éireann, Department of Industry and Commerce. *Commission on Emigration and Other Population Problems: Report 1948–54* (Dublin: Stationery Office, 1956), pars. 277–282.
25. T. Breathnach. 'Social and Economic Problems of Western Ireland', *Christus Rex*, Vol. 20, No. 2, 1966, pp. 125–133.
26. Ibid.
27. M. O'Riordan. 'Technical-vocational Education, 1922–52: The Cultural Emphasis', in *The Proceedings of the Education Conference Held in University College Cork*, 24–26 March 1977, pp. 194–199.
28. The following account is based on that in S. M. Pegley. The Development and Consolidation of the Gaeltacht Colony Ráth Cairn, Co. Meath 1935–48 (Unpublished M.Litt. Thesis, Department of Modern History, National University of Ireland Maynooth, 2007), 20thesis.pdf.
29. Ibid., p. 59.
30. Ibid.
31. Ibid., p. 79.
32. *Dáil Éireann Debates*, Col. 82, 3 April 1941.
33. *Meath Chronicle*, 25 July 1936.
34. *Irish Press*, 7 May 1936.
35. Ibid., 25 October 1935.
36. Ibid., 7 May 1936.
37. Ibid., 17 January 1938.
38. *Meath Chronicle*, 16 July 1938.
39. *The Drogheda Independent*, 31 August 1946.
40. *Irish Independent*, 19 June 1936.
41. Coimisun Talmhan na Éireann. *Annual Report, 1 April 1938 to 31 March 1939* (Dublin: Stationery Office, 1939), p. 6.

42. S. M. Pegley. The Development and Consolidation of the Gaeltacht Colony Ráth Cairn, Co. Meath 1935–48, p. 127.
43. L. de Paor. 'Ireland's Identities', *The Crane Bag*, Vol. 3, No. 1, 1979, p. 25.
44. T. Browne. *Ireland: A Social and Cultural History, 1922–1985* (London: Fontana Books, 1985).
45. SPO. Cabinet Files. File S8 230A entitled 'Irish History Films—General File' and Files S13 115(A) and S1a3115(B).
46. *Scéala Éireann*, 30 April 1937.
47. SPO. Cabinet Files. File S6 308, entitled 'Preparation of Local Histories'.
48. Ibid.
49. Ibid.
50. Department of Education. *Irish Folklore and Tradition* (Dublin: Stationery Office, 1937), p. 3.
51. Seán Ó Súilleabháin. 'An béaloideas agus and t-oideachas', *Oideas*, Vol. 2, Earrach 1969, p. 47.
52. The following statistics are taken from the annual reports of the Department of Education for the school years in question.
53. An Bráthair Ó Coileáin. 'No Good Purpose Would Be Served', *Combar*, Nollaig 1949, p. 5.
54. Ibid.
55. T. Browne. *Ireland: A Social and Cultural History*, p. 146.

CHAPTER 7

"You Don't Want to Be a Gaelic Dafty in This Town": Memories of Gaeltacht Residents on Their Schooling

Introduction

This chapter draws upon autobiographical works in which memories of growing up in the Gaeltacht, including in relation to one's schooling there, and primarily for the period from national independence to the mid-1960s, are related.[1] It is organised under three main themes. The opening two relate to a range of memories of the experience of schooling by individuals who grew up in the Gaeltacht that, while instructive, do not, at the same time, have a unique Gaeltacht element to them. The first of these relates to student's memories of local expectations of them in relation to schooling and the second relates to memories pertaining to the particular culture of schooling in Ireland at the time. Attention is then focused on school-related memories of individuals from the Gaeltacht that are associated specifically with the fact that Irish was their first language.

Students' Memories Related to Local Expectations of Them in Relation to Schooling

Cathal Ó Searcaigh is one of Ireland's best-known poets writing in the Irish language. Born in 1956, he grew up on a small hill-farm at the foot of Mount Errigal in the County Donegal Gaeltacht. He was educated locally at Caiseal na gCorr national school and then at the vocational

T. O'Donoghue and T. O'Doherty, *Irish Speakers and Schooling in the Gaeltacht, 1900 to the Present*,
https://doi.org/10.1007/978-3-030-26021-7_7

school at Ghort a' Choirce. In his memoir, *Light on Distant Hills*,[2] he describes his childhood in what he characterises as having been a remote Irish-speaking community.

Ó Searcaigh did not commence primary school until he was six years of age. A dominant recorded memory of his of what soon followed was an experience of having a somewhat idyllic childhood playing in the countryside interrupted abruptly. The associated experience of then struggling to come to terms with having to attend primary school daily and being corralled in a classroom, he recalls, intensified, because he had not been alerted to what would be entailed. Indeed, he makes clear that his mother, being a "free spirit", would not have cared if he had never gone to school.

Not so in the case of Gearóid Cheaist Ó Catháin, who lived on An Blascaod Mór, or the Great Blasket Island, in the Kerry Gaeltacht, before its population was evacuated in 1953, and was relocated to Dún Chaoin (Dunquin), the nearest district on the mainland. The island community had been declining for many decades and when the final group of 22 inhabitants moved to the mainland, Gearóid was the only child amongst them. While he did not attend school until then, he knew for some time beforehand that it was going to happen eventually:

> One man on the island decided it was time to curb my wayward ways and put an end to my rambling. His name was Seán Tom Kearney….One day being the rascal that he was, he stopped me in my tracks and told me to sit down again. He landed a big leather-bound book on the table, banged it with his cane and said, "we must out you to school". I ran home to my mother screaming.[3]

This experience, he related, also prodded his mother into action. Already, he stated, she had been concerned about his schooling and now began to teach him "how to recognise words by linking them with pictures". On this, he said that when she read to him in the late 1940s, she

> ….moved her finger slowly from one word to the next. Every now and then she pointed to the picture by the text to explain certain words. She taught me how to count numbers on my abacus…When it came to teaching me how to write numbers she had her own special way. To draw the number eight, she said to me, 'Gearóid, just draw two seagulls eggs one on top of the other'.[4]

As a result, he stated, when he started to attend the national school at Dún Chaoin, he was motivated to read all of his school books, as he put it, "from cover to cover".[5]

Parental interest, guided by his mother, continued throughout Ó Catháin's schooling. For example, when he was about to enter his final year in primary school his parents took him out of the local school and enrolled him at the Christian Brothers' primary school in the town of Dingle, 10 miles away, where he lived with relations during the school week. The feeling in his household was that the Brothers' school had the facilities and expertise to maximise his chance of being successful in the examinations set by Kerry County Council for the award of a scholarship to attend a secondary school. And he was successful, going on to spend a number years at the boarding school run by the Mill Hill Fathers in Freshford, County Kilkenny, before returning to study for his Leaving Certificate examination at the Christian Brothers' secondary school in Dingle.

As is clear from the accounts in the previous chapters, Ó Catháin was unusual for the time in that he attended a secondary school at all, not to mention a boarding school. Such an experience became somewhat more prevalent following the introduction of "free" second-level education in 1967. This was revealed in 1974, in a documentary on Telefís Éireann,[6] the national television station, on attendance at Coláiste Einde, a secondary school, and former preparatory college, where pupils learnt their subjects through Irish. While a large number of the pupils came from Galway city, there were many first-language speakers of Irish enrolled who came from Gaeltacht areas throughout Connemara and the Aran Islands.

The documentary, at the same time, also related that the education choices for boys on the islands in the Aran group in Galway Bay in relation to attending a post-primary school were still few. Those from Inis Mór, the largest of the three islands, could study up to Intermediate Certificate level at the local vocational school, and then, if possible, move on to the mainland for second-level schooling. For those from Inis Meáin or Inis Oírr, however, once they had left primary school, it was boarding school or nothing. Furthermore, for those who chose to stay at home, the only employment options available to them were fishing or working on very small farms.

Fr. Breathnach, Latin master and the school principal at Coláiste Einde, argued that second-level schools should be built in Connemara and the Aran Islands. It was important for students from there, he held, that they be educated locally. This, he argued, was because it was not psychologically healthy for young teenagers to have to leave their families, their homes and their local communities at such a young age.

Not all, however, were keen on studying at primary-school level in order to maximise their chances of obtaining a scholarship to attend a secondary school. On this, Maidhc Dainín Ó Sé,[7] from the West Kerry Gaeltacht, commented as follows on the urgings of his parents that he studies at home each night with such an end in mind:

> An dá bhliain dheireanacha a thugas ar scoil Bhaile an Mhúraigh do bhí gach seift á n-úsáid ag m'athair agus mo mháthair chun go luífinn leis ne leabhra. Is é an scrúdú a thabharfadhdh isteach go dtí an gColáiste Ullmhúcháin mé a bhí sa cheann acu dom. Theastaigh ó gach tuismitheoir an uair sin múinetóirí a dhéanamh dá gclann. 'Féach an saol a bhéadh agat dá mbeifeá i do mhúinteoir', a deireadh mo mháthair liom. 'Bheifeá críochnaithe le do chuid oibre aga trí a chlog gach lá. Bheadh léine bhán agis tie fút. Ná feiceann tú an feola atá orthu ar fad.'
>
> (During the last two years I spent at the school in Baile an Mhúraigh, my father and my mother tried everything to get me to study. They wanted me to prepare for the examination that would give me a scholarship to attend a preparatory college. At that time, every parent [in the district] wished for their children to become teachers. 'Look at the nice life you would have if you were a teacher', my mother said. 'Your work would finish at 3.00 pm each day. You would wear a while short and tie. And look at how well fed teachers are'.)

Others did respond more positively to their parents' promptings, and not just in relation to the possibility of becoming teachers. The problem for many of these, though, was that until the advent of State-provided free transport to second-level schools from 1967 onwards, it was not often physically possible to get to such a school daily even if one's parents could pay the fees.

Seán Seosamh Ó Coistín, one of eight children who grew up in the parish of Rinn Ua gCúanach (Ring) in the County Waterford Gaeltacht, recollected along such lines when recalling how he came to attend a secondary school, having completed his primary schooling at Scoil Náisiúnta na Rinne, the parish national school.[8] There were, he stated, two constant refrains at home from his parents, namely, "You all have to go to school and do your Leaving Certificate" and "none of you should have to emigrate". "These mantras", he went on:

> .... were forged from my parents' life experiences. To stiffen our resolve and prepare us for the effort required, my mother repeatedly told us of the heroics of Frank Murphy from [nearby] Grange who cycled 16 miles each way, each day for 5 years to the Christian Brothers in Dungarvan in order to sit his Leaving Certificate. Each evening he faced the daunting task of climbing the Sweep, a steep 2-mile climb through a series of hairpin bends, frequently against western gales, a task that would break the resolve of an Arctic explorer.[9]

The difficulty, however, was, as he put it, that "when the time came to turn their aspirations into deeds, the cost implications were both formidable and forbidding". The solution was provided when the lay secondary school in the parish, whose foundation has already been considered in Chapter 6, was opened at the end of the 1950s. He communicated his memory on this as follows:

> When Nioclás Mac Craith [the principal of the school] knocked on the door of my parents, Jim and Peig Costin, Baile Uí Cuirrín in the summer of 1959, inquiring if there was anyone in the house eligible to attend the newly to be opened Meánscoil, my late mother was overcome with relief and disbelief. Forever more she said it was the answer to her prayers.[10]

"No longer", he concluded, was secondary school education in the district "limited to those who could muster fees for boarding schools or those few who were awarded scholarships. Meánscoil San Nioclás had democratised education. It was a cathartic change".

Others recalled along similar lines, with some indicating that the decisions they arrived at were based more on their own reflections on possibilities, rather than on encouragement by parents. Evidence available from the West Cork Gaeltacht districts is instructive on this. Cáit Ní Rouirc recalled as follows regarding her final year at primary school at Scoil Náisiúnta Ceapach Buí (Cappabue National School), outside Bantry, in 1959:

> Bhí rang a seacht críochnaithe agam i Scoil Náisiúnta Ceapach Buí. Ní raibh aon deimhneacht ann ar cad a bhí romham. Ba mhian liom leanúint ar scoil ach ní raibh aon mhéan scoil níos cóngaraí ná Beanntraí - dhá

mhíle déag uaim. Ní raibh aon ghluaisteán againn, mar ba gnáth an tam sin. Bhí an leictreachas againn ar feadh bliana. Bhí radio againn ach ní raibh aon teilifís....Ní raibh aon seans agam dul ag feirmeoireacht mar bhí beirt deartháir níos sinne ná mise.

(I had finished my final year at Cappabue National School. I had no idea what I was going to do. I was keen to continue my schooling but the nearest secondary school was at Bantry, 12 miles away. As was usual at the time, we did not have a car. We had had electricity for a few years. We had a radio but no television. I had no chance of becoming a farmer as I had two brothers who were older than me.)

She then went on to state that her life changed when she heard that Fionnbarra Ó Murchú was about to open a small secondary school in Béal Átha'n Ghaorthaidh (considered already in Chapter 6). "B'fhéidir go mbeadh seans ann, nach mbeadh orm dul ag obair, nó dul ar an mbád go Sasana, ba iad san an dá rogha a bhí ar fáil i 1959", she recalled (Maybe I now would have a chance in life that did not involve taking the boat to seek work in England, or to look for a job locally). She enrolled as a student and found it possible to pay the annual fee of £10.

Until the introduction of the "free" second-level education scheme in 1967, however, the great majority of students in many of the Gaeltacht districts never went beyond primary school. Many also were acutely aware it was out of their reach, sometimes for reasons of geographical location, sometimes for lack of money to pay fees, sometimes because the family could not do without whatever income or labour they might be able to contribute to the home and sometimes for all of these reasons combined. Tomás Ó Munghaile, born in 1918, in Ros Dubh, in the Gaeltacht district in North-West County Mayo, attended the local primary school in the early years of the new independent State. In recalling his final days there, he said he was aware that the number of scholarships available at the time was no way near sufficient to cater for many who wished to attend a secondary school but could not afford to do so. "Bhíodh daoine a raibh airgead acu, lucht siopaí nó rudaí mar sin, ag dul ag coláiste ag íoc a mbealach. Ní raibh sé ró-dhaor, ach ní raibh aon fhocail air sin againne....aghaidh ar Shasana ag go leor acu",[11] he stated. ("People who had money, shopkeepers and the like, used to pay for their children to go to secondary school. It was not too expensive but we could not afford it....off to England with most".)

Some have claimed also that the scholarship system spawned practices that operated in such a manner it resulted in certain students being disadvantaged in the classroom. Ó Searcaigh, for example, has recorded that the effort some teachers put into preparing a small number of senior students in primary school for scholarship examinations could sometimes be at the expense of attending to the great majority in a class. His own memory of this regarding when he was 12 years of age was that he was "in the authoritarian care" of the headmaster, "a severe unsmiling man entirely focused on getting his students through the scholarship hoops". "I wasn't brainy enough and showed no flair for arithmetic", he went on, "which at the time was the real test in rating intelligence. And I had no aptitude to trot out the facts that were given me in a neat, coherent order and so was not considered fit to sit the exams".[12]

Máirtín Ó Direáin, who is widely held to have been one of the foremost Irish-language poets of the twentieth century, was also someone who, in his adult years, thrived in the field of the creative arts while living in Dublin, despite never having attended a secondary school. He was born in Sruthán on Inis Mór, the largest of the Aran Islands, and he grew up on a small farm. He attended the national school nearby, at Eoghnaght. While he worked as a public servant from 1928 until 1975, he had not had a formal schooling ended when he left primary school.[13] However, he educated himself from the time he obtained his first position in Galway City; "As soon as I could lay my hands on books in the library, I grabbed the opportunity of going in [there]. The first book I ever read was a book by Annie M. P. Smithson. I continued on then, reading most of the Irish short stories".[14]

Ó Direáin's recollections highlight a matter sometimes overlooked by historians of education, namely, that memory of schooling need not necessarily be amongst one's most memorable experiences of youth. This point also becomes clear on considering Ó Catháin's reminiscences, as it does on also considering those of Tomás Ó Munghaile, who put the situation very simply when he stated: "Ní raibh mórán aire againn ar mhúinteoirí an uair sin, ach ag 'play' agus ag imirt a bhí inár gcloigeann".[15] ("At that time we paid little attention to our teachers. Rather, engagement in play was what uppermost in our minds".) Seán Sheáin Í Chearnaigh, who attended primary school on the Great Blasket Island in the years immediately prior to the advent of national independence, commented in similar terms when writing about a new teacher who arrived at the school. In particular, he recalled that he and his fellow students were keen to leave school as quickly as possible: "Bhíomar chomh mór léi féin an uair sin. Ní raibh uainn ach dul fé láimh an Easpaig, ansan bheimis réidh leis an scoil agus le muinteóiri".[16] ("We were as grown up as herself. We were only waiting to be confirmed by the bishop and that would be the end of school and teachers for us".)

In relation to all of the individuals mentioned above, memories of experiencing nature were also much more notable than attendance at primary school. Ó Direáin recalled his childhood on the Aran Islands as being, more than anything else, "all magic, with moonlit nights in summer when you would never want to come in and [one had] the sea all around you all the time, and the sound of the waves under the rocks keeping you from sleep in the night".[17] He also emphasised that his non-formal education during his school years was in the oral literary tradition, with the seanachaí or local storyteller telling "an awful lot of ghost stories and I'd be afraid to go back to the room for a candle". Further, he stated that "there was some poetry-making too by people who wrote satires and songs, trying to make two families fight, or something like that and laughing about it afterwards".[18] All of this activity, he made clear, was undertaken using the Irish language alone. In a similar vein, Ua Maoileóin recalled his evenings visiting neighbour's houses with his elders in the West Kerry Gaeltacht. Here, "i bpoll an iarta agus ar lic an tinteáin"[19] ("on the hob and the edge of the fireplace"), he absorbed the stories told in the Irish language by local storytellers, along with the poetry they recited and the folklore they related.

Ó Direáin placed particular emphasis on the part that religion played in the life and education Scoil Caep. Amongst his recollections on this is the following:

> We lived about four or five miles away from the church and we had to walk, rain, hail or snow. The older men were the best attenders and were usually there about half an hour before everybody else, lying down on the green sward that came down from the chapel to the road. There was a parish priest there who came over from Kilronan [Cill Rónáin, the main island settlement], every five or six weeks when he had something important to say. But he used to say it in English and nobody understood it. He was a great speaker if only you knew what he was saying.[20]

At the same time, he held that the teaching of religion in school had played a role in the general education of his character. In particular, he recalled that priests, family and school teachers gave him "a good outlook", explained to him why he should be "a good citizen" and brought him to believing that one needs to ensure that one's "neighbours are treated well".[21]

Memories Related to the Culture of Schooling in Ireland

In Chapter 1, it was pointed out that the new programme prescribed for primary schools in Ireland in the early 1920s was a radical departure from the child-centred programme that had been in operation during the last two decades of British rule.[22] This was reflected not only in the narrow range of school subjects taught, but also in the emphasis placed on the imparting of facts and the maintenance of strict discipline. Classroom dynamics, however, were, at least to some extent, influenced also by the personalities and social backgrounds of teachers and students, as well as by the cultural milieu in which each school was located.

At the time when he wrote them down, Cathal Ó Searcaigh's memories were of having had a very depressing experience in primary school. He opened up on this as follows:

> The school had windows, but, looking back on it now, it seems to me that no light got into brighten the grim, dispiriting rooms where we sat in fear....I was lucky in that my parents had no aggressive social ambitions for me...my father had no choosy expectations for me. Being a success with myself was, I think, what he hoped the most for me; in other words, a genuine desire to see me happy.[23]

Clearly, his reminiscences indicate that primary school was not a place that fulfilled his father's expectations for him. On the contrary, the memory he carried with him for many years was of the all-pervasiveness of an atmosphere of fear there. The threat and execution of corporal punishment both to maintain strict order and as a form of pedagogy, he claimed, generated this. He also conjures up a picture for us of the first teacher he had as being "a thin, bony woman in a black fleece skirt and a dull red patterned cardigan, [who] sat on a spindly stool in front of my class and glared at us with unblinking eyes". He went on:

> There would be no codding she said. No giving cheek to the teacher and no gabbing to each other. She swished a sally rod in the air and then thwacked it impatiently against her skirt, giving little oohs and aahs of agony to show how painful it was to get a lash of it.[24]

His description specifically of the use of corporal punishment as a form of pedagogy is also evocative:

> At school, learning was not a graceful pursuit of knowledge, but a ruthless head-plunge into a pit of facts. Everything was beaten into us. It wasn't entirely the teachers; fault. They themselves were the victims of a cruel and brutal schooling and, as is often the case with victimization, they perpetuated and passed it on with the same rigour the pain inflicted on them. Declensions and set expressions; formulas and fractions; tables, totals and tenses; lists, rules and litanies. It was a fact-based curriculum, a syllabus of algebraic tediousness that did not encourage creativity.[25]

The overall view, he concluded, was that "knowledge was no more than factual cleverness".[26]

Others have recorded similar memories of much physical punishment being meted out in primary school. "Bhíos cúig bhliana ar scoil ag Tomás Ó Sábháin sara haistríodh ón mBlascaod é agus ba mheasa iad ná cúig mbliana fé dhiansclábhaíocht", recalled Seán Sheáin Í Chearnaigh, when reflecting on his schooling on the Great Blasket Island. "Mar múinteóir cruaidh ab ea é".[27] ("I spent five years in school being taught by Tomás Ó Sábháin before he left the Great Blasket Island. The experience was worse than if I had had five years of hard labour. He was a very tough teacher".) In a similar vein, Micil Chonraí,[28] reflecting on his school days in the Connemara Gaeltacht, drew attention to the use of corporal punishment both to keep order in the school and to try to motivate students to learn:

> Bhí dhá mháistir ag múineadh in aon tseomra amháin. Bhí seanfhear ann agus fear óg. Is é an chaoi a mbeadh comórtas idir iad hé bith cé acu is mó a bhuailfeadh gasúr, cheapfainn, a chuirfeadh ag obair an tslat, go b'in é an chaoi a raibh sé ag an am. Dhá bfhanfá sa mbaile ón scoil bhí do ghreadadh lé fail agat agus mara mbeadh a fhios agat do chuid cheachtanna bhí an oiread ceanna le fáil agat….Sin é an sciúirséil a bhí gasúr a fháil an t-am a raibh mise ag goil ar scoil Thír an Fhia.

(Two male teachers taught us in the one schoolroom. One was elderly and the other was young. It was as if there was a competition going on between them to see who would use the stick most often on the young male pupils. If you stayed away from school for a day you received your physical punishment, and if you did not know the material you were required to learn, you also received it. That is the scourging that was given to us when attending school at Tír an Fhia.)

"Is iomaí gasúr a tháinig amach as an scoil a raibh mise aici agus ní raibh sé in ann a ainm a scríobh agus chaithfidís a bheith ag goil ag an scoil go mbeidís cheithre bliana déag",[29] he went on. ("It is many a youngster who left the school I attended and he was not able to write his name, yet all had to continue to attend school until they were 14 years of age".)

At the same time, Micil Chonraí, like some others, recognised that not all primary school teachers were cruel. On this, he described a Máirtín Ó Conámha who taught in a number of other Gaeltacht schools in the Connemara Gaeltacht, as being well known as a "fear iontach…muinteoir iontach…agus níor bhuail sé aon pháiste ríamh"[30] ("a wonderful man, a wonderful teacher, and he never struck any-one"). In a similar vein, Seán Sheáin Í Chearnaigh spoke of one of his teachers on An Blascaod Mór, a Pádraig Mac Gearailt, as a "fear breá sochma agus múinteóir gan cháim" ("a gentleman and a teacher without blemish").

Reminiscences of others who also grew up in the West Kerry Gaeltacht are even more effusive about teachers who taught there. For example, quite a number of islanders from the Great Blasket Island related fond memories of those who taught them in the 1920s. Seán Ó Mainín recounted as follows the teaching approach of a Pádraig Mac Gearailt, who took up a position on the island in 1925: "Bhí leanaí an Oileáin ana-mhór ar fad leis mar níor bhuail sé buille ar dhuine acu faid a bhi sé ann. Mhúin sé an Béarla go maith dóibh agus Gaelainn chomh maith céanna".[31] ("The children of the Island were very fond of him because as long as he was there he never hit any of them. He taught them both English and Irish".) Nic Craith has documented similar accounts relating to later years and to other teachers in her study of primary school education on the Great Blasket Island during the years 1864–1940.[32] Further, in his account on life at the national school in nearby Dún Chaoin, on the mainland, Ó Catháin recalled the introduction of a certain amount of novelty to his schooling on becoming an altar boy: "Every single day without fail, Father Harrington popped into the school to teach us altar service and pump us with Latin phrases".[33]

Those from the Gaeltacht who went on to attend a second-level school had experiences as wide and varied as those outlined already on primary schooling. What is particularly striking in the case of memories of some, however, is the intensity with which they remembered how their interpersonal relationships with teachers improved radically at this stage. Ó Searcaigh has placed a strong emphasis on this in relating how his experience of schooling took a dramatic turn for the better when he enrolled at the local vocational school, whose official curriculum he depicted as follows:

> You went there to pick up a trade. Unsurprisingly, the curriculum was largely practical and geared towards those who needed a solid grounding either in woodwork or metalwork. Good, useful, workaday training that prepared you for work 'across the water' or, if you were lucky, an apprenticeship at home. Similarly, girls were instructed in domestic and apprenticeship skills, giving them a good footing so that they could easily step into hotel and office jobs. Irish, English, maths, technical drawing and agricultural science were the other subjects on my course of studies when I signed on in September 1969.[34]

This curriculum, he has said, was as he expected it would be. What came as a great surprise to him, however, was when, on his first day at school, his teacher of English impressed on him and his peers that there would be no use of fear in the classroom. Soon also, he said, he found that "whatever you said was received gracefully, weighed and pondered by our smiling teacher".[35] "For the first time ever", he stated, "I had been praised at school and made to feel special. It was a lovely moment of joy, and I let it seep into me like a sudden burst of warm sunshine". Further, while he pointed out that he had little ability when it came to practical subjects, those teachers who taught them did not ridicule him. On the contrary, they treated him well and with respect.

Others recalled having had a similarly unexpected and pleasant experience on also attending their local Gaeltacht vocational school. Ó Sé, who, it will be recalled, did not like primary school and did not take heed of his parents' advice to prepare for the examinations that could have led to admission to a preparatory college, eventually decided to attend the vocational school nearby in Dingle, with no preconceptions about what would be involved. Like Ó Searcaigh, although for a different reason, he claimed that within a short time as a student there, he was pleasantly surprised:

> Ba dheacair é a chreidiúnt ach tar éis cúpla mí a bheith caite agama ar scoil is amhlaidh a bhíos ag baint sásamh as mo chuid scolaiochta den chéad uair riamh. Is docha gurb é an fáth le sin ná gur ag obair le mo lámha a bhínn trí lá sa tseachtain. Bhí ag eiri réasúnta maith liom i líníocht chomh maith. Ní raibh an mhatamaitic féin ag teacht róchruaidh orm....Is dócha gurb é an rud is mó a thug an cheardscoil dos na buachaillí agus na cailíní a bhí uirthi ná misneach a thabhairt dóibh chun aghaidh a thabhairt ar an saol mór lasmuigh.[36]
>
> (It was difficult for me to believe, but after attending the vocational school for a few months I was enjoying school for the first time ever. I think the reason for that is that I spent three days a week there working with my hands. I also found I was doing reasonably well in drawing. Even mathematics was not too difficult for me....I think the main thing the vocational school did for boys and girls was give them courage to face the great big world that lay before them.)

Donnchadh Ó Luasaigh recalled along the same lines in relation to attending the vocational school in Béal Átha'n Ghaorthaidh in the West Cork Gaeltacht, following his enrolment there in 1948.[37]

Similar memories have been related by some who attended Fionbarra Ó Murchú's secondary lay school in Béal Átha'n Ghaorthaidh. One of these was an Eibhlín Ní Lúasa, who enrolled there in its first year of operating. She was, she said, very surprised to discover that, unlike the general pattern in most secondary schools, it was a co-educational institution. She added that it had been difficult for many years previously to come to terms with the fact that the possibility of attending any secondary school was remote. Now, however, she had one located, as she put it, "i ngiorracht scread asail de mo thig féin....ní raibh le déanamh agam ach pocléimnigh síos an bóthar"[38] ("it was within an donkey's roar from my home and all I had to do was to skip up the road to get to it"). She went on to relate the pleasure she got from attending a school where all subjects were taught through Irish, her first language, and Irish was the "normal" language of conversation in and around the school, and where she took part "i ndráma Gaeilge" (Irish-language drama productions). Cáit Ní Rúairc, who attended the same school at the same time, had similar fond memories:

> Bhí oideachas leathan á fháil againn. Bhí cómhrá éigin againn geall leis gach lá, nár bhain leis na h-ábhair scoile. Thug Fionnbarra le tuiscint dúinn muinín a bheith againn asainn féin. Thug sé idéalachas, misneach, creideamh, dóchas don lá a bhí le teacht, agus bródúlacht as ár dteanga, cultúr agus as ár dtír féin dúinn. Spreag sé sinn chun oibre, go háirithe lena shampla féin....Bhí suim aige i ngach gné dár scoláireacht agus oideachas i.e. drámaíocht, spórt, amhránaíocht agus ár gcreideamh.[39]
>
> (We received a broad education. Our every-day conversations were very pleasant. Fionnbarra [the headmaster] impressed upon us the importance of having confidence in ourselves. He imparted idealism, strength [of mind], religious faith to us, helped us to have hope for our futures, and helped us to develop a pride in our national language, our Gaelic culture and our nation. He also motivated to work hard at school, and led by example....He was interested in all aspects of our schooling and our education, including drama, sport, music and religion.)

Máire Bean Uí Mhurchú, another pupil at the same school and at the same time, declared as follows regarding the first day the school opened: "lasadh coinneal beag bídeach, coinneal an dóchais, do ghlúin óg Bhéal Átha'n Ghaorthaidh" ("a small slender candle, the candle of hope, was lit for the young people of Béal Átha'n Ghaorthaidh on that day").[40]

Ó Searcaigh, in his account of schooling at his local Gaeltacht vocational school, recalled that, while enrolled in the second (and normally final) year, the national Department of Education permitted those enrolled to remain on and to study for both the Intermediate and Leaving Certificate examinations, which had been the sole preserve of the secondary schools up until then. What followed, he concluded, was a fabulous "voyage of discovery"[41] in doing creative writing in both English and Irish, and being exposed to the Irish-language poetry of the giants of the era, namely, Seán Ó Ríordáin, Máire Mhac an tSaoi and Máirtín Ó Direáin.

This mention of Ó Direáin also serves to recall that poet's own memories of the primary school curriculum he experienced in Inis Mór. On the one hand, his account on this, when he states that it involved "doing arithmetic and reading, including English poems like 'The Burial of Sir John Moore', Irish, history and geography" and that "mastery in all of the subjects depended on innate memory" is similar to that of Ó Searcaigh.[42] On the other hand, his recollection was not one of feeling miserable about the experience. Rather, he related it in a very matter-of-fact way, stating: "school life was something apart on one side, and the home life was something other than that. It seemed natural enough to me that it should be different, a different outlook".[43]

In cogitating the latter quotation, it is instructive to consider Ó Direáin's memories related to the great respect he developed for some of his teachers. He left primary school when he was only 11 years of age in order to obtain a salary by breaking stones on a road-making scheme on the island. Two of his former teachers, however, encouraged him to re-enrol in primary school so that they could tutor him for a nationwide examination held in 1924. Success in this led to him gaining a position as a post office clerk. These teachers, he remembered, were "very diligent and very nice people". On one, a Mr. Flanagan, he said, "if he found there was anything in you at all, he'd continue to make you get down to it".[44]

Seán Seosamh Ó Coistín who, as mentioned earlier, attended his local primary school in Rinn Úa gCúanach in the County Waterford Gaeltacht, was luckier than Ó Direáin in that he had the opportunity to attend a local secondary school. He has also related his positive memories of his experiences of his teachers:

> [Our teachers were] locals and seemed to be impossibly young. Nioclás Mac Craith was still playing Senior football with the Brickey Rangers. He wore a cap, high fashion at the time and played at full back, a position where you take no prisoners but encounter the opposition at their roughest. It was the perfect position to acquire the life skills to instil confidence in his [school-teaching] team, to provide leadership and make the many tough decisions that is a school principal's responsibility, duty and lot. His younger sister, Eibhlín Nic Craith, a consummate lady, compassionate and maternal, was the ever available fountain of kindness and comfort, to offer succour to worried or upset pupils and the perfect ballast to her brother's robustness. The late Séamus Ó Braonáin, the son of the creamery manager in Old Parish, a former seminarian commanded great respect. He was elegant, decorous mannered and urbane. He was trusted and the fairness of his judgements was respected.[45]

The complementary skills and personalities of these teachers, Ó Coistín, concluded, "made the three of them as near as is possible, an ideal team".

Education-Related Memories of Individuals from the Gaeltacht That Are Associated with Irish Having Been Their First Language

Autobiographical works also reveal memories of individuals from indicating that by the period under consideration, students were not leaving primary school unable to speak any English whatsoever, although research in the future may reveal otherwise. Thus, it appears as if the situation that prevailed in the latter half of the nineteenth century, when some monolingual Irish speakers like Seán Dhónaill Mhuiris Ó Conaill (who had been born 1853 in Cill Rialaigh, Baile na Sceilge, in the South-West County Kerry Gaeltacht) had not even been able to attend a primary school had passed. A consequence of the situation in Ó Conaill's time, and related by him, was that when he attended the fair or market in the nearby town of Caherciveen, he could not sell his cattle or horse without the assistance of fear an Bhéarla. While literally the latter term means "the man with English", it was used locally to refer to someone who could speak English well enough to be able to negotiate the purchase and sale of animals and goods on behalf of a monolingual Irish speaker.[46]

People in the Gaeltacht, then, not only from the time of Ó Conaill, but for long before, had been aware that a good command of spoken and written English was necessary in order for themselves and their children to be able to advance economically and socially in the world. During the relatively short period that the Bilingual Programme of Instruction operated in pre-Independence days, they had little reason, once they understood properly what was involved, to seek to abandon Irish. State policy following national independence on promoting Irish at the expense of English, however, led them to worry they might be condemned to being an underclass in Irish society. Joseph O'Connor, a Department of Education inspector of primary schools who spent a certain amount of his time examining children resident in the Gaeltacht to determine if they were eligible for the government grant paid to those who demonstrated fluency in Irish,[47] commented in 1949, on the attitude of the parents of these children as follows:

> To them Irish is as ordinary as their working clothes – a threadbare thing which cost them nothing, gained them nothing, and is ready for the discard. They find that it puts them to shame in public places and leaves them

> at a disadvantage in shops and markets. It must not be forgotten they, like you and me, live for their children. One lively matron of Derriana left me in no doubt as to her attitude to Irish. "I will tell you where they'd be [our grown-up children who have managed to get good occupations if they only spoke Irish] Below there in the bog footing turf or above in the heather at the tail of a sheepdog".[48]

"And yourself too", she concluded, "Would you be coming here in your fine car and your fine clothes to tell us what's good for our children, if you had no English?"[49]

Former students' experiences of poor teaching of English in primary schools in the Gaeltacht have also been recalled, and with some bitterness. Ó Catháin recalled that when he commenced school in Dún Chaoin, he and his peers were "taught how to write in English but not how to speak it, which was a shame as that proved to be a huge drawback in later years. We never spoke English among ourselves".[50] The regret was not about the teaching of Irish in the school. Rather, it appears to have been that thinking in the independent Irish state had not been on the lines of that underpinning the Bilingual Programme of Instruction of 1904–1922.

The problem associated with the situation portrayed by Ó Catháin, he held, did not become apparent to him until he attended a boarding school. On this, he recalled as follows:

> I felt the other boys were way ahead and that I had learned next to nothing in primary school. I felt backward, frustrated and isolated. Not being fluent in English was a huge drawback, as I couldn't express myself well when the teachers asked me a question. I tried to understand how it came to be that I could not speak English fluently.[51]

He was lucky, he claimed, as one of the priests who taught him gave him lots of extra tuition and this resulted in his spoken English improving greatly. His confidence was also boosted, he offered, when his teacher of Irish praised him "to the hilt",[52] because of how well he was progressing in his study of Irish as a school subject. He also hinted that if such affirmation had not been forthcoming, his secondary schooling could have been disastrous for him.

Others have related more upsetting experiences. Pádraig Ua Maoileoin from the West Kerry Gaeltacht is particularly evocative on this in his reminiscences. Certainly, he had great praise for "an seana-Mháistir Ó Dálaigh"[53] (his primary school teacher named Ó Dálaigh), stating:

> Aon Bhéarla bhí i measc na ndaoine, is ar scoil a phiocadar suas é. Compulsory English na Gaeltachta [a bhí ann], rud ná cloisfeá puinn tráchta tharéis ríamh....Do mhúin sé go maith duit é agus Gaeilge, agus gach aon ní chomh maith.
>
> (Any English that was spoken in the community it was because it had been taught to them [by him] in school. This was because there was the 'compulsory teaching of English' for the people of the Gaeltacht, something that is never spoken about. He taught it well, as he did Irish and everything else also.)

Accordingly, the problem he had when enrolled in St. Brendan's Secondary School in Killarney, which was run by priests from the Diocese of Kerry, was not that he did not have a command of English. Rather, it was that, unlike the majority of his peers at the school, he did not, as he put it, have a command of "Béarla mín, ceannsaithe, go raibh níos mó baint le léann aige ná le saol na ndaoine. Ana-stróinsaithe ar fad a fuaireas é nuair a thosnaíos ag teacht isteach air".[54] ("Gentle disciplined English that had more to do with learning than with the lives of the 'ordinary' people. I found it very strange indeed when I was confronted by it".)

Ua Maoileoin has also stated that difficulty turned into great embarrassment as a result of the response of his peers to the manner in which he spoke English: "Nuair a thosnaínn ag léamh ós ard, do chloisinn fear anso and fear ansúd thar mo ghualainn ag sciotaráil gháirí fúm. Do lasainn suas le náire".[55] ("When I used to read aloud I used to hear my [English-speaking] peers laughing cynically about me behind my back. My face used to light up with shame".) This shame, in turn, he has related, prompted him to become determined to learn to speak, read and write English better than anyone in his class. From then on, he said, "do chuireas mo chuid Ghaeilge laistiar díom ar fad" ("I abandoned my relationship with Irish totally"). This, however, was not the position he adopted later in life; on the contrary, he had a very successful career in the Garda Síochána (the Irish police force), rising to the rank of sergeant, a position that required an excellent command of English. He also became one of the best modern prose writers in Irish, along with Máirtín Ó Cadhain, Diarmuid Ó Súilleabháin and Seosamh Mac Grianna.

Some reminiscences indicate also that difficulties arose when teachers who spoke one dialect of Irish taught students residing in Gaeltacht districts where they spoke a different one. Séamus Ó Grianna, from the Donegal Gaeltacht, spoke of the frustration he felt as a visiting teacher in other Gaeltacht districts, summing up his experience by saying: "Bhí sé chomh maith agam a bheith ag caint leis an ghealaigh" ("I might as well have been speaking to the moon"). The use of what came to be known as "an caighdeán", or "official standard Irish", did not, in certain cases, help to improve communication between teachers and students. Conchúr Ó Síothcháin from Oileán Cléire (Cape Clear Island), in the County Cork Gaeltacht, for example, recalled the confusion created in the minds of himself and fellow schoolgoers because of the lack of agreement between the vocabulary, phraseology and grammar of the dialect they spoke and the "standard" or "official" spoken- and written-Irish that school teachers were obliged to teach.[56]

More traumatic may have been the experiences of those Irish speakers who were disadvantaged in the workplace as adults because of their poor command of spoken and written English. In the oral tradition of County Kerry, the outrage expressed by John Kerry O'Donnell, the most prominent GAA official in the USA until the early 1990s, is spoken about.[57] Born in Gleann na nGealt, near Camp, Co Kerry in 1899, he emigrated as a young man to Montreal in Canada where he became a lumberjack. He regularly spoke about a young man from the Kerry Gaeltacht who had travelled to New York about 1967, where he now resided himself. In providing him with assistance when he was trying to obtain a job, he discovered that this young man had had a primary school education and a few years of secondary school education, yet when asked to write a letter to apply for a position, he was unable to do so. This led John Kerry to rail against schooling in the Gaeltacht that was, as he saw it, unable to provide a young person with the necessary skills in English to take the first step in attempting to get a job.

While more research in the field is required, it seems clear that many young men from Gaeltacht regions came to decry what they remembered as the State's policy of simultaneously promoting their first language in their local schools while significantly downgrading their education aimed at acquiring English language skills. Many of them considered that this policy disadvantaged them. Some also indicated they developed an inferiority complex about their spoken English and there were those who, on returning to Ireland to live after getting married, took whatever steps they could to ensure their children would get the best possible chance to learn to speak, read and write English fluently. Testimony on this is very striking in relation to those who never proceeded beyond primary school and had to go to Britain to work as labourers.

Ó Searcaigh, while working in England in his late teens, was very attentive to people there from the Gaeltacht who had managed to overcome their difficulties yet greatly resented having had to struggle with language difficulties to do so. Regarding one navvy who had grown up on Achill Island in the County Mayo Gaeltacht, he noted:

> He was a native Irish speaker but declined to speak it. Once when I stuck up for the language, he got quite ratty with me. 'If I were you, kiddie, I'd keep it to myself. You don't want to be a Gaelic dafty in this town'. He felt demeaned by it, as if the language was some odious deformity, a cloven hoof or a straggly tail that he had been born with and had to conceal for fear of ridicule.[58]

O'Searcaigh also recalled regularly meeting a labourer from the Dingle Peninsula in the West Kerry Gaeltacht, who, he said, "felt equally ashamed of the language and wouldn't utter a word of it". "For him", Ó Searcaigh concluded, it was "a down-in-the-mouth language and in his yearning for success and respectability he couldn't countenance it".[59]

Some first-language speakers of Irish have also declared that because of their own language-related struggles, they developed empathy with their peers who spoke English as their first language and who experienced difficulties trying to learn Irish, which, it will be recalled, was taught as a compulsory subject in primary and second-level schools throughout the nation. Ó Catháin, for example, indicated that, while in secondary school, he came to realise that "the teaching of Irish had gone astray in some form, as the boys from the non-Irish-speaking areas didn't have a clue and lacked a basic understanding of the language". He went to say that "the sheer terror on their faces as they walked into the Irish class was disturbing" and "their suffering" had such an impact on him that when, as an adult, he gave after-school tuition in Irish to students, he "bent over backwards" to help them. Ó Searcaigh also states that while in Britain, he met with Irish people who were first-language speakers of English and who abhorred Irish because of the severe approach taken by those who tried to teach it to them while in school.

"They were", he said, "hostile to the language and hit out at it any chance they got". Accordingly, he made it a practice not to comment on the matter while in their presence: "I felt sympathy for them. They had been gratuitously hurt by brutes".[60]

Ó Direáin came to reflect on the same matter during his adult years. He had formed very clear views on the policy the State had been promoting to try to maintain and revive Irish. "I [would like to have] an Irish-speaking Ireland with any other language coming down the line", he said, but "that's only an ideal of mine and I'm afraid it's impossible without bloodshed and tears and we have enough of that in this country as it is". He also attributed the demise of the language to the strategies of those State and non-State organisations that, as he put it, "despite their sincerity and good intentions, wasted their time by sending organisers to the Gaeltacht districts to encourage locals not to abandon the speaking of Irish without giving any consideration to their material conditions". To this, he added:

> At the same time [as the visitors used to arrive], the people in the Irish-speaking districts were either running away to America or trying to eke out an existence [at home]....I think a lot of the thing about a language is economic but they never thought of that at all. The poor unfortunate 'man in the street', as we'll call him to illustrate a point, he never bothers about a second language at all. He doesn't even bother about his own. He doesn't think about it, he just uses it. Language doesn't mean anything to him except as a way of making known what he wants.[61]

He then asked how sensible was it for people to be going around talking about their love of the Irish language. "What is that?" he asked. His reply was that his parents had no self-consciousness about speaking Irish. "If a Chinaman came up the road and said Bail ó Dhia oraibh" ("God be with you") he stated, "they might lift their eyes a bit but they'd say: 'Sure damn it, what else would he say?'" He then concluded by saying that, over the decades following independence, the State should have tried to foster the different historical and cultural strands in Ireland and equally have tried to ensure that, above and beyond all else, children should have received a schooling "that might have brought a little happiness into their lives and to the lives of other people".[62] This was a very different view to the narrow one which had informed much of primary and post-primary schooling in Ireland for most of the period considered in this chapter.

Notes

1. Overall, this field of study is greatly under-researched. Yet, given the potential of the material currently available to put a somewhat more "human face" on the accounts presented in the previous chapters, which are in rather traditional historical-exposition format, it was felt that it would be remiss to ignore it.
   Within the corpus of available works, the testimony of females is greatly under-represented in comparison with that of males. One would need to be mindful of this if planning any extensive research projects on the matter in the future, so that a gender balance can underpin accounts. Furthermore, the presentation in this chapter is not oral history. Rather, it is in the life history tradition, where the concern is with the stories of individuals' lives given by the people who have lived them. It should also not be assumed that one can generalise from the account given here (which is based on a small corpus of work), in the sense of suggesting that it is representative of the memories of schooling of all students from the Gaeltacht for the period in question. Rather, the intention is that, on reading the chapter, one may develop a sense of the possible range of memories of how education was experienced at the time both in the Gaeltacht and in rural Ireland more generally.
   We can imagine many a reader legitimately saying "I had a totally different experience and I went to a similar type of school". Far from being a weakness of the chapter, we see responses like this as indicating a strength of the exposition. To put it another way, disagreements that may arise should be encouraged in order to stimulate cogitation of alternatives and contribute to debate on them. The outcome could be the sowing of the seed for engagement in a much wider project, the aim being to capture not only the full range of memories of Gaeltacht people who attended school, but also to generate from the resultant knowledge base some notions regarding memories that were general, that were specific and that were idiosyncratic.
2. C. Ó Searcaigh. *Light on Distant Hills* (London: Simon and Schuster, 2009).
3. G. C. Ó Catháin. *The Loneliest Boy in the World: The Last Child of the Great Blasket* (Dublin: The Collins Press, 2014), p. 55.
4. Ibid., p. 56.
5. Ibid.
6. https://www.rte.ie/archives/2014/0408/607579-leaving-the-aran-islands-for-school/.
7. M. D. Ó Sé. *A Thig Ná Tit Orm* (Dublin: C. J. Fallon, 2011), p. 39.
8. This testimony is in an unpublished account by Ó Coistín and given by him to the first-named author of this book.

9. Ibid.
10. Ibid.
11. T. Ó Munghaile. *Ó Bharr Thrámh go Baile Ghib* (Baile Átha Cliath: Coiscéim, 2008), p. 12.
12. C. Ó Searcaigh. *Light on Distant Hills*, p. 111.
13. This account is based on that in D. Murphy. *Education and the Arts: The Educational Autobiographies of Contemporary Irish Poets, Novelists, Dramatists, Musicians, Painters and Sculptors* (Dublin: School of Education, Trinity College Dublin, 1987), pp. 18–22.
14. Ibid., p. 19.
15. T. Ó Munghaile. *Ó Bharr Thrámh go Baile Ghib* (Baile Átha Cliath: Coiscéim, 2008), p. 10.
16. S. S. Uí Chearnaigh. *An tOileán a Tréigeadh* (Baile Átha Cláith: Sáirséal agus Dill, 1974), p. 19.
17. Ibid., p. 20.
18. Ibid.
19. P. Ua Maoileóin. *Na hAird Ó Thuaidh* (Baile Átha Cláith: Sáirséal agis Dill, 1970), p. 35.
20. Ibid., p. 19.
21. Ibid.
22. T. Walsh. 'Conceptions of Childhood in Ireland in the Twentieth Century: A View from the Primary School Curriculum 1900–1999', *Child Care in Practice*, Vol. 11, No. 2, 2005, pp. 253–269.
23. Cathal Ó Searcaigh. *Light on Distant Hills*, p. 116.
24. Ibid., p. 37.
25. Ibid., p. 114.
26. Ibid.
27. S. S. Uí Chearnaigh. *An tOileán a Tréigeadh*, p. 9.
28. p. 71.
29. p. 73.
30. C. Ó Giollagáin. *Stair Sheanchais Mhicil Ó Chonraí: Ón Máimín go Ráth Chairn* (Indreabhán, Co. Galway: Cló Iar-Chonnachta, 1999).
31. S. Ó Mainín. 'Scoileanna an Oileáin'. In A. Ó Muircheartaigh (Ed.). *Oidhreacht an Bhlascaoid* (Dublin: Coiscéim, 1989), p. 42.
32. M. Nic Craith. 'Primary Education on the Great Blasket Island 1864–1940', *Journal of the Kerry Archaeological and Historical Society*, Vol. 28, 1995, pp. 77–137.
33. G. C. Ó Catháin with Patricia Ahern. *The Loneliest Boy in the World: The Last Child of the Great Blasket*, p. 135.
34. C. Ó Giollagáin. *Stair Sheanchais Mhicil Chonraí*, p. 153.
35. Ibid., 149.
36. M. D. Ó Sé. *A Thig ná Tit Orm*, p. 42.

37. D. Ó Luasaigh. 'Ceardscoil Bhéal Átha'n Ghaorthaidh', *Cumann Staire Bhéal Átha'n Ghaorthaidh*, Vol. 1, 1999, http://ballingearyhs.com/journal1999.html.
38. E. Ní Luasa. 'Scoláire bocht na seascaidí', *Cumann Staire Bhéal Átha'n Ghaorthaidh*, Vol. 1, 1999, http://ballingearyhs.com/journal1999.html.
39. C. Ní Rouirc. 'Mo smaointí ar Mheánscoil Mhuire', Vol. 1, 1999, http://ballingearyhs.com/journal1999.html.
40. M. B. Uí Mhurchú. 'An máistir. Cérbh é?' *Cumann Staire Bhéal Átha'n Ghaorthaidh*, Vol. 1, 1999, http://ballingearyhs.com/journal1999.html.
41. C. Ó Searcaigh. *Light on Distant Hills*, p. 116.
42. D. Murphy. *Education and the Arts: The Educational Autobiographies of Contemporary Irish Poets, Novelists, Dramatists, Musicians, Painters and Sculptors*, p. 20.
43. Ibid.
44. Ibid.
45. This testimony is in an unpublished account by Ó Coistín and given by him to the first-named author of this book.
46. S. Ó Conaill and S. Ó Duilearga. *Leabhar Sheáin Uí Chonaill: Scéalta agus Seanchas Ó Uibh Rathach* (Dublin: Educational Co. of Ireland for the Folklore of Ireland Society, 1948).
47. J. O'Connor. 'The Teaching of Irish', *The Cappuchin Annual*, 1949, pp. 205–220.
48. Ibid., p. 214.
49. Ibid.
50. G. C. Ó Catháin with Patricia Ahern. *The Loneliest Boy in the World: The Last Child of the Great Blasket*, p. 109.
51. Ibid., p. 168.
52. Ibid., p. 170.
53. P. Ua Maoileóin. *Na hAird Ó Thuaidh*, p. 34.
54. Ibid.
55. Ibid.
56. C. Ó Síothcháin. *Seanchas Chléire* (Cork: Mercier Press, 1975).
57. Personal communication between the first-named author and Dr. Patrick Donovan, Tralee, Co. Kerry, on 2 March 2019.
58. C. Ó Searcaigh. *Light on Distant Hills*, p. 223.
59. Ibid.
60. Ibid., p. 224.
61. D. Murphy. *Education and the Arts: The Educational Autobiographies of Contemporary Irish Poets, Novelists, Dramatists, Musicians, Painters and Sculptors*, p. 21.
62. Ibid., p. 22.

CHAPTER 8

From Cultural Nationalism to Human Capital Production: Schooling in the Gaeltacht in a Changing Ireland, 1967–1998

Introduction

By the middle of the 1950s, the ability of the Irish State to continue to function as a viable economic and social entity was coming into question as it became starkly apparent the search for economic independence that had dominated State policy since 1922, had failed.[1] The decade 1948–57 was characterised by economic stagnation, continual balance of payment problems, rising unemployment and the emigration of 400,000 people. The situation was approaching crisis proportions when the Fianna Fáil party came to office after winning the general election held on 5 March 1957. The new government created a spirit of hope, enterprise and innovation, embodied in the nation's first *Programme for Economic Expansion*, published in November 1958.[2] This and a second programme introduced in 1963[3] were direct responses to the condition of the nation and brought about a turning point in Irish economic policy and annual growth rates.

Seán Lemass succeeded Mr. De Valera as An Taoiseach in 1959, and the implementation of the State's new economic policies were overseen by him. The State established a number of organisations to assist in the associated developments. These were orientated towards the application of expertise, particularly in the economic sphere. They included the Institute of Public Administration, An Foras Talúntais (the Agricultural

T. O'Donoghue and T. O'Doherty, *Irish Speakers and Schooling in the Gaeltacht, 1900 to the Present*,
https://doi.org/10.1007/978-3-030-26021-7_8

Institute), the Economic Research Institute, and the National Industrial and Economic Council.

As economic improvement became a national objective,[4] a growing awareness that improvement in education was also necessary emerged.[5] A central argument was that while the nation's declining population retarded the growth of national production, the high levels of emigration that gave rise to this situation would not decline until a high rate of economic development and competitive efficiency became evident. Related to this was the contention that increased capitalisation without expansion in the provision of education would not be sufficient to improve productivity. The State's view was that if such expansion took place, it would have to play a major part in directing the future role of schools and schooling.

Two major forces were shaping the new ideas evolving on the provision of education throughout the nation. One force originated in the international contacts being forged through Ireland's membership of such international organisations as UNESCO and the Council of Europe,[6] and through an awareness of the likelihood that the country was about to join the European Economic Community. The second force originated in the increasing awareness within the Department of Education of the importance of planning when it came to the provision of education facilities and that the associated level of expansion envisaged was going to be an expensive undertaking.

Between 1957 and 1962, Jack Lynch and, to a lesser extent, Patrick Hillery, as ministers for education, adopted a new approach to the development of education policy. Prior to this point, there had been no major driver for change in education in Ireland, with the Department of Education being unwilling to become involved in any activity that might lead to confrontation with Church authorities, both Catholic and Protestant. Thus, when, on 30 May 1963, Dr. Hillery stated in the Dáil that matters of fundamental policy had to be formulated on the sole responsibility of the Minister concerned, with, where necessary, government approval, and that there could be no question of submitting such matters to outside bodies prior to their promulgation, he heralded the birth of a new era.[7]

Following the attendance of officials of the Irish Department of Education at an OECD conference in Washington, USA, in 1961, the government decided to open all aspects of education in Ireland to international review. The resulting report, entitled Investment in Education,[8] conducted under the auspices of the OECD, and published in 1965, shifted the national policy agenda from one of cultural nationalism to one of human capital production. It proposed that the purpose and content of education be reformed to meet the needs of the national economy. It also illustrated the social and geographic inequalities of education opportunity that existed in Ireland, where one-third of all children left full-time education on completion of primary schooling and only 59 per cent of all 15-year-old children were in school. By 1973, however, the situation had changed to such an extent that, following the introduction of a "free" post-primary education and free school transport scheme in 1967, three-quarters of all 15-year-olds were attending school.

Developments in the Gaeltacht in the Late 1960s and Early 1970s

Between 1926 and 1971, the population of the Fíor-Ghaeltacht decreased by 35 per cent and that of the Breac-Ghaeltacht by 30 per cent. This decrease was follows:

Number of Irish Speakers in the Fíor-Ghaeltacht and the Breac-Ghaeltacht 1926–61

	Fíor-Ghaeltacht	*Breac-Ghaeltacht*	*Total*
1926	128,440	116,464	244,904
1936	123,125	115,213	238,338
1946	104,449	89,125	193,574
1961	83,145	81,084	164,229

Source *Statistical Abstract of Ireland 1967.* Dublin: The Stationery Office, p. 55

In 1963, a State-appointed commission, the Commission on the Restoration of the Irish Language,[9] was established. The government of the day agreed with the position of the members of this body that the preservation and strengthening of the Gaeltacht were essential in trying to restore the Irish language throughout the nation. Relatedly, the members of the commission argued that the State should encourage and expand suitable economic activities and take action to improve social conditions so that those residing in the Gaeltacht and who used the Irish language as their normal medium of communication would be facilitated in securing gainful employment and in enjoying reasonable living standards.

The Commission's definition of the Gaeltacht was that laid down by the Gaeltacht Areas Order, 1956. This identified widely scattered districts in counties Donegal, Mayo, Galway, Kerry, Cork and Waterford. Together, they constituted an area that, at approximately 1860 square miles, was less than 6 per cent of the land surface of Ireland. They contained 142 district electoral divisions grouped into 21 reasonably compact units of widely differing size and population.[10] These were outlined as follows in English:

Gaeltacht Districts

		Population
Co. Donegal:	Fanad	1269
	Rossguill	1638
	West Central	18,329
	Glenculombkille	4173
	Arranmore	948
Co. Mayo:	Blacksod Peninsula	4327
	Carratigue-Rossport	6464
	Achill	3877
	Tourmakeady	1607
Co. Galway:	North Connemara	2523
	Carna-Rosmuc	4432
	Lettermore	5932
	Cois Fharraige	3731
	Moycullen	1400
	Carnmore-Claregalway	3208
	Aran Islands	1651
Co. Kerry:	Corkaguiney	5986
	Iveragh	2750
Co. Cork:	Muskerry	3252
	Clear Island	235
Co. Waterford:		792
Total		78,524

In 1972, Professor Kevin C. Kearns of the Department of Geography at the University of Northern Colorado, USA, pointed out that, even by minimal standards of the day, many of the dwellings in most of the

Gaeltacht districts were not very suitable for habitation.[11] He also noted that, back in 1961, fewer than 20 per cent of dwellings had a piped water supply and only about 70 per cent had electricity. Furthermore, by 1968, only 24 per cent of Donegal Gaeltacht households had piped water, only 18 per cent had a flush toilet and only 12 per cent had running hot water, while in the Galway Gaeltacht, only 10 per cent of houses had a public water supply.

Roinn na Gaeltachta, which had had the melioration of such conditions as a major goal, had been having some success. Kearns pointed out that about 150 new houses were now being built annually, and major renovations were being conducted, primarily in relation to bathrooms and kitchens, in 300 homes.[12] Nevertheless, he added that for a total Gaeltacht population that exceeded 70,000, such progress was diminutive. This situation was attributed primarily to Roinn na Gaeltachta not generating sufficient awareness amongst the people of the programmes it conducted to facilitate improvements.

At the time, there were 12,172 farmers in the Gaeltacht overall, along with 4266 landholders who did not derive their livelihood solely or mainly from farming. Just over half of the farmers had holdings of less than 15 acres each, while slightly more than one-fifth had holdings of between only 15 and 30 acres. Furthermore, almost 80 per cent of the total area of the Gaeltacht was mountain, bog and marshland. Thus, it was suitable primarily for grazing sheep and cattle, as opposed to cultivation. At the same time there was variation, with the proportion of mountain, bog and marshland in the country's smallest Gaeltacht in County Waterford being only 24 per cent, while that in the relatively large Carna-Rosmuc Gaeltacht in County Galway being over 90 per cent.

The *Report of the Commission on the Restoration on the Irish Language* also pointed out that there was a considerable amount of underemployment at certain times of the year on farms in the Gaeltacht, as in many other rural areas. In recognition of this situation, farmers with small amounts of land were paid unemployment assistance at various stages during the year. In most Gaeltacht districts also, some of the population earned some form of additional income from fishing and from labouring jobs with the county councils, the forestry sectors and other public bodies.

Taking all kinds of employment into consideration, the total number at work in the Gaeltacht at the time was 27,282, of whom 22,450 were men and 4832 women. Almost 75 per cent of all of these were engaged in agriculture, as compared with 36 per cent in the State as a whole. Of the remaining number, about 5 per cent were working in manufacturing industry, with over two-thirds of these being employed by Gaeltarra Éireann which, it will be recalled, had its powers augmented dramatically in 1965, when it was granted the liberty to develop new industries and to enter into development schemes with non-government organisations and firms.

The *Report of the Commission on the Restoration on the Irish Language* presented a very "matter-of-fact" outline of the types of State assistance available to the 18,669 private households in the Gaeltacht, including that outlined already.[13] The work of Gaeltarra Éireann at 34 centres in or near the Gaeltacht for the production of tweed, knitwear, embroidery and toys had led to 760 people being in full-time employment, and almost 1000 being in part-time employment. A company in which the State had a majority shareholding also provided employment for about 50 people in the processing of seaweed and gave part-time employment to collectors of seaweed along the western seaboard.

The report drew attention to the annual capitation grant that families had received for quite some time for each Irish-speaking child in a Gaeltacht household, and which at that stage stood at £10.[14] The grants paid by Roinn na Gaeltachta through recognised committees in respect of students from outside of the Gaeltacht spending a period of 24–28 days in the Gaeltacht during the summer holiday season in order to seek to improve the quality of their spoken and written Irish were also detailed. It was estimated that Gaeltacht families derived an income of more than £120,000 from these grants in 1964 from accommodating almost 7000 students.

While not contradicting any of the data outlined in the *Report of the Commission on the Restoration on the Irish Language*, Professor Kearns did adopt a much more evaluative and critical stance towards the prevailing situation.[15] He opened his exposition by noting that the precipitous population decline in the Gaeltacht was due largely to emigration. This he saw as being attributable largely to poor employment opportunities. He pointed to recent studies that had revealed that more than three-quarters of those surveyed said they would remain in the Gaeltacht if they had employment there. He also pointed out that while the national population trend had finally reversed itself—in 1971, Ireland's population was 2,978,248, an increase of nearly 3.3 per cent over the 1966 population of 2,884,002—the decade between 1956 and 1966, saw the overall population of the Gaeltacht diminish by 14 per cent, from 85,630 to 73,630. Between 1966 and 1971, the latter decline continued, but at a slackened pace of only 4.2 per cent.

Lack of employment was not the only factor deemed to be encouraging emigration from the Gaeltacht. In a study of secondary school students in the Galway Gaeltacht, for example, some 12 per cent of them gave dissatisfaction with their social life as the primary reason for wanting to leave.[16] This dissatisfaction related to such matters as the shortage of movie theatres, libraries, dance halls, playing fields and restaurants. While such young people there and in other Gaeltacht districts may have had some sense for quite a long time of what amenities were unavailable to them, their discontent is likely to have been amplified greatly following the establishment of Ireland's national television station in 1961.

Kearns certainly recognised the level of effort made by Gaeltarra Éireann to try to dilute the pronounced agrarian character of employment in the Gaeltacht in order to go some way towards addressing the forces encouraging emigration. However, he also did not ignore the obstacles it faced in its efforts.[17] These included poor roads, poor utilities, poor communications' facilities, remoteness from major ports and airports and the absence of urban amenities. He lauded the efforts made to overcome such obstacles through the provision of cash grants to Irish and overseas industrialists of up to 66 per cent for factory construction and for the purchase of machinery, compared with the maximum of 50 per cent available for other underdeveloped parts of the country. Training grants for industrial workers were also available, and full relief from income tax for a period of 15 years, followed by another five years of partial relief, on profits earned, was available to companies. Furthermore, Gaeltarra Éireann was able to assist incoming management personnel in their efforts to locate suitable housing, in helping to pay expenses involved in moving to a new home, and in recruiting labour.

Most of the firms availing of the incentive schemes were Irish, but a number of companies from the USA, Great Britain, West Germany, Denmark and Belgium also located factories in the Gaeltacht.[18] Amongst the major industries were the production of finished tweed clothing, knitwear, toys and plastics. These were concentrated in two modest industrial estates established in Gaeltacht districts in County Donegal and County Galway, with single factories spread strategically throughout the other Gaeltacht districts. In general, the extent of allocation of these single factories corresponded with the size of the districts. Thus, most of them were located in County Donegal and County Galway, while County Waterford and County Meath hosted the least amount.

One of the advantages of the dispersion of the industries, as Kearns noted, was that it allowed residents to take factory jobs near home while continuing to farm on a part-time basis.[19] As a result, they were able to maintain private land ownership, acquire some savings and even consider building new homes. Surprisingly, he also noted that, under this arrangement, many farm owners employed in industry managed to also increase their agricultural output.

Overall, 34 different factories throughout the Gaeltacht districts manufactured tweed, knitwear and toys.[20] The manufacturing of tweed was a well-established industry in the Donegal Gaeltacht. Here also, and in the County Mayo Gaeltacht, knitwear (most notably hand-knit sweaters) was equally well established. Together, these two industries were the largest providers of jobs, employing 1124 people. Furthermore, of the 982 persons employed in manufacturing knitwear, 932 were women. The toy business, however, had been incurring heavy losses for some time, but the opening of a new factory at An Spidéal, in the County Galway Gaeltacht held hope for the future. The manufacturing of plastics was both the youngest and the smallest industry, with a concentration being on producing fibreglass furniture.

In 1972, Gaeltarra Éireann was assisting 123 minor industrial projects.[21] These included the manufacturing of garments, embroidery, carpets and souvenirs; the processing of fish, seaweed and wood; meat processing and packaging; boat building, and electronic engineering. There was also a factory in the Donegal Gaeltacht producing "fancy yarn" and a processor of marble in the County Galway Gaeltacht was using techniques developed in Italy.

Kearns praised the progress made by Gaeltarra Éireann, noting that in mid-1972 nearly 1900 people were working in Gaeltacht industries. At the same time, he argued that this figure fell short of meeting employment needs. On this, he pointed out that Roinn na Gaeltachta predicted that the population of the Gaeltacht would increase to 77,400 by 1976, and, as a result another 3000 industrial positions would need to be created by then. Further, he highlighted work undertaken to train Irish language speakers for managerial positions and a willingness on the part of some foreign personnel to learn Irish. Indeed, he concluded, "industrial personnel from continental Europe have been more sympathetic to and respectful of the Irish language than have the English speakers".[22]

Kearns adopted a rather controversial position in stating there was a pronounced reluctance on the part of some people in the Gaeltacht, as well as in non-Gaeltacht rural areas, to accept jobs as factory workers. He attributed his view partly to observations on the difficulty people had in adjusting to the regimentation of industrial life. Equally, he held, social stigma had long been attached to factory work, and that people were often willing to take a lower paying position to "put on a tie and push a pen",[23] as he put it, since this brought greater prestige. Overall, while one is not inclined to accept such reasoning by Kearns uncritically, his related position that the influx of non-Irish-speaking managers and technicians was frequently increasing pressure for the use of the English language by those working in factories is quite convincing.

Kearns concluded his review by indicating that developments in tourism in the Gaeltacht had been minuscule. Tourists, he pointed out, were content to travel through Gaeltacht districts, but had no incentive to stay there for periods of time due to a great lack of restaurants, shops and banks, and to a scarcity of decent water supplies of sewerage, and of telephone services. Tourism could become an integral sector of the economy, he argued, if assistance was available to help local populations overcome these deficiencies. The dilemma this would then create, however, he noted, was that "an unbridled onslaught of outsiders could wreak havoc on local culture by bringing increased pressures for English speech". "Unchecked", he concluded, "this could exact a terrible sociolinguistic toll".[24]

Recommendations in the 1960s in Relation to Education in the Gaeltacht

While the Commission on the Restoration on the Irish Language made a number of recommendation on education in the Gaeltacht, most of these were concerned largely with suggesting minor improvements in the status quo.[25] A recommendation for primary school education, for example, was that "more attention should be paid to the writing of Irish in the primary schools in the Gaeltacht than outside it", and that "it should be taught to the children there at an earlier age".[26] There was nothing radical about this. There were also other non-radical recommendations. One of these stated was while reading books in Irish for use in both Gaeltacht and non-Gaeltacht schools should aim at giving children a conversational knowledge of the language, teachers should also keep in mind that because children in the Gaeltacht already possessed such knowledge at a higher level, they should be provided with "a special series of graded readers, including works by local authors".[27] Furthermore, while members of the Commission may have considered they were being innovative in recommending that children in the higher standards in school in the various Gaeltacht districts should be "given a little acquaintance with dialects other than their own",[28] they were probably unaware this had already been a practice in Gaeltacht schools in the final decades of the pre-independence era.

The very low level of secondary school provision throughout the Gaeltacht districts was barely mentioned, again indicating a desire not to confront the power of the Catholic Church in education. Indeed, the Commission went little further than stating it welcomed the fact that a larger number of secondary school scholarships than previously were now available for Gaeltacht children. It added that "the Department of Education should constantly review the position and should increase the number according as further secondary schools are opened in the Gaeltacht".[29]

The Commission adopted a similar position in the case of the provision of education in vocational schools. While this sector was the one making most strides in trying to provide for the education of children in the Gaeltacht since the early 1930s, little was proposed by way of new policies. An exception was a recommendation that "the services of woodwork teachers and building instructors stationed in vocational schools in the Gaeltacht should be made available to the local people to provide advice on and direct improvements in housing and the installation of modern conveniences".[30] Presumably, an associated statement that "an arrangement to facilitate this should be made between the Department of the Gaeltacht and the Department of Education"[31] was "code" for saying that the teachers should receive extra-remuneration for performing such additional duties, but this was not stated explicitly.

In relation further to vocational education, it is difficult to understand why it was even deemed necessary to recommend that "vocational schools in the Gaeltacht catering for boys should provide more courses which would equip them for entrance to the various apprenticeship schemes of State-sponsored bodies and of other interests"[32]; this had always been very much their function anyway. On the other hand, some food for thought may have been provided for the relevant authorities in the proposal that special provision should be made for the provision of higher technical courses for students from the Gaeltacht within a "regional technical college" about to be built in Galway city. This was to be one of a number of new sub-university colleges to be established by the State around the country with the aim of providing semi-professional and technical education for second-level school graduates.

Recommendations were also made by the Commission on the Restoration on the Irish Language perpetuating a view that education policy for the people of the Gaeltacht, as for the population nationally, should be concerned with taking conservative steps to raise the social class levels of the lower classes to just a little above those into which they were born, rather than with seeking radical social transformation. Concurrently, there was an assumption that traditional gender roles would continue. It was stated on these related matters, "that because of a great dearth of Irish speakers with an accurate knowledge of the written language for clerical and secretarial posts", all vocational schools in the Gaeltacht catering for girls should "provide a good course to equip them for such posts in the public service, in State-sponsored bodies and in private concerns".[33]

VECs had offered a number of courses over the previous three-to-four decades for young women. These aimed at providing certain "refinement" skills so that graduates could "serve" middle-class families, including in the cities and larger towns, and in so doing, help their children to become fluent speakers of Irish. The same aims were reflected in recommendations of the Commission, one of which stated that "one vocational education committee serving a Gaeltacht area should institute a course for the training of girls from the Gaeltacht as governesses" and such training should "include instruction in baby care, children's ailments and first-aid, cookery and house-crafts" and "the elements of the teaching of Irish to children".[34] The fact that there was no questioning whatsoever of recommendations like this suggested that the international movement for "women's rights", that had by now only being sprouting some shoots in a small number of quarters in Ireland, had, as yet, hardly any voice whatsoever in the Gaeltacht, or if it had, it was not being heeded at government level.

Developments in the Gaeltacht from the Early 1970s, Including in Relation to Education

In 1988, Ó Gadhra, reflecting on developments that had taken place in the Gaeltacht over the previous 25 years, argued that while achievements were praiseworthy, they were also modest. As he put it, "dynamic development policies were not forthcoming, even in the booming 1960s, while the unsuitability of most mainly English-speaking structures to deal with the special sensitive problems of the Gaeltacht communities themselves only led to increasing English-language influence".[35] Yet, a small but committed group of Gaeltacht people who had benefited from education at different levels in the preceding years began to become more assertive of what they saw as the rights of their fellow Gaeltacht inhabitants. It may also be that vibrant youth politics and civil rights agitation internationally in the late 1960s inspired them as they began to contest the official cultural rhetoric of the State.

A significant outcome of the latter development was Cearta Sibhialta na Gaeltachta (the Gaeltacht Civil Rights Movement), which became particularly strong in Connemara in the County Galway Gaeltacht. Ó Gadhra commented on this development as follows:

> The population of this Gaeltacht was big enough to have some political clout so that for the first time since the foundation of the state perhaps, the Gaeltacht itself, as a community, began to make demands that could not go unheeded. The new generation of Gaeltacht agitators spoke less about the language, which they used in any case without any revival effort, and more about jobs, development at home and civil rights of all sorts.[36]

Through the avenue of a pirate Irish language local radio station, they agitated for the establishment of a national counterpart funded by the State. They also campaigned for increased local autonomy as a key, as Fennell put it, "to the development of a self-reliant, Gaeltacht-based approach to local issues and concerns".[37]

The new movement had some results that pleased agitators. The State-funded radio service, Raidió na Gaeltachta, was established in 1972, to service all of the Gaeltacht districts throughout the country, as well as to broadcast on national and international issues, and all through the medium of the Irish language. Gaeltacht cooperatives were also set up to promote social and economic improvement for communities through the construction of water schemes and bulk buying of raw materials. Ó Tuathaigh detailed additional developments:

> A network of parish councils improved communication and morale between Gaeltacht parishes; sporting and cultural events improved cohesion between the different Gaeltacht areas; a newspaper specifically for the Gaeltacht (though mainly Connemara-centred) was a further sign of the new confidence. Above all, there was a demand for a specific Gaeltacht Authority, to give some cohesion (and a democratic basis) to integrated social and economic development in the Gaeltacht.[38]

Much debate took place on what a Gaeltacht Authority might be. Some demanded that it accommodate a form of democratically elected local bodies that would link the various Gaeltacht communities together in various ways. Further, much discussion took place on the possible value of harnessing such concepts as federalism and decentralisation to this end. What eventuated in 1979 was entitled Údarás na Gaeltachta (The Gaeltacht Authority), while Gaeltarra Éireann now ceased to exist.

The majority of the members of the board of the new authority was to be elected by adult Gaeltacht suffrage, although the franchise was extended to many first-language English speakers since the geographical definition of what constituted the Gaeltacht districts was still that of 1956, and these now contained large areas that were not "real" Gaeltachts at all. Moreover, the industrial and community development powers of Údarás na Gaeltachta were no different from those of Gaeltarra Éireann. Furthermore, no local government structures were developed to try to address specific issues of Gaeltacht communities in health, roads, planning and education. As a result, the Gaeltacht communities were not given any new statutory powers to help them take control over their own lives, a situation which, as Ó Gadhra pointed out, was not in accord with views on integrated regional development as envisaged by the European Community.[39]

Matters were looking healthier on the demographic front, with the population of the Gaeltacht as a whole stabilising between the mid-1960s and the late 1970s, and several Gaeltacht districts even experiencing an increase in population. This did not mean, however, that the Gaeltacht was succeeding in retaining its native-born population. On the contrary, a significant number of young adults continued to emigrate. Thus, the population situation was due in part to in-migration, some by married couples where at least one partner had grown up locally but whose children were often monolingual speakers of English. On this, Ó Gadhra pointed to some regional variation as follows:

> The out-migration of young adults was highest from the Kerry Gaeltacht, where industrialisation and general economic development was weakest during the period 1965–81. The Gaeltacht [districts] of Galway and Donegal were most successful in retaining their young adults, but because of industrialisation and economic development (including tourism) these areas also experienced a high incidence of in-migration.[40]

Overall, he concluded, the situation had serious implications for language behaviour in homes, schools and shops in the Gaeltacht, and in social interaction there. In a similar vein, he declared that, while back in the early 1970s, the proportion of school-going children in the Gaeltacht registered as being Irish speaking was over 80 per cent, at least 35 per cent to 40 per cent of these were not learning Irish in the family home. This, he held, meant that a substantial number of parents in the Gaeltacht were relying on the schools to give their children a knowledge of Irish. In the absence of specific countermeasures, the situation, he argued, did not bode well for the continuation of Irish as the dominant language in the Gaeltacht.

Education Developments Since the Early 1970s

One of the main administrative policies on the Irish primary school system during the late 1960s and into the 1970s was the closure of small schools. The belief was that larger schools would result in better use of teacher resources and enable the State to provide new equipment that would assist in the implementation of a new child-centred curriculum. Additionally, the provision of free school transport was to make travel to school easy for students. Nevertheless, there was much resistance around the country because communities viewed local schools as their focal points and they worried about the lack of cohesion that might follow closure.

A most celebrated case of local protest was that related to Scoil Dhún Chaoin (Dunquin National School) in the Corca Dhuibhne Gaeltacht district in West Kerry.[41] Telling the full story of this case could result in a separate book. However, a very brief account is appropriate here.

In the early 1970s, the then Fianna Fáil government announced it was closing the school and that the pupils would have to be bussed daily to and from the school in the not-too-distant village of Baile An Fheirtéaraigh. Locals objected vehemently, stating that such action would be the death knell of the Dún Chaoin community. A national campaign featuring protest marches followed. On one occasion, protesters organised a march to Dublin, meeting up in Naas and walking from there into the city, where they staged a sit-in, during which the Gardaí Síochána arrested and jailed a number of them.

Local people kept the school open and volunteer teachers taught the children. Some of these were national celebrities and worked for no remuneration, while others received some remuneration out of locally raised funds. When a Fine Gael-Labour coalition government came to power in 1973, one of its first acts was to reopen the school officially. By now, the case had achieved such a high profile nationally, that Richard Burke, the new Minister for Education, who later became a European commissioner, visited Dún Chaoin for the official reopening. While there is no empirical research on the matter, it is likely that the resolution of the case in favour of the local community provided inspiration to other Gaeltacht communities and encouraged them to become more assertive in the preservation of their distinctive cultural inheritance.

The early 1970s also witnessed the introduction of a new child-centred curriculum for primary schools throughout the nation.[42] While a wide range of obligatory school subjects was prescribed, teachers were encouraged to adapt the programme to meet the needs and education environment of the district in which each school was situated. At face value, this gave great latitude to teachers in Gaeltacht districts to develop the curriculum in harmony with local geographical, social and cultural environments. The problem was that the Department of Education provided no related special teacher preparation of any significance, no more than had been the case since the establishment of the State. Rather, all students in initial teacher preparation programmes, as with practising teachers attending courses in continuing professional development, continued to be prepared as if the same pedagogical approaches were appropriate for use in schools in Gaeltacht and non-Gaeltacht districts.

By now, the Department of Education had introduced a new approach to the teaching of Irish nationally, although it did not distinguish very much between its use for Gaeltacht districts and in non-Gaeltacht districts. Its origin was a research project entitled Buntús

Gaeilge that commenced in 1962, with the aim of investigating how to make the learning of Irish easier and more enjoyable than had been the case up to then.[43] Vocabulary, structures and syntax patterns of the Irish language were investigated, with a view to formulating graded programmes for use in primary schools. Conversation courses were prepared, as were handbooks, audio tapes, pictures, audio-visual aids and carefully graded reading books based on oral work.

Starting in the junior-level primary school classes in the school year 1967–68, and in the senior classes from the school year 1969–70, the graded courses were trialled for one year and revisions based on feedback took place. Short courses were conducted nationwide by a cohort of 150 teachers who themselves had been given special training during a four-day course. Teachers and educationists throughout the land welcomed the new curriculum and pedagogical approach, along with its structure, and also welcomed the provision of all necessary materials within one pack.[44] Each series consisted of 40 lessons and was designed to be taught over one year, with one individual lesson for each week and a revision lesson after every four. There were five steps to each lesson (hearing and recognition, imitation, repetition from stimulus, speech mould and vocabulary exercises, and free creative conversation), with a recommendation that half of the time be dedicated to steps four and five.

The Department of Education deemed the new approach to be appropriate for the teaching of Irish in a new primary school curriculum introduced in 1971. While this curriculum had separate sections on the teaching of Irish in the Gaeltacht and on the teaching of Irish outside of the Gaeltacht, only a small number of additional Gaeltacht-specific matters were detailed for consideration. In particular, emphasis was placed on the importance of preventing the entry of English terms into spoken Irish in the Gaeltacht and on the onus being on the teacher to be familiar with the traditional terms. Also, for the infant classes, stress was to be placed on oral aspects of the language, along with reading and writing. This was to be extended in the senior classes to include storytelling, poetry, grammar and project-work.[45] Furthermore, as in statements like the following, emphasis was placed on the importance of creating an atmosphere for the teaching of Irish to ensure continuity with the experiences of the child:

> B'fhurasta, trí ghníomhachtaí oiriúnacha, imeachtaí an bhaile a athchruthú chun teacht ar chumas na bpáistí chun labhairt faoina saol féin.[46]

(It is easy, through appropriate activities, to recreate the events of the home to enable children to speak about their own lives.)

To this end, the use of puppets, mime and drama was recommended. It was also emphasised that Irish was not just a subject for use within formal lessons in Gaeltacht schools, but also in informal communication, in the playground, and for greetings.

A section within the new curriculum had five pages allocated to teaching English in the Gaeltacht. It opened by stressing the importance of not equating the teaching of English there with the teaching of Irish in non-Gaeltacht schools since, it argued, radio, television and tourism supported the learning of English in the Gaeltacht. What was emphasised was the desirability of the child in the Gaeltacht learning English as complementary to mastering Irish as his or her first language.

In 1980, the Minister for Education formed An Chomhchoiste um Oideachas sa Ghaeltacht[47] (the Joint Committee for Education in the Gaeltacht) to examine education issues in the Gaeltacht. This Committee drew attention to the existence of small and ill-equipped schools in the Gaeltacht, poor training for teaching there, and a dearth of suitable textbooks and resources in Irish. It also recommended the appointment of a group of specialist schools' inspectors for the Gaeltacht, the provision of training in modern language teaching methods for application in the teaching of Irish and a strengthening of the position of Irish within the colleges of education. Further, it called for an entirely different curriculum to be devised for Gaeltacht schools, a point also made in a separate report prepared by Comhar na Múinteoirí Gaeilge[48] (The Irish Teachers' Partnership). The latter group also asserted that the existing syllabus for Irish (which was similar to that for non-Gaeltacht schools) was unsuitable for pupils with a native command of Irish. Consequently, it proposed the introduction of a specific reading series and oral language programme for Gaeltacht areas.

No concerted action, however, was taken on foot of the recommendations of both reports noted above. The Department of Education policy makers also took no heed of a reiteration of these recommendations in reports on the teaching of Irish issued by the INTO in 1985 and 1989.[49] Rather, the Buntús Gaeilge programme devised in the 1960s remained the core curriculum for the teaching of Irish to both Gaeltacht and non-Gaeltacht pupils throughout the nation.

This is not to argue that individuals working in the Department of Education were unconcerned about the situation. On the contrary, members of its Curriculum Unit established in 1976, with a brief to coordinate, evaluate, diagnose and prescribe the curriculum at both primary and post-primary level, had tried to highlight the issues mentioned above. The unit consisted of six inspectors, a member of the Department's psychological service, and senior administrative and professional officers.[50] While never adequately resourced, it did produce individual reports on all aspects of the primary school curriculum between 1979 and 1988. They were not available, however, for public consideration.

One report of the Curriculum Unit that would have been informative for many if it had been disseminated, dealt with the teaching of Irish in both Gaeltacht and non-Gaeltacht districts.[51] Specifically regarding the former, it drew attention to all of the issues outlined in the other reports mentioned already. It also highlighted the need for teachers in schools in the Gaeltacht to be well prepared in approaches that could help improve the quality of spoken Irish of those pupils who did not speak Irish at home. Further, it argued that Gaeltacht schools needed to have appropriate textbooks, library books, reference books and other resources in Irish.

With the establishment of a national Curriculum and Examinations Board in 1984,[52] there was reason for a little more optimism that something might change. The intention was that future policy and practice in all areas of schooling would come largely under this body, and that it would be independent of the Department of Education, yet would have to operate with the approval of the Minister for Education. The following year, 1985, in a wide-ranging document entitled *Language in the Curriculum: A Curriculum and Examinations Board Discussion Paper*,[53] a "crisis facing Gaeltacht schools requires immediate attention"[54] was highlighted. What was being referred to here was that the language-centred approach of the Buntús Gaeilge programme was in conflict with the child-centred philosophy of the primary school curriculum and also did not accommodate the diverse categories of pupils attending Gaeltacht primary schools. The solution proposed was that a learner-centred communicative approach to the teaching of Irish be developed for use in all schools, both in Gaeltacht and in non-Gaeltacht districts, and that it be accompanied by achievable objectives and by appropriate materials for implementation. Again, however, little came of this, and the Buntús

Gaeilge programme continued to form the basis of instruction over the years ahead.

Another body, the Review Body on the Primary Curriculum, was established in October 1987, to examine aspects of the implementation of the primary school curriculum, to identify weaknesses in design and implementation, and to recommend amendments.[55] Its terms of reference placed a particular focus on the teaching of Irish, English and mathematics, on assessment within the curriculum, on the aims and objectives of primary school education, and on the need for close alignment between the primary school curriculum and that of post-primary schools. Once more, a recommendation that a flexible curriculum should be developed for Gaeltacht schools to ensure that the language needs of all pupils would be met, and that a set of readers for Gaeltacht pupils and an adequate supply of textbooks, library books and reference books in the Irish language be provided for the teachers, was made.

The same year the Review Body was established, the State abolished the Curriculum and Examinations Board. It was replaced by a new agency, the National Council for Curriculum and Assessment.[56] Being a purely advisory body, decisions on curricula and examinations were now firmly back under the control of the Department of Education. At the same time, the Council did adopt a proactive approach. It produced various reports that led to curriculum changes, especially at the post-primary school level. However, it was not until 1999 that it conducted a review of the primary school curriculum.[57] The next chapter considers the review and subsequent developments, including in relation to schooling in the Gaeltacht.

Changes in School Structures During the Period, Including in the Gaeltacht

This chapter has concentrated largely on the period 1967–98. In dealing with education in the Gaeltacht, the focus has been primarily on developments in relation to primary schooling. Developments, however, were also taking place in relation to second-level schooling during the period. As in the primary school sector, many second-level schools were absorbed into larger regional units, the State provided capital grants for secondary school expansion, small secondary schools (meán scoileanna) and vocational schools (gairmscoileanna) were encouraged to cooperate, and fees for attendance at the great majority of schools were abolished. The secondary schools continued, as before, to be owned and managed by religious communities or private organisations, and the vocational schools continued to be owned and run by "vocational education committees", which later were replaced by what are now termed "education and training boards".

The State also introduced new models of school governance with greater levels of State and parental involvement than previously. The first model was termed the comprehensive school (scoil choimsitheach) model. When conceived, the idea was that this type of school would be co-educational and would offer a very wide range of subjects to those of all social classes and ability levels. The intention was that only a small number of them, each catering for a minimum of 150 pupils, would be established and that they would be situated in regions where there was already a great lack of second-level schools. One of the first of these schools, and the only one ever built in a Gaeltacht district, was Scoil Chuimsitheach Chiaráin, An Cheathru Rua in County Galway, which opened in 1966.

Over time, various amalgamations also resulted in the emergence of two other models, namely, the community school (pobalscoil) model and the community college (coláiste phobail) model. Both types of schools offer the same broad curriculum as the comprehensive schools. However, while the boards of both include representatives of parents and teachers, variations came to emerge between them in relation to the number of representatives of religious authorities and representatives of "education and training boards" on them.

A complicated set of activities involving restructuring and realignment of the five school types took place throughout the country over the three decades under consideration in this chapter, and even afterwards, including in Gaeltacht districts. To document all of the associated developments would be a tedious and unnecessary exercise. At the same time, it is instructive in relation to second-level schooling in the Gaeltacht to outline the following overall pattern that had eventuated by 2015. Here it is important to recall that a meán scoil is a secondary school, a gairmscoil is a vocational school, a scoil chuimsitheach is a comprehensive school, a pobalscoil is a community school and a coláiste phobail is a community college:

Co. Donegal

Gairmscoil na Carraige
Gairmscoil Mhic Diarmada, Árainn Mhór
Pobalscoil Ghaoth Dobhair
Pobalscoil Chloich Cheannfhaola
Pobalscoil na Rosa

Co. Mayo

Coláiste Acla (meán scoil)
Coláiste Mhuire, Tuar Mhic Éadaigh (meán scoil)

Co. Galway

Coláiste Chroí Mhuire, An Spidéal (meán scoil)
Coláiste Cholm Chille, Indreabhán (coláiste phobail)
Gairmscoil Éinne, Inis Mór, Árainn
Scoil Chuimsitheach Chiaráin, An Cheathru Rua
Coláiste Phobail Mhic Dara, Carna
Gairmscoil na bPíarsach, Ros Muc

Co. Kerry

Coláiste Íde, Daingean Uí Chúis (meán scoil)
Pobalscoil Chorca Dhuibhne, Daingean Uí Chúis

Co. Cork

Coláiste Ghobnatain, Baile Mhic Íre (meán scoil)

Co. Waterford

Scoil San Nioclás, Rinn Ua gCúanach (meán scoil)

Co. Meath

Coláiste Pobail Rath Chairn

In 1990, Ó Tuathaigh expressed concern about the events taking place that eventually resulted in changes in the general pattern of primary school provision in the Gaeltacht noted earlier, and in the eventual pattern of second-level school provision outlined above, in terms of how they might be having quite a disruptive impact on the status of Irish in the education of Gaeltacht people.[58] Particularly concerning for him was that, as he saw it, school amalgamations, the provision of transport to schools and the introduction of new syllabi were all taking place without adequate planning aimed at safeguarding the place of the Irish language amongst Gaeltacht communities. The removal of the requirement that one needed to pass Irish in the second-level school examinations in order to obtain a pass overall, he argued, amplified the precarious situation. To this, he added the removal of the requirement to demonstrate a competent standard in Irish for employment in the civil service and to be eligible for the offer of a place as a student in a number of new third-level institutions.

In the next chapter, the extent to which the concern of people like Ó Tuathaigh that the Gaeltacht would continue to shrink is considered. At this stage, however, it is instructive to consider the testimony given in 2016, to the authors of a publication that became available in that year commemorating 50 years of education at Scoil Chuimsitheach Chiaráin, An Cheathru Rua. In it, it is claimed that Irish was, from the outset, the language not only of the classroom, but also of the playground and when travelling to and from school. One former pupil stated:

> Gaeilge uilig a bhí sa scoil an t-am sin. Níor labhair muid riamh ach Gaeilge lena chéile amuigh sa gclós. Bhi meas againn uirthi ach ní raibh an oiread sin suime again inti mar ábhar scoile.[59]
>
> Only Irish was used in the school at the time. We never spoke anything other than Irish in the schoolyard. We had great regard for the language, but we had little interest in it as a school subject).

Another stated:

> Sa scoil an uair sin ní raibh tada eile ach Gaeilge le cloisteáil ag na scoláirí. Ní raibh deoraí ag Béarlóireacht. Má bhí cuid de na scoláirí fiú a rugadh agus a tháinig as Sasana ní raibh baol ar bith gur ag Béarlóireacht a bheadh muid leo.[60]
>
> (In school at the time one never heard pupils speaking anything other than Irish. Also the migrants did not speak English. And with those pupils who were born in England and had returned there was no way we would speak English to them.)

These are but two examples of a corpus of testimony replete with similar memories, at least in relation to this particular school.

Conversely, it is true that the number of schools outside of the Gaeltacht using Irish as a medium of instruction fell dramatically throughout the period under consideration. Yet, the number of declared Irish language speakers reported in national census reports continued to rise, thus reflecting a trend from 1926. In 1971, for example, 789,429 citizens (28 per cent of the population) stated that they were Irish speakers,[61] while a report of the "Committee on Irish Language Attitudes Research" found that four per cent of the population outside of the Gaeltacht used Irish both frequently and intensively.[62]

In 1969, the State established Comhairle na Gaeilge to advise on how best to further the Irish language throughout the country and how to assist the government in relation to policy formulation.[63] It was replaced in 1978 by Bord na Gaeilge, whose aim was to promote the Irish language nationally, particularly by extending its use by the public as a living language.[64] A *White Paper on Educational Development*[65] published in 1980, also advocated increased levels of continuing professional development in relation to teaching methods and the provision of materials and resources for the teaching of Irish in all schools throughout the nation. Further, there was a plea made to colleges of education to dedicate more time to improving student teachers' standard of spoken Irish and to provide them with opportunities to engage in teaching through Irish. There was also a movement from the 1970s to accelerate the establishment of gaelscoileanna, or all-Irish-medium schools, outside of the Gaeltacht. While the first gaelscoil had appeared in 1954, the second did not open until 1969. From then on, the number of them increased rapidly, reaching 13 in 1974 and 68 in 1990. In the 1980s, also there was no great government enthusiasm for the development.

Ó Tuathaigh's relatively pessimistic conjectures expressed in 1990, regarding the position of Irish in schools both in the Gaeltacht and outside of it, as noted already, were also mirrored in some of his statements in relation to the place of the language in other aspects of Irish society. On this, he constructed the following inventory:

> There is no thriving indigenous Irish language cinema, despite some brave and creative initiatives by Bob Quinn; the Irish language theatre produces only an occasional flicker in the Gaeltacht; publishing is rather healthier, with the volume and variety of books for adults and young children (though not for adolescents) showing improvement in recent years. There is no satisfactory Irish language newspaper with a decent circulation in the Gaeltacht. Gaeltacht-orientated newspapers have been short-lived, while no "national" Irish language newspaper has yet succeeded in simultaneously serving its mission to the scattered constituency of Irish speakers throughout the country as a whole and serving a Gaeltacht community of faithful readers. The same is true of Irish language magazines.[66]

Yet, he then went on as follows to say that the situation was not "uniformly bleak":

> If we accept that, in addition to key institutions, there are also key roles for public events, rituals, and social customs in sustaining a sense of community, then the revival of interest in (and respect, nationally and internationally, as well as locally, for) séan-nós (traditional) singing, currach-racing and traditional sailing vessels, pattern-days in Gaeltacht parishes, may be considered affirmative of the general Irish language culture in the Gaeltacht. Most important of all, however, has been the influence of the Gaeltacht radio service, Radio na Gaeltachta, in allowing the Gaeltacht communities to speak to each other (with some diminution of dialect difficulties) and to the Irish-speaking public in the country as a whole; in re-affirming the status of the language as a community language, and in producing a general accretion of self-confidence to the people of the Gaeltacht.[67]

"Not surprisingly", he concluded, "the demand for a Gaeltacht television service has been based on the assumption that it would significantly magnify the benign impact of Radio na Gaeltachta, given the pervasiveness and potency of television as a mass medium of information and entertainment".[68]

Finally, throughout the 1970s, 1980s and 1990s, surveys amongst the population nationally reported a growing positive attitude towards the Irish language amongst the Irish population over time. In particular, they reported support for the teaching of Irish in schools, an increase in positive perceptions of the importance of the language as a cultural and ethnic symbol, and support for providing increased state investment for the promotion of the Irish language. Where all of this was leading, including in relation to schooling in the Gaeltacht from the late 1990s is the central concern of the next chapter.

Notes

1. T. K. Whitaker. 'Economic Development. The Irish Experience', *The Irish Times*, 20 September 1982.
2. Department of Finance. *Programme for Economic Expansion* (Dublin: Stationery Office, 1958).
3. Department of Finance. *Second Programme for Economic Expansion* (Dublin: Stationery Office, 1958).

4. T. K. Whitaker. 'Capital Formation, Saving and Economic Progress', *Journal of the Statistical and Social Inquiry Society of Ireland*, Vol. 19, 1955–56, pp. 185–188.
5. The Survey Team. *Investment in Education: Report of the Survey Team* (Dublin: Stationery Office, 1966).
6. For an overview on developments in Europe during the period in question, see V. Mallinson. *The Western European Idea in Education* (Oxford: Pergamon Press, 1980).
7. Dáil Éireann Debates. Vol. 203, Col. 598, 30 May 1963.
8. The Survey Team. *Investment in Education: Report of the Survey Team.*
9. Commission on the Restoration of the Irish Language. *Athbheochan na Gaeilge. The Restoration of the Irish Language* (Dublin: The Stationery Office, 1965).
10. Ibid.
11. K. C. Kearns. 'The Resuscitation of the Irish Gaeltacht', *Geographical Review*, Vol. 64, No. 1, 1974, pp. 82–110.
12. Ibid.
13. Commission on the Restoration of the Irish Language. *The Restoration of the Irish Language.*
14. Ibid.
15. K. C. Kearns. 'The Resuscitation of the Irish Gaeltacht'.
16. B. S. Mac Aodha. *The Galway Gaeltacht Survey: 1968–69* (Galway: Social Sciences Research Centre, University College Galway, 1971).
17. K. C. Kearns. 'The Resuscitation of the Irish Gaeltacht'.
18. Ibid.
19. Ibid.
20. Ibid.
21. Ibid.
22. Ibid., p. 97.
23. Ibid.
24. Ibid., p. 101.
25. Commission on the Restoration of the Irish Language. *The Restoration of the Irish Language.*
26. Ibid., p. 90.
27. Ibid.
28. Ibid.
29. Ibid., p. 92.
30. Ibid., p. 86.
31. Ibid.
32. Ibid., p. 92.
33. Ibid.
34. Ibid.

35. N. Ó Gadhra. 'Irish Government Policy and Political Developments in the Gaeltacht', *Language, Culture and Curriculum*, Vol. l, No. 3, 1988, p. 251.
36. Ibid., p. 257.
37. D. Fennell. 'The Last Years of the Gaeltacht', *The Crane Bag*, Vol. 5, p. 11.
38. G. Ó Tuathaigh. *The Development of the Gaeltacht as a Bilingual Entity* (Dublin: Linguistics Institute of Ireland, 1990), p. 9.
39. N. Ó Gadhra. 'Irish Government Policy and Political Developments in the Gaeltacht', *Language, Culture and Curriculum*, p. 258.
40. G. Ó Tuathaigh. *The Development of the Gaeltacht as a Bilingual Entity*, p. 10.
41. See 'Scoil Dún Chaoin Celebrates Landmark in Its History', *The Kerryman*, 14 March 2019. https://www.independent.ie/au/regionals/kerryman/localnotes/scoil-dn-chaoin-celebrates-landmark-in-its-history-27369613.html.
42. This account is based on that in Thomas Walsh. A Critical Analysis of Curricular Policy in Irish primary Schools 1897–1990 (Unpublished Ph.D. Thesis, National University of Ireland Maynooth, 2006).
43. T. Ó Domhnalláin. 'Buntús Gaeilge: Cúlra, cur le chéile, cur i bhfeidhm', *Teangeolas*, Vol. 13, 1981, pp. 24–32.
44. N. A. 'Buntús Gaeilge and Buntús Cainte', *An Múinteoir Náisiúnta*, Vol. 12, No. 7, 1967, p. 3; Conradh na Gaeilge. 'The Language and the National Identity', *An Múinteoir Náisiúnta*, Vol. 11, No. 11, January 1967, pp. 30–31; NA. 'Linguistic Research and Its Application', *An Múinteoir Náisiúnta*, Vol. 12, No. 7, 1967, p. 27.
45. Department of Education. *Primary School Curriculum: Teacher's Handbook: Part 1* (Dublin: The Stationery Office, 1971).
46. Ibid., p. 30.
47. An Roinn Oideachas. *Tuarascáil an Chomhchoiste um Oideachas sa Ghaeltacht* (Baile Átha Cliath: Oifig an tSoláthair, 1982).
48. Comhar na Múinteoirí Gaeilge. *Bunoideachas trí Ghaeilge sa Ghaeltacht: Tuarascáil* (Baile Átha Cliath: Comhar na Múinteoirí Gaeilge, 1981).
49. Irish National Teachers' Organisation. *The Irish National Teachers' Organisation and the Irish Language: Discussion Document* (Dublin: Irish National Teachers' Organisation, 1985); Irish National Teachers' Organisation. 'The Irish National Teachers' Organisation and the Irish language', *Tuarascáil*, No. 3, March 1989, pp. 29–31.
50. Department of Education. *Report of the Committee on Primary Schools Inspection* (Dublin: The Stationery Office, 1981); Department of Education. *Programme for Action in Education* 1984–1987 (Dublin: The Stationery Office, 1984).

51. This account is based on that in Thomas Walsh. A Critical Analysis of Curricular Policy in Irish Primary Schools, 1897–1990 (Unpublished Ph.D. Thesis, National University of Ireland Maynooth, 2006).
52. Ibid.
53. Curriculum and Examinations Board. *Language in the Curriculum: A Curriculum and Examinations Board Discussion Paper* (Dublin: Curriculum and Examinations Board, 1985).
54. Ibid., p. 28. See also: Comhar na Múinteoirí Gaeilge. *Bunoideachas Trí Ghaeilge sa Ghaeltacht: Tuarascáil* (Baile Átha Cliath: Comhar na Múinteoirí Gaeilge, 1981).
55. Review Body on the Primary Curriculum. *Report of the Review Body on the Primary Curriculum* (Dublin: Department of Education, 1990).
56. G. Granville. 'Politics and Partnership in Curriculum Planning in Ireland'. In C. Sugrue (Ed.). *Curriculum and Ideology: Irish Experiences: International Perspectives* (Dublin: The Liffey Press, 2004), pp. 67–99.
57. Ibid.
58. G. Ó Tuathaigh. *The Development of the Gaeltacht as a Bilingual Entity.*
59. C. Ó Comhraí (Ed.). *Scoil Chuimsitheach Chiaráin: Caoga Bliain ag Fás* (Indreabhán, Conamara: Cló Iar-Chonnacht, 2016), p. 249.
60. Ibid.
61. https://www.cso.ie/en/census/censusvolumes1926to1991/historicalreports/census1971reports/census1971volume8-irishlanguage/.
62. Committee on Language Attitudes Research. *Report* (Dublin: The Stationery Office, 1975).
63. D. Mac Giolla Chríost. 'Micro-Level Language Planning in Ireland.' In A. Liddicoat and R. B. Baldauf (Eds.). *Language Planning in Local Contexts* (Bristol: Multilingual Matters, 2008), pp. 75–94.
64. Ibid., p. 82.
65. Department of Education. *White Paper on Educational Development* (Dublin: Stationery Office, 1980).
66. G. Ó Tuathaigh. *The Development of the Gaeltacht as a Bilingual Entity*, p. 15.
67. Ibid.
68. Ibid., p. 8.

CHAPTER 9

A New Multilingual Ireland and Schooling in the Gaeltacht: 1998 to the Present

Introduction

Developments in relation to education in general in Ireland for the years considered in the previous chapter, and particularly in relation to education in the Gaeltacht, took place during one of bleakest times in the history of the State.[1] Poor government policies combined with global economic problems contributed to this situation. The outcome was high unemployment and mass emigration for most of the 1980s. The decade was also one of political instability, with power alternating between the major political parties, and some governments not even lasting a year. The tide began to turn in 1987, when the major political parties began to promote economic reform, tax cuts, welfare reform and a reduction in borrowing to fund current spending.

By 2000, the nation had become one of the wealthiest in the world, unemployment stood at 4 per cent and income tax levels were almost 50 per cent less than they had been in the 1980s. During this time, the Irish economy grew by five-to-six per cent annually, dramatically raising Irish monetary incomes to equal, and eventually surpass, those of many states in the rest of Western Europe. Yet, within eight years, the country became the most indebted state in the European Union following the global financial crisis. It took until the start of 2015 for a series of austerity measure introduced in the interim, to lead eventually to economic growth and low unemployment.

T. O'Donoghue and T. O'Doherty, *Irish Speakers and Schooling in the Gaeltacht, 1900 to the Present*,
https://doi.org/10.1007/978-3-030-26021-7_9

Developments in relation to the place of the Irish language in the nation continued throughout both the high and low periods of the country's economy noted above. As detailed in the previous chapter in relation to the years 1967 to 1998, some of these developments related to the place of the Irish language in Irish society generally, while others related to social, economic, and Irish language developments in the Gaeltacht, and others yet again related to the place of Irish in the education system across the country. This chapter now addresses each of these developments in relation to the period from 1998 to the present.

Developments in Relation to the Irish Language in Ireland

During the economic boom in Ireland during the 1990s, a great influx took place not only of EU citizens to the country, but also of non-EU citizens, in order to meet labour requirements. On this, Ó Laóire[2] has drawn attention to the numbers of migrant workers that came from countries as far apart as the Czech Republic, Latvia, Poland, the Philippines, Lithuania and South Africa. To these can be added asylum seekers and refugees who arrived in the 1980s and early 1990s, from many countries, including Algeria, the Democratic Republic of Congo, Nigeria, Romania, the Republic of Moldova, Poland, the Russian Federation and Ukraine.

A major outcome of migration is that Ireland has experienced in recent years a growth in ethnic and cultural diversity and a huge increase in multilingualism.[3] Cognisance of this situation is likely to have been a major stimulus for a significant amount of media discussion that has taken place on the Irish language in the country.[4] Furthermore, much of the associated debate has been controversial, with the expression of a wide range of opinions and emotions, including by those who reject out of hand arguments that the Irish language and national identity are intimately connected.[5]

The State, nevertheless, took a renewed interest over the period under consideration in taking steps to try to halt the loss of the Irish language nationally and re-establish it as a language of everyday communication. A major landmark was a statement in the Good Friday Agreement of 1998[6] on the establishment of a joint North of Ireland/Republic of Ireland body to promote Irish. The following year, Foras na Gaeilge (the Irish Language Institute), a cross-border inter-government agency was set up to carry out this vision. Its main work is to facilitate and encourage the speaking and writing of Irish in public and in private arenas in accordance with part three of the European Charter for Regional and Minority Languages.

By now, the Republic of Ireland's *Education Act* (1998) had been passed. It states that every person covered by the Act shall:

> …. contribute to the realisation of national policy and objectives in relation to the extension of bilingualism in Irish society and in particular the achievement of greater use of the Irish language at school and in the community [and] contribute to the maintenance of Irish as the primary community language in Gaeltacht areas.[7]

Further, Section 31 of the Act sets out the structure for the provision of education services for schools in the Gaeltacht, for gaelscoileanna, and for the teaching of Irish.

In 2002, An Chomhairle um Oideachas Gaeltachta agus Gaelscolaíochta (COGG) (the Advisory Body for Education in the Gaeltacht and in gaelscoileanna) was established under the provisions of the Act. Amongst its functions are planning for the provision of textbooks and for pedagogical resources to assist in teaching through Irish, advising on the promotion of education through Irish in schools (including gaelscoileanna and schools in the Gaeltacht), providing support services to each of these types of schools, and engaging in research on language planning and language promotion in them. It also developed a website containing a comprehensive directory of resource material to support teachers in their teaching through Irish.

Shortly afterwards, the *Official Languages Act* (2003)[8] was passed which established the statutory framework for providing public services through the medium of Irish. The Act also provided the legal basis for the office of An Coimisinéir Teanga (Language Commissioner), with responsibility for monitoring and enforcing compliance by public bodies with the Act.

Under the *Official Languages Act*, each Irish citizen is guaranteed the right to engage with all state services in either Irish or English, and the Act outlines mechanisms to ensure that this provision is delivered by public officials. It articulates the requirement that all important documents, such as annual reports and policy statements, are published simultaneously in both languages, while it also addresses the sensitive issue of place names in Gaeltacht districts, by enabling the designation of Irish versions of place names and thereby removing the official status of English place names in the Gaeltacht.

Three years after the passing of the Act, the Irish Government issued a *Statement on the Irish Language*. The statement emphasises the importance of both preserving and promoting the language in the Gaeltacht, in Irish society broadly, and amongst the Irish diaspora in many parts of the world.[9] It outlined thirteen key objectives to guide practices aimed at achieving these ends.

The following year, 2007, Irish became an "official language of the European Union". This had been a long time coming. When the country joined the EEC, Irish became "a Treaty language" rather than "a working language". It is generally considered that the Irish Minister for Foreign Affairs at the time told the EEC that the situation reflected the wish of the Irish government. This, it appears, was because of a lack of desire on the part of the government, given the constitutional status of Irish as an official and national language, that it be simultaneously a minority language. This same position also goes some way towards explaining why Ireland was not a signatory to the "European Charter for Regional or Minority Languages" of 1992, even though representatives of the Irish government played an active role in the associated drafting process.

Back in 1974, Comhairle na Gaeilge had highlighted "a potential for increased realisation of a diversity and richness of language in an enlarged community".[10] In the 1980s, this view became more widespread with the establishment of a EU documentation centre, the "Bureau for Lesser Used Languages" in Dublin. Following the accession of new states to the Union in 2004, and the subsequent inclusion of their languages as working languages, a lobby group seeking similar recognition for Irish became active. In April of that year, over 5000 supporters marched in Dublin, calling on the government to pursue its aims, and an online petition on the matter, with up to 80,000 signatures, was presented to the government, which then tabled a proposal in the EU Parliament seeking official and working status in the EU for Irish. The EU foreign ministers unanimously approved the proposal in June 2005, and it came into effect in January 2007.

Government action continued with the development of *The 20-year Strategy for the Irish Language 2010–2030*. A key objective set down in this document is to heighten visibility of Irish in society and to encourage its increased use in public discourse and services. The hope is that, following from this, associated action can lead to an incremental increase in "the use ... of Irish as a community language"[11] and in bilingualism in society. The rejuvenation of Irish in Gaeltacht areas is also an objective emphasised in the document.

The stated expectation is that *The 20-year Strategy* will lead to an increase in the number of people in Ireland with a knowledge of Irish from the 1.66 million in 2010 to 2 million in 2030, and in an increase in the number of daily speakers of Irish from 83,000 to 250,000 over the same period. The implementation process adopted to try to meet this ambitious challenge, however, hit some obstacles. Plans to establish a new authority, Údarás na Gaeilge agus Gaeltachta (the Irish Language and Gaeltacht Authority), which was to be one of the key players in the process, were abandoned. Instead, responsibility was placed in the hands of Údarás na Gaeltachta, in conjunction with the Department of Arts, Heritage and the Gaeltacht, Foras na Gaeilge, and a number of other government departments, including the Department of Education and Skills.

Various reports published over the period under consideration drew attention to concerns expressed that unless concrete and practical steps are taken, appropriate financial resources are allocated and appropriate timeframes regarding completion, evaluation, enforcement and cross-checking of goals are laid down, then much of what is envisaged may not be achieved. Those expressing views along these lines are acutely aware that while some shift towards the use of Irish occurred following the implementation of practices associated with language policy and planning, bilingual reproduction in the home and intergenerational transmission are far from being common practices. A major challenge regularly related to this is to try to find ways to build on favourable attitudes towards the language in Irish society so that they translate into motivation for deliberate and active use in the home.

Social, Economic and Language Developments in the Gaeltacht

A report published in 2018 contained a comprehensive socio-economic profile of the seven Gaeltacht districts in the country,[12] providing key baseline data to support future policy development. It opened by indicating that the overall population increase across the State between 2006 and 2016, was 12.3 per cent, or 500,000. According to the national census of 2016, the total population residing within the Gaeltacht that year was 99,617. This accounted for 2.1 per cent of the State's population of 4.76 million and was equivalent to the total population residing within County Kilkenny, including Kilkenny City. On a county-by-county basis, the relative population of each of the Gaeltacht districts was as follows: Galway (50,570), Donegal (23,346), Mayo (9340), Kerry (8756), Cork (3932), Meath (1857) and Waterford (1816). Much of the growth—5213 people—took place between 2006 and 2011, whereas there was a decline of 1099 between 2011 and 2016. Further, by far the largest increase in population in the Gaeltacht districts in both number and percentage terms between 2006 and 2016 was in County Galway (4472 people or 9.9 per cent).

The most notable population declines in both number and percentage terms in the Gaeltacht districts between 2006 and 2016 were in County Donegal and County Mayo. Since 2006, the population of the Donegal Gaeltacht fell by 437 (1.8 per cent). The decline of 482 people in Mayo was significantly higher, at 4.4 per cent. Further, this latter decline was a continuation of a decline in the Mayo Gaeltacht since the 1960s. Here, the population in 2016 was 29.6 per cent lower than that of 14,762 in 1966.

Relative to the State average, the combined Gaeltacht areas in 2016 had a much older population profile. With 16.6 per cent or 16,511 residents aged 65 years or older, this contrasted with 13.4 per cent of the residents in the State in the same age group. At the same time, there were substantial variations in the age profile across the seven Gaeltacht districts, with Mayo (22.8 per cent or 2131 people), Donegal (21.7 per cent or 5055 people) and Kerry (18.6 per cent or 1626 people) having by far the highest rates of population aged 65 or over. Rates were much lower in the Meath Gaeltacht (10.6 per cent or 196 people), the Galway Gaeltacht (13.2 per cent or 6657 people) and the Waterford Gaeltacht (13.2 per cent or 239 people). It was concluded, however, that the changing demographic trend in the Gaeltacht overall will have a significant impact on future service delivery and community well-being in the future.

Across the seven Gaeltacht districts, there was also a high level of variance in employment figures, with over a fifth of the labour force classed as unemployed in both the Donegal and Mayo districts, at 22.5 per cent or 2181 people and 22.3 per cent per cent or 864 people, respectively. The other five areas combined had a much lower rate overall, at 13 per cent.

The lowest of all was in the Cork Gaeltacht, which recorded an unemployment rate of only 6.7 per cent.

In relation to education attainment, in the 25-year period leading up to 2016, that of 15 year olds across the nation had greatly improved. Trends in overall education attainment in the Gaeltacht also showed improvement. However, the situation was behind that of the State average; of 11,293 persons residing in the Gaeltacht in 2016, 17 per cent had an education level classified as being "no formal or primary only". This was much higher than the State average of 12.5 per cent. The situation varied also across the Gaeltacht districts, with those in Donegal and Mayo having approximately a quarter of their populations classified as having an education level termed "no formal or primary only". All other Gaeltacht areas recorded rates of less than 13 per cent. Further, regarding frequency of speaking Irish, of the 73,803 daily Irish speakers outside the education system, 20,586 people (27.9 per cent) lived in Gaeltacht areas. All Gaeltacht areas had rates in excess of 25 per cent, with the highest being in the Donegal Gaeltacht (37.3 per cent or 5929 people). In sharp contrast to this, the rate in the Mayo Gaeltacht was 13.8 per cent or 743 people.

In the *Comprehensive Linguistic Study on the Use of Irish in the Gaeltacht*[13] conducted in 2007, three distinct types of language community were deemed to exist within the statutory limits of the Gaeltacht as then defined, namely Categories A, B and C. Category A Gaeltacht districts referred to electoral divisions where more than 67 per cent of the total population (3 years+) were daily speakers of Irish. These electoral divisions evidenced the broadest spectrum of Irish language use and exhibited stable levels of Irish language use except in the language behaviour patterns of the younger age groups.

Category B Gaeltacht districts referred to electoral divisions where between 44 per cent and 66 per cent of the total population (3 years+) were daily speakers of Irish. Although English was the predominant language, these areas still contained some relatively strong Irish-speaking networks. The census data for these areas also indicated clear signs of language shift in the levels of Irish use between different age groups: it was usual that the number of daily speakers of Irish was higher amongst the school-going age cohorts than in the adult age cohorts. This implied that the use of Irish had declined as a communal language in the area and its use amongst young people occurred predominantly in an education context. The statistical data also indicated that Irish was still a community language to a certain degree, but that this tended to be limited to specific age groups, specific institutions and specific social networks.

Category C Gaeltacht districts referred to electoral divisions where less than 44 per cent of the total population (3 years+) were daily speakers of Irish. This category included a majority of Gaeltacht electoral divisions. In general, those in school-going age cohorts reported the highest level of usage of Irish in these districts, indicating weak communal use of the language. Nevertheless, some electoral divisions in the category contained small Irish-speaking enclaves that did not readily conform with the sociolinguistic traits common to the rest of Category C. The data also indicated that in particular areas people still used Irish in some social networks and in community and education institutions.

An overall conclusion of the 2007 study was that without urgent remedial work, the Irish language might disappear as a community or household language in the Gaeltacht within 15–20 years. In response, the *Gaeltacht Act* (2012)[14] was passed, with a principal aim being to modify the structure and functions of Údaras na Gaeltachta which, it will be recalled, is the regional authority responsible for the social, cultural and economic development of the Gaeltacht. Overall, the function of the authority now is to stabilise the current patterns of language shift and to ensure the future of the Gaeltacht as a distinct Irish-speaking community.

Another objective of the *Gaeltacht Act* is to provide for a new definition for a Gaeltacht based on linguistic criteria (as proposed in the 2007 study noted above), instead of on geographic areas, as had been the case up to this point in time. In tandem with this, it made clear that areas located outside the existing statutory Gaeltacht districts are to be given the opportunity to achieve statutory recognition as "Irish language networks" or as "Gaeltacht service towns", as long as they fulfil certain criteria.

Education and the Irish Language, Including in the Gaeltacht Including in the Gaeltacht

General Overview of Education in Ireland

The private, voluntary and community sectors provide "early childhood care and education" outside families and junior and senior infants' classes in primary schools. Service provision is diverse and fragmented. Settings include crèches, playgroups, nurseries, preschools and day care services. Some settings operate with no explicit philosophy, while others market themselves as embracing the education ideas of such famous educationists as Froebel, Montessori, Steiner, Piaget and Dewey.

Ireland's primary and post-primary education sectors, as indicated in previous chapters, include state-funded schools and private schools. Primary education consists of an eight-year cycle: junior infants, senior infants and first-to-sixth classes. Although children are not obliged to attend school until the age of six, almost all children begin school at the age of four or five. The curriculum for primary school education covers the following key areas: Irish, English, mathematics, social, environment and scientific education, arts education including visual arts music and drama, physical integration, social personal and health education.

The post-primary education sector, again as pointed out in previous chapters, comprises secondary schools, vocational schools, comprehensive schools, community schools and community colleges. The differences between these schools, as also indicated, relate to their management structures. In all of them, the first three years is termed the "junior cycle". Students usually begin this "cycle" at 12 years of age and study a broad and balanced curriculum. At the end of the three years, they sit for the Junior Certificate examination. The senior cycle, which usually caters for students in the 15–18 age group, follows the junior cycle. In some cases, the senior cycle is of two years' duration, while in schools that offer the optional "transition year", it is of three years' duration. The transition year follows immediately after the junior cycle and provides an opportunity for students to experience a wide range of educational experiences over the course of a year free from formal examinations.

During the final two years of senior cycle, students take one of three programmes, each leading to a State Examination, namely the established Leaving Certificate, the Leaving Certificate Vocational Programme, or the Leaving Certificate Applied. The established Leaving Certificate examination is the terminal examination of post-primary education and is taken when students are typically 17 or 18 years of age. Syllabi are available in more than 30 subjects and students are required to study at least five subjects, one of which must be Irish.

Irish in English-Medium Schools Outside of the Gaeltacht

From 1992 until 1960, while all Irish governments emphasised the importance of the Irish language in the education system, the emphasis was often on the written rather than on the spoken language. As indicated in previous chapters, the Department of Education issued a circular in 1960, which explained to teachers that they had permission to lessen this emphasis if they considered that it would be beneficial for their students. Following this, as Ní Fhearghusa[15] has pointed out, the number of schools teaching through the medium of Irish fell drastically, to the point where, at the beginning of the 1970s, there were only 11 primary schools and 5 post-primary schools outside of the Gaeltacht that fitted into this category.

Nevertheless, the Department took steps to try to improve the quality of spoken Irish in primary schools. It introduced a new course to this end, Cúrsaí Comhrá (Conversational Matters), in 1969. In the 1960s, it followed up by introducing a compulsory oral examination in Irish for those taking the Leaving Certificate examination. Initially, it decreed that one-sixth of the marks for the examination were for this component. Later on, it increased this proportion to one quarter. In 2012, the situation changed yet again, with Leaving Certificate students sitting, for the first time, a new examination in Irish where 40 per cent of the marks were awarded for the oral examination, 10 per cent for an aural examination, and 50 per cent for the written examination.

Irish-Medium Schooling Outside of the Gaeltacht

In any one year, around 4000 preschool services, including those where all activity is conducted through Irish, are registered, either with the national Child and Family Agency (a State agency established which in 2014 and responsible for improving the well-being of children) or with the Irish Montessori Educational Board. Two organisations, Forbairt Naíonraí Teoranta[16] (Development of Irish-medium Playgroups Limited) and Na Naíonraí Gaelacha[17] (Gaelic playgroups), developed Irish-immersion early childhood care and education courses for children outside of the Gaeltacht. By the year 2017–18, there were 130 naíonraí operating in Ireland, catering for more than 4000 preschool children. Concurrently, gaelscoileanna continue to grow as a result of a "ground-up" movement driven by parents, and in 2017–18 there were

145 gaelscoil and 43 gaelcholáiste (second-level schools) operating outside of the Gaeltacht, catering for almost 36,000 pupils and 10,000 students, respectively.[18]

Students attending gaelscoileanna normally do not speak Irish as their first language. From the 1980s, however, research began to demonstrate that they achieve much higher levels of proficiency in Irish than do those who only study the language as a regular school subject in English-medium schools.[19] At the same time, while they display fluency and confidence in their use of Irish, the level of accuracy and the range of language competencies achieved are less than that of native speakers.[20] This is understandable, since, as has been pointed out, "a full language context cannot be created within the classroom because the natural context is not there".[21]

Education in the Gaeltacht

Eagraíocht na Scoileanna Gaeltachta,[22] the organisation that coordinates and lobbies for Gaeltacht schools, stated in a submission in 1998, to the "National Forum on Early Education", that providing all-Irish education in the Gaeltacht presents many difficulties.[23] Those highlighted included the following: administering a school in Irish in a surrounding world working in English only; English being used increasingly by families who traditionally had spoken Irish only at home; a mixture of language abilities in Irish in all preschool and primary school classes; and a lack of appropriate teaching materials. By now, studies undertaken on pupils' achievements in Irish[24] had found it was not correct to assume that teachers in all Gaeltacht schools taught exclusively or mainly through Irish.

The results of a study of all primary and post-primary schools in the Gaeltacht[25] also indicated the existence of a wide variety of practices. In general, the language of instruction in each school reflected the proportion of pupils fluent in Irish on entry and the position of the Irish language in the school's community. However, the policy of the school itself towards the use of Irish as the teaching medium, and on whether the amount of Irish used should increase or not as the child progressed through the school, was found to be of equal significance.

There was also a slow but steady decline in Irish-only education in Gaeltacht schools. Further, a substantial minority of teachers were teaching at least some of their classes through English only. The frequent use of English language texts and materials used while teaching through Irish, especially in second-level schools, was another characteristic of Gaeltacht schooling. Moreover, anecdotal evidence indicated it was widely known in Gaeltacht areas which schools had particular attitudes to teaching in Irish and that, where there was a choice, and particularly at primary school level, parents often selected a school that matched as close as possible their own linguistic and education priorities for their children.

At the end of the 1990s, also, studies indicated that pupils who commenced preschool as dominant Irish speakers were by now in a minority throughout most of the Gaeltacht districts and that a substantial minority of Irish speakers in the Gaeltacht, and even a majority in certain age groups and professions, did not support Irish-only education.[26] At the same time, it was clear that a combination of community language usage and the education system was still succeeding in bringing a significant proportion of children for whom English was their dominant language, to competence in Irish at an early age. It is difficult, however, to see how this situation will continue in the long term if high competence in Irish amongst the younger cohorts declines and Irish-medium schooling does not command full community support from Gaeltacht Irish speakers themselves.[27]

In *The 20-year Strategy for the Irish Language 2010–2030*, certain policies existing at the point of its publication were abandoned, including the abolition of scholarships provided for Gaeltacht students to attend university. The State also abolished allowances for teachers teaching through Irish and teaching in island schools. On the other hand, the State gave support for the provision of early childhood education through naíonraí. This was channelled through Comhar na Naíonraí Gaeltachta (CNNG) (the Early Childhood Education Partnership), a company founded specifically by Údarás na Gaeltachta in 2004, to provide the necessary infrastructure for provision.

In recent years, the preparation of teachers for early childhood education has been receiving more attention than previously, both in official government policy and in the teacher preparation programmes. Two of the nation's providers of programmes leading to "certificates in childcare" have courses that qualify graduates to work in naíonraí. In addition, CNNG produced two additional mandatory modules—Saibhriú na Gaeilge (Enriching the Irish Language) and Sochtheangeolaíocht agus an Páiste (Sociolinguistics and the Child) specifically for those working with children in naíonraí in the Gaeltacht. Furthermore, in collaboration with the Dublin Institute of Technology (DIT), it has produced a number of books and CDs featuring traditional rhymes and songs in Irish.[28]

In order to cater for the mixed language backgrounds of children in Gaeltacht schools, and particularly in primary schools, CNNG and DIT also collaborated in the design of a thematic, differentiated curriculum entitled *Borradh* (Development/Expansion). This development is designed to assist teachers who are experiencing difficulties due to the increasingly diverse pupil intake in terms of language background. In addition, since 2012, it has been mandatory to conduct standardised Irish language reading tests in all Irish-medium primary schools both in Gaeltacht districts and outside of them. They are taken by students at the end of second class, fourth class and sixth class, and it is a requirement that the results be reported to parents, to school boards of management, and to the national Department of Education and Skills.

Those teaching through Irish at the primary school level, including in the Gaeltacht, are now also reasonably well-served with teaching materials through output from the An Gúm publishers, COGG, voluntary organisations and commercial publishers. Some materials prepared for the teaching of Irish in schools in the Northern Ireland education system are also used. Further, the digitisation of Séideán Sí, an integrated material-reading scheme for use in Gaeltacht primary schools and in gaelscoileanna, is a joint initiative supported by bodies in both jurisdictions.

While commercial publishing companies have been producing a wide variety of materials for the teaching of Irish as a school subject in secondary schools, there are still quite a few gaps in relation to the provision of appropriate materials for teaching through Irish across a range of other subjects. An Gúm and COGG, however, are acutely aware of this and continue to address it as best they can. In doing so, they are also cognisant of the challenge to move away from the traditional textbook and towards providing flexible resources to meet changing curricula and student expectations. Indeed, to this end, COGG maintains an online database of resources, including some located in Northern Ireland.

Breacadh (Dawn), a group that is active in Gaeltacht districts has, since 2000, provides adult education services through Irish to adults; working in collaboration with the respective Education and Training Boards, these programmes focus on literacy in Irish, on communication skills, on computer skills and on family learning. They also produce resources in the nation's three main dialects for use in literacy classes and publish vocabulary lists in areas of work integral to Gaeltacht life. While these programmes aim at improving the quality of adults' spoken and written language, they also provide them with knowledge and skills to assist in the education of their children.

Whether working in Irish-medium schools within the Gaeltacht or outside the Gaeltacht, teaching content to pupils who have a limited proficiency in a language requires teaching strategies unlike those required when teaching in pupils' mother tongue. Teachers need not only a highly developed competence in the language themselves, but also deep understandings and key competencies in immersion teaching.

In 1998, a one-year initial teacher education postgraduate programme for second-level teachers, Ard Dioplóma san Oideachas (Higher Diploma in Education), conducted through the medium of Irish, was established at the National University of Ireland Galway. Later, in 2014, it became a two-year programme and was renamed An Máistir Gairmiúil san Oideachas (Professional Masters Degree in Education). This higher diploma programme (H.Dip) was to prepare teachers to teach second-level school subjects through Irish in both Gaeltacht schools and in gaelscoileanna.[29] Mary Immaculate College Limerick also designed and commenced in 2015 offering of a two-year part-time professional development programme at master's level for already qualified professionals teaching in Irish-medium settings, entitled An M. Oid. san Oideachas Lán-Ghaeilge (Master of Education in Irish-medium Education).

In response to the shortage of teachers competent to teach in Irish-medium settings, and as part of the implementation of the *Gaeltacht Education Policy 2017–2022,* the Department of Education and Skills established Aonad un Oideachas Gaeltachta (Gaeltacht Education Unit) in 2017, which published tenders for two new teacher education programmes. The first initial teacher education, four-year bachelor of education degree, which will be delivered completely through the medium of Irish and will prepare primary teachers, was launched in 2018. Offered by Marino Institute of Education, Dublin, this programme will enrol its first students in 2019, who will complete all their placements in Irish-medium settings and undertake their final 10-week practicum in a Gaeltacht school. In addition, a master's programme for practising primary and post-primary teachers teaching in Irish-medium settings is being offered by Mary Immaculate College, Limerick. Over the period 2018–2024, it is anticipated that this blended programme (30 per cent of the provision is online) will graduate 150 teachers and principals who are capable of leading Irish-medium schools. The government has committed to increase significantly the funding to support the Policy on Gaeltacht Education, from 1 m Euro in 2017 to 2.3 million in 2018, and almost 5 million in 2019. Expenditure is committed to supporting a number of new projects, including the e-Hub which allows post-primary Gaeltacht schools experiencing difficulties securing teachers of subjects, competent to teach in Irish, to access online and distance programmes. The Gaeltacht School Recognition Scheme is a further project which is being funded by the Department—this scheme supports and encourages schools to engage in community-based activities with a view to extending the use of Irish in the Gaeltacht.

The National Council for Curriculum and Assessment (NCCA) introduced in 2018 a revised language programme, which is being applied in English medium, Gaeltacht schools, and Irish-medium schools and special schools. There are two versions of the *Primary Language Curriculum*, one for English-medium schools, where English is the schools' first language and Irish is the second, and one for Irish-medium schools, where Irish is the schools' first language and English is the second. This new programme, which prioritises children's oral language skills, identifies learning outcomes and stages in the progression of children's language acquisition (progression continua), with a view that the language expectations for children in their first language, should be the same whether that is Irish or English. The progression continua allow children to move at their own pace, and teachers to track the children's success at each step and milestone. In English-medium schools, children are exposed to Irish in their Irish lessons from junior infants onwards, while in gaelscoileanna and Gaeltacht schools, schools may choose to teach through Irish for the full day, and children will not be exposed to English lessons until they are in their third year at school. The new programme emphasises the transferrable skills children acquire in their first language (Language 1) with a view to supporting their development of a second language (Language 2). This programme is at an early stage of implementation and its impact on the level of children's competence in Irish in both settings is set to be assessed.

To conclude, it is clear that the State continues to recognise that the nature of the education provided in Gaeltacht schools is critical to the maintenance of Irish as a family and community language in the Gaeltacht. Over the decades, however, the manner in which support is given has changed. For example, the State-funded scheme in operation since the 1930s, under which Gaeltacht families received an annual grant for each child deemed on inspection to be an Irish language speaker, was replaced in 1993, by Scéim Labhairt na Gaeilge (the Spoken Irish Scheme). The State awards grants of Euro 260 per annum to families that were deemed to be Irish-speaking following an inspection to determine the language fluency of their homes.

Scéim Labhairt na Gaeilge was replaced by another scheme in 2011. Fundamental to the new scheme is the provision by the Department of Culture, Heritage and the Gaeltacht of language support packages for families in the Gaeltacht to assist them in raising their children aged up to 5 years of age, through the Irish language. It also involves developing an awareness campaign in conjunction with the Health Service Executive (HSE) through distributing an information leaflet to expectant mothers and mothers of babies in the Gaeltacht, detailing the advantages of raising children through Irish. Údarás na Gaeltachta also supports a youth organisation, Óige na Gaeltachta. This organisation, founded in 2006, seeks to promote and develop services, through the medium of Irish, for young people in the Gaeltacht. This is part of a larger movement aimed at trying to develop an Irish language "youth culture". The establishment of Raidio na Gaeltachta (Gaeltacht radio station) in 1972 and in particular TG4 (Irish-medium television station) in 1996 has done much through its coverage of culture and sports, to bring the Irish language to the wider population, with an average of 650,000 viewers watching the channel each day.

It is evident over that there has been a renewed vigour on the part of government agencies over the last decade to promote Irish within the Gaeltacht and across the state. The role of education and schooling in particular in the preservation of Irish has been underscored during this period, and the growth of Irish-medium schools, outside of the Gaeltacht regions, has been a cause for much optimism. While the number of first-language Irish speakers has been in decline within the Gaeltacht regions, the huge growth in the number of Irish-medium schools at primary and post-primary levels outside of the Gaeltacht has done much to reverse this decline in Irish speakers and offers new shoots of promise for the language.

Notes

1. The account in this opening section is based on that in K. O'Rourke. 'Independent Ireland in Comparative Perspective', *Irish Economic and Social History*, No. 44, 2017, pp. 19–45. https://doi.org/10.1177/0332489317735410. hdl:10197/8246.
2. M. Ó Laoire. 'The Language Planning Situation in Ireland', *Current Issues in Language Planning*, Vol. 6, No. 3, 2005, pp. 251–314.
3. T. J. Ó Ceallaigh and Á. Ní Dhonnabháin. 'Reawakening the Irish Language Through the Irish Education System: Challenges and Priorities', *International Electronic Journal of Elementary Education*, Vol. 8, No. 2, 2015, pp. 179–198.
4. See, for example, C. Nic Pháidín and S. Ó Cearnaigh (Eds.). *A New View of the Irish Language* (Dublin: Cois Life, 2008) and P. Ó Duibhir. The Spoken Irish of Sixth Class Pupils in Irish Immersion Schools (Unpublished Ph.D. in Applied Linguistics, Dublin, Trinity College, 2009).
5. See I. Watson. 'The Irish Language and Identity'. In C. Nic Pháidín and S. Ó Cearnaigh (Eds.). *A New View of the Irish Language* (Dublin: Cois Life, 2008), pp. 66–75.
6. This was the peace agreement between the British and Irish governments, and most of the political parties in the North of Ireland, on how Northern Ireland should be governed.
7. Government of Ireland. (1998). Education Act. http://www.irishstatutebook.ie/1998/en/act/pub/0051/.
8. See http://www.irishstatutebook.ie/eli/2003/act/32/enacted/en/html.
9. P. Ó Flatharta. *A Structure for Education in the Gaeltacht: Summary* (Dublin: An Chomhairle um Oideachas Gaeltachta agus Gaelscolaíochta, 2007).
10. Comhairle na Gaeilge. *Implementing a Language Policy* (Dublin: Comhairle na Gaeilge, 1974).
11. Government of Ireland. *The 20-year Strategy for the Irish Language 2010–2030*, p. 3. http://www.ahg.gov.ie/en/20YearStrategyfortheIrishLanguage/Publications.
12. The account in this section, and all of the statistics quoted, are based on P. Ó Céidigh. *Socio-economic Profile of the Seven Gaeltacht Districts in Ireland* (Dublin: Irish Research Council, 2018).
13. C. Ó Giollagáin. *Comprehensive Linguistic Survey of the Use of Irish in the Gaeltacht* (Maynooth: National University of Ireland Maynooth, 2007).
14. Seehttp://www.irishstatutebook.ie/eli/2012/act/34/enacted/en/html.
15. J. Ní Fhearghusa. Gaelscoileanna. Stair na hEagraíochta. 1973–1988 (Unpublished M.Ed. Thesis, University College Dublin, 1998).

16. See https://www.activelink.ie/content/irish-links/education/forbairt-na%C3%ADonra%C3%AD-teoranta.
17. http://www.gaelscoileanna.ie/en/na-naionrai-gaelacha/.
18. http://gaeloideachas.ie/i-am-a-researcher/statistics/.
19. See J. Harris. *Spoken Irish in Primary Schools* (Dublin: Institiúid Teangeolaíochta Éireann, 1984); J. Harris and L. Murtagh. 'Irish and English in Gaeltacht Primary Schools'. In G. Mac Eoin, A. Ahlqvist, and D. Ó hAodha (Eds.). *Third International Conference on Minority Languages: Celtic Papers: Multilingual Matters* (Clevedon: Multilingual Matters, 1988), pp. 104–124; J. Harris, P. Forde, P. Archer, S. Nic Fhearaile, and M. O' Gorman. *Irish in Primary Schools. Long-term National Trends in Achievement* (Dublin: Government Publications, 2006).
20. See P. Ó Duibhir. The Spoken Irish of Sixth Class Pupils in Irish Immersion Schools (Unpublished Ph.D. Thesis in Applied Linguistics, Trinity College Dublin, 2009); F. Genesee and K. Lindholm-Leary. 'Two Case Studies of Content-Based Language Education', *Journal of Immersion and Content-based Language Education*, Vol. 1, No. 1, 2013, pp. 3–33.
21. N. Ní Mhaoláin. *Ár bPolasaí Gaeilge: Polasaí na Gaeilge do Ghaelscoileanna* (Dublin: Gaelscoileanna, 2005), p. 25.
22. See http://www.gaelport.com/eagra%C3%ADochtnascoileannagaeltach-taeng.
23. See T. Ó hIfearnáin, 'Raising Children to Be Bilingual in the Gaeltacht: Language Preference and Practice', *International Journal of Bilingual Education and Bilingualism*, Vol. 10, No. 4, 2007, pp. 510–528.
24. As for notes 17 and 18 above.
25. See S. Mac Donnacha, F. Ní Chualáin, A. Ní Shéaghdha, and T. Ní Mhainín. *Staid Reatha na Scoileanna Gaeltachta* (Baile Átha Cliath: An Chomhairle um Oideachas Gaeltachta agus Gaelscolaíochta, 2005).
26. See T. Hickey. *Luathoideachas Trí Ghaeilge sa Ghaeltacht* (Galway: Údarás na Gaeltachta, 1999) and P. Ó Fiannachta. *Stair na Gaeilge ó Thús* (Corcaigh: Mercier Press, 1974).
27. The following account is based on that in European Research Centre on Multilingualism and Language Learning. *The Irish Language in Education in the Republic of Ireland* (Ljouwert/Leeuwarden, The Netherlands: Fryske Akademy Doelestrjitte, 2016).
28. See http://www.comharnaionrai.ie/; http://gaeloideachas.ie/i-am-a-researcher/statistics/.
29. S. Ó Grádaigh. 'Who Are Qualified to Teach in Second-Level Irish-Medium Schools?' *Irish Educational Studies*, Vol. 34, No. 2, 2015, pp. 165–182.

CHAPTER 10

Looking Backwards

The principal focus of the exposition presented throughout this book is the schooling of children living in the Gaeltacht, with particular reference to the period from 1900 to the present. The origin of the terms, "An Ghaeltacht" in the Irish language and "the Gaeltacht" in the English language, and an overview on the conditions of life in Gaeltacht districts at the beginning of the twentieth century were considered by way of geographical and language background. A presentation outlining the broader national historical context followed, with the concentration being on the fate of the Irish language in Ireland, and specifically in education, up to the last decades of the nineteenth century. The Gaelic League's campaign over the next two decades aimed at the introduction of a bilingual programme for schools in the Gaeltacht was then detailed. This was accompanied by a consideration of steps taken regarding the promotion of the Irish language, including in the Gaeltacht, by the Sinn Féin leaders who took their seats in the First Dáil in 1918, up until the publication in 1926 (four years after the establishment of the independent Irish State), of the report of the State-initiated Coimisiún na Gaeltachta (Commission on the Gaeltacht).

The remainder of the book deals with the provision, nature and content of schooling in the Gaeltacht from 1922, until the present. We considered a variety of issues in relation to a number of periods over the time span. This involved taking account of broad developments in Irish society nationally, including developments in relation to the promotion

T. O'Donoghue and T. O'Doherty, *Irish Speakers and Schooling in the Gaeltacht, 1900 to the Present*,
https://doi.org/10.1007/978-3-030-26021-7_10

of the Irish language throughout the country in general, in the schools for the majority English-speaking population, and in the Gaeltacht. Considered also were Gaeltacht people's memories of schooling. On cogitating all of this, we came to hold in relation to schooling, with Mac Giolla Chríost's judgement on the Gaeltacht in general, namely that "the relentless contraction and fragmentation of the Gaeltacht during the course of the 20th century underscores the inescapable conclusion that [native] Irish speakers did not benefit from equal social citizenship in the Irish nation state".[1]

We leave it to others, including sociologists and applied linguists, to provide a detailed overview of current developments in relation to Irish in Ireland, to economic and social life in the Gaeltacht and to the education of students there. We hope, however, that our work provides them with a historical context that can be of assistance to them. On this, we subscribe to a long-held view that those who ignore history condemn themselves to not understanding contemporary situations, since studies of historical developments alone permit us to weigh and evaluate in their respective relations the elements of the present. To put it another way, a historical perspective is useful, not because it provides a basis for prediction but because an understanding of human action in the past makes it possible "to find familiar elements in present problems and thus make it possible to solve them intelligently".[2]

The remainder of this final chapter indicates certain patterns extrapolated from our overall exposition that go some way towards addressing the above-stated aspiration. Firstly, patterns that help to provide an understanding of the current situation in relation to the Irish language throughout the country are considered. Secondly, patterns that help to provide an understanding of the current social and economic situation in relation to the Gaeltacht are detailed. Thirdly, patterns are outlined that help to provide an understanding of the current situation in relation to schooling in the Gaeltacht.

Historical Patterns and the Current Situation on Irish in Ireland

The population of the 26-county Irish state in 2017 was 4,757,956. In the same year, it was recorded that only 1.5% (73,803) spoke Irish on a daily basis outside of the education system, with a third of that figure (20,586) residing in the Gaeltacht.[3] Thus, it is not surprising that UNESCO has classified Irish as an endangered language.[4] This, by definition, means that the great majority of children in Ireland do not learn Irish as a mother tongue in the home.

For decades, it has been common to lay the blame for the decline in the number of Irish speakers at the feet of teachers, given the emphasis placed by the State on teaching the language in schools since 1922. In 1988, however, Ó Gadhra, argued that this was unfair. It is important in the first instance, he held, not to lose sight of "the catastrophic decline [in the number of Irish speakers] that had set in by the time the Gaelic League was founded in 1893, and the further rapid decay in genuinely Irish-speaking communities by the time the Irish Free State was founded in 1922".[5] Equally, he held, the folly of the language revival lobby in arguing that "Irish was the unique heritage of all Irish people, including those whose background had never had a Gaelic element of any significance and a much larger segment of 'native Irish' who had abandoned Irish in the nineteenth century",[6] needs to be kept in mind. An outcome of this folly, he stated, was the adoption of a compulsory Irish policy for schools in the post-Independence era that served to alienate a large proportion of the population who might otherwise have had enthusiasm for learning it.[7]

The teachers in the primary schools, despite the best efforts of many, were also, with some exceptions, not prepared or sufficiently qualified to negotiate the vicissitudes of revitalising any level of interest in the Irish language amongst the student population in the schools. Many teachers also had limited proficiency in spoken and written Irish. Yet, they were compelled to teach it, and their related hostile attitudes were certainly not conducive to adopting creative teaching approaches. The expectation of most parents that their children would achieve upward social mobility through emigration was also a major influence. In other words, a focus on their children's economic situation rather than on any government or minority middle-class proposals with regard to revitalising the Irish language was central in the minds of many.

Government policy on compulsory Irish in the schools had long-lasting deleterious effects on generations of Irish people. This is hardly surprising if one accepts that compulsion rarely works in any sphere of human endeavour. To put it another way, coercion, as opposed to providing individual choice, can act to enable negativity to linger on in the mind, to fester and to contribute to the process of associated attitudes being passed on to succeeding generations. Thus, from the point of view of those enthused by language revivalism, it is unfortunate for the fate of Irish that twentieth-century government education policy did not embrace a more liberal curriculum for the language, without compulsion.[8]

As Ó Gadhra has also stressed, it is important not to underestimate the extent of achievements.[9] On this, he pointed to the absence during the early decades of independent Ireland scientific knowledge on language revival, of insights from post-colonial studies, of the application of linguistics to the development of second-language language teaching methods and of approaches to social, cultural and economic policy development based on scholarship in the social sciences. It is easy, he stated, to

> … be wise after the events, to make over-simple comparisons and, with true Irish modesty, to underestimate the achievements of our own efforts in more difficult times, when neither the modern attitudes to language toleration nor the advances in education, mass media and modern social planning techniques were as developed as they are today.[10]

"The fact", he went on, "is that the Irish revival effort … was one of the most ambitious, idealistic and perhaps revolutionary undertakings in modern times".

Given this situation, one is tempted to speculate on whether the notable increase in interest in Irish in Ireland in recent years is due to a late influence of earlier education policies and the earlier work undertaken by various language revival movements or whether it has very different origins. Certainly regarding the latter possibility, a great influx of people to the country over the last number of decades from different ethnic and cultural backgrounds has resulted in a situation whereby more than half a million Irish residents now speak a language other than Irish or English at home.[11] It is possible that this change stimulated amongst the Irish people an awareness of the importance of the Irish language as an element of national identity. Concurrently, a large increase in gaelscoileanna outside of the Gaeltacht has taken place. Both those attending and supporting these schools, along with other Irish language enthusiasts, now also have support in maintaining and enhancing their language-based identity as a result of the advent of TG4 (Irish-medium television station), the *Official Languages Act, 2003* and, since 2007, the official working status of Irish in the EU.[12]

The new view of the Irish language under consideration emerged at a time when the government's national Irish language policies had moved away "from their leading role in the early decades of the 20th century of stimulation and regeneration that envisaged full national language revival".[13] Instead, as Ó hIfearnáin has put it:

> ... there was a steady and consistent move to sound out popular opinion on issues of policy, with a series of commissions and surveys that were intended to inform government of the needs and desires for Irish in the population. The result has been a gradual retreat from obligations for competence in Irish for state sector employees and a relaxing of some of the requirements in schooling, while at the same time seeking to respond to demand from organised groups.[14]

Various individuals have outlined what they have seen as a concurrent change in public attitudes towards Irish. In 2004, for example, one individual stated as follows:

> When I speak in Irish to my young son on today's Dublin bus, I no longer feel that I am stared at because these days we're surrounded by people speaking Latvian, Russian, French and Portuguese. Being different, in whatever way, is a more comfortable experience when lots of people are different too.[15]

More recently, Seán Bán Breathnach, Irish language broadcaster and celebrity from the Connemara Gaeltacht, has spoken about how many non-Gaeltacht people are now willing and able to converse with him in Irish on national radio and television stations, unlike the case 20 or 30 years ago. This, he has said, is particularly the case in relation to people residing in Dublin.[16]

Social media are also playing a significant role in popularising the language across the country, bringing many to a proud realisation that there is great interest in Irish internationally. YouTube videos, for example, broadcast scenes of large numbers of people across the world studying the language at university level and in special classes for adults. The sean-nós or traditional singing style in Irish of Muhammad Al-Hussaini,[17] a London-born imam, and the fluency in spoken Irish of Dr. Bayda,

Russian-born lecturer at Moscow State University who, in 2019, took up a position as language planning officer in the Gaeltacht in south-west of County Kerry, have enthralled others.[18]

A recent and very popular development is that termed "pop up Gaeltacht". Prior to this, various social events aimed at promoting the language amongst young speakers outside of the Gaeltacht had met with little success. The pop-up Gaeltacht concept, however, has helped to change the situation. It is a simple notion that commenced in Dublin and has resulted in 200–300 attendees meeting in pubs at least once a month.[19] The underlying assumption is that Irish is not dead or useless, and that there are thousands of people across the country who are keen to speak it with each other, but do not live in concentrated language communities. By harnessing Facebook, Twitter and Snapchat, they are able to follow up invitations and meet in relaxed settings around the country and in many cities across the world.[20]

None of what we have stated above means we are unaware of continuing concerns about low level of proficiency in Irish attained by many students during their schooling. We are also not oblivious to the statistics on the number of students seeking and gaining exemption from studying Irish for their Leaving Certificate on various official grounds, and about the lack of language and pedagogical proficiency amongst some primary school teachers. At the same time, there appears to be cautious room for optimism. The Irish Teaching Council, for example, which regulates the registration of teachers, recognises the need for high standards of Irish amongst both primary and post-primary teachers in terms of language and teaching proficiency.[21] As the final section of this chapter indicates also, various developments are underway aimed at preparing teachers with special qualifications to teach in gaelscoileanna and in Gaeltacht schools. Above all else, however, unprecedented opportunities to use Irish in ways that appeal to growing numbers of individuals continue to arise in settings other than those of formal education.

Historical Patterns and the Current Social and Economic Situation in the Gaeltacht

While the situation with regard to the Irish language in Irish society generally seems to have been strengthening over the last number of decades, the Gaeltacht has continued to shrink.[22] The economic and social situation in a number of Gaeltacht districts deteriorated badly following the economic crisis that beset the nation in 2008, and the enormous cuts to State spending that followed. Údarás na Gaeltachta had its budget cut by 73.7 per cent between 2008 and 2015.[23] Also, as Ó Ceallaigh has put it, "in a classic example of the neoliberal 'rolling-back' of the State, the *Gaeltacht Act, 2012* saw much of the responsibility for language planning transferred to voluntary community groups which are operating with only minimal resources".[24] Concurrently, a dramatic drop in the number of Irish speakers in the Gaeltacht was taking place; the 2016 census showed that the drop since 2011 was 11.2 per cent. A number of Gaeltacht areas also witnessed large-scale emigration during this time.

The developments noted above were particularly disheartening for those who had started to believe during the Celtic Tiger era that there might be a bright social and economic future for Gaeltacht residents, including through the establishment of information technology industries.[25] Other developments also seemed to hold out the possibility of economic improvement. Reporting in 2007, for example, the West of Ireland newspaper, the *Connaught Telegraph*, announced that for the Gaeltacht overall, the previous year had been the best year for job creation since 1998, and that Údarás na Gaeltachta was continuing "to make considerable progress in the 'transition' from manufacturing to services employment in a broad spectrum of areas".[26] Referring specifically to the County Mayo Gaeltacht, it pointed to the development of shellfish farming there, the opening of an enterprise arts-and-administration centre, the establishment of a fibre-telecommunications network in an industrial park in Béal a' Mhuirid and the construction of a 1.6 million Euro call centre in Acaill (Achill).

Certain Gaeltacht communities resisted State financial cutbacks when they were introduced, thus following an earlier tradition noted in previous chapters. The nature of this resistance has been summarised as follows:

> The fightback has materialized in a number of ways, whether it be local communities opposing the withdrawal and downgrading of transport and postal services, parents forming collectives which guarantee their children develop first class fluency in the language, people coming together on a voluntary basis to devise language plans for their districts, or young people joining radical activist organizations such as Misneach which calls for a complete overhaul of the class structures in the country and the

establishment of Gaeltacht workers co-operatives with a view to salvaging the language from the brink.[27]

Amongst the resistance groups was one entitled Guth na Gaeltachta (Voice of the Gaeltacht), that agitated between 2009 and 2013. Established in Donegal, it "helped politicise Irish speakers, who, like much of Irish society, had been largely de-politicised during the 'Celtic Tiger' boom years".[28]

While existing for only five years, Guth na Gaeltachta provided inspiration for other campaigns. In 2014, Irish speakers from both within and outside of the Gaeltacht, organised successfully to resist an amalgamation of the office of An Coimisnéar Teanga (the Language Commissioner) with that of the State Ombudsman. Operating under the title of Dearg le Fearg (Red with Anger) they conducted protest marches in Dublin, Belfast, and in the Galway Gaeltacht. With over 10,000 Irish speakers taking part, the government abandoned its plan for the proposed merger.

In 2015, people living on Oileáin Árainn (the Aran Islands) in County Galway, also mounted a protest, this time to attempt to maintain the quality of their air service to the mainland. The government planned to replace the aeroplanes that serviced the islands with a helicopter. A major worry for the islanders was that this was just the beginning of action that would eventually lead to the total discontinuation of their air service. The scale of their resistance efforts, however, led to the government continuing with the status quo.

Another population of Gaeltacht islanders, those living on Oileán Toraí (Tory Island) in County Donegal, engaged in a number of protests in 2018, aimed at ensuring that the ferry that connected them to the mainland was not replaced by one that was much older and less seaworthy. Their most publicly visible protest was when they vented their anger outside State buildings in Dublin.[29] Many of the public, aware that these people constitute one of the strongest Irish-speaking communities in the Gaeltacht, offered them strong support.

Gaeltacht populations have also been enthused by reporting on, and visits to, the neo-Gaeltacht established in Belfast, in Northern Ireland. At various times since national independence, attempts to establish other neo-Gaeltacht districts in the Republic were undertaken, but they all petered out.[30] Only in the Shaw's Road, Belfast, in the Northern Ireland State, did such a development survive.[31] It has been thriving in recent years after expanding to become An Cheathrú Ghaeltachta (the Gaeltacht Quarter).[32] At its heart are three primary schools (Gaelscoil an Lonnáin, Gaelscoil na bhFál, Bunscoil an tSléibhe Dhuibh) and one secondary school (Coláiste na Feirste). There is also an Irish language cultural centre there named after a nineteenth-century Presbyterian Irish language revivalist.

Gaeltacht populations are also having their language and cultural world connected to a wider Gaelic world through being able to view BBC Alba, which broadcasts in Scottish Gaelic. This connection is also starting to transcend religious differences as members of the Gaeltacht population, whose background is Catholic, are coming to realise that "the vast majority of Scotland's Gaels are not only Protestant, but seriously Presbyterian".[33] A new complexity has arisen in relation to these connections across Sruth na Maoile (the Straits of Moyle) with the growth of interest in learning and speaking Irish on the part of Protestant and Unionist individuals and groups in Northern Ireland,[34] and especially in Belfast, notwithstanding the lack of support afforded the language by the Democratic Unionist Party.[35] Groups on both sides of the religious divide are now also starting to realise that plenty of Protestants spoke Irish in Northern Ireland a hundred years ago.

Historical Patterns and the Current Situation in Relation to Schooling in the Gaeltacht

A serious issue since Irish independence that Irish-speaking parents in the Gaeltacht had to deal with regarding the education of their children, at least until recent decades, was the State's main concern that their children should, above all else, be Irish speakers. The indications are that many of these same parents wished for their children to be bilingual. In particular, they did not favour any language policy that could diminish the quality of their children's spoken and written English.[36] Fear has led parents in the Gaeltacht, Ó hIfearnáin has argued, to speak English with their children as they believed it was not being used sufficiently in the schools.[37] The results of his research also led him to conclude as follows:

> … as children grow up their parents wish that they had both spoken more Irish to them in their youth and that their education should have been as far as possible through the medium of Irish. Despite the bulk of opinion built on the experience of older parents that favours the reinforcement of the institutional support for Irish in the community so as to promote

> wider bilingualism, younger parents and some of the most strongly Irish-speaking sectors of society still doubt the merit of Irish-medium education.[38]

It would be folly to contend that this conclusion holds true for all Gaeltacht parents over the total period considered in this book. Nevertheless, it does go some way towards explaining why schooling in the Gaeltacht was not able to reverse the never-ending decline in the number of "native" speakers of Irish there in any decade.

Another likely influence on the perspective of parents was an awareness of the gap that existed between the level of education attainment of students residing in Gaeltacht districts and those residing in much of the rest of the country. Recently published data available indicate that such a gap still exists.[39] What stands out in particular is that, in 2016, while a State average of 12.5 per cent of the population nationally were classed as "no formal or primary education only" being their highest level of education attainment, 17 per cent of those residing in the Gaeltacht fitted into the classification. Cognisance of this reality is helpful in trying to arrive at some understanding of the origins of a conflict that erupted in the town of Daingean Uí Chúis (Dingle), in the Corca Dhuibhne Gaeltacht in West Kerry and that got headlines in the national media.[40] A group that styled itself the "Concerned Parents of Corca Dhuibhne" was pitted against those who supported the all-Irish language medium education policy adopted by the newly opened post-primary community school, Pobalscoil Chorca Dhuibhne. While a resolution was eventually secured, whereby the Department of Education and Skills provided additional tuition to those students who needed support to reach the appropriate standard to allow them to benefit from an Irish-medium education, the debate created an unpleasantness amongst the community.

Again, however, matters are far from gloomy overall for those who are committed to Irish-medium schooling throughout all of the Gaeltacht districts. In 2015, *The Irish Times* reported that most of the Gaeltacht second-level schools had significantly improved their rankings amongst all second-level schools nationally in terms of the numbers of their graduates who were proceeding to third-level education.[41] By now, the Department of Education and Skills, as part of the State's *20 Year Strategy for the Irish Language 2010–2030*,[42] had developed a range of research-informed policy proposals to strengthen Irish-medium education in the Gaeltacht. A policy document entitled *Policy Proposals on Educational Provision in Gaeltacht Areas* contains an outline of these proposals.[43] Major related developments took place in relation to preparation of teachers specifically for teaching in schools in the Gaeltacht and in gaelscoileanna. All programmes for the initial preparation of teachers for primary school teaching were restructured and developed to incorporate specific modules focusing on both Irish-medium immersion pedagogy and theory, and bilingual pedagogy and theory.

Education policy makers in Ireland were now also keeping abreast of research results published around the world on language teaching and were becoming increasingly sensitive to the changing nature of the language background of students residing in the Gaeltacht. This, in turn, brought them to realise the importance of teachers teaching in Gaeltacht schools and in gaelscoileanna knowing how to differentiate teaching and learning approaches in classrooms in order to cater for the specific needs of native speakers of Irish, particularly in the multi-grade or multi-class context. Such new thinking on providing high-quality Irish-medium schooling was central in an Irish government policy document of 2016, entitled *Polasaí don Oideachas Gaeltachta 2017–2022* (Policy on Gaeltacht Education 2017–2022). This was the first comprehensive State plan since 1922, aimed at addressing the education needs of students in the Gaeltacht.

What followed early in 2018 was the creation of two new Irish-medium teacher education programmes for the preparation of teachers to teach in Gaeltacht schools and in gaelscoileanna.[44] Concurrently, An Chomhairle um Oideachas Gaeltachta agus Gaelscolaíochta (COGG) continues to provide teaching resources and support services aimed at catering for the diverse Irish language needs of the education sector and also promotes research initiatives on these and related areas. While current policy is still identifying teachers and schools as pivotal to the revival of the language, it is imperative that the language does not remain trapped in the schools, but is spoken in the community.

We stated at the beginning of this chapter that we have not been concerned with providing a detailed overview of current developments in relation to Irish in Ireland, to economic and social life in the Gaeltacht and to the education of students there. Rather, by reflecting on the considerations of previous chapters, we have sought to provide a synthesis of some key developments historically that might help those attempting such a task. In similar vein, we have not seen it as part of our research agenda to speculate on the future of the Gaeltacht itself. Nevertheless, we have become acutely aware of the studies of others who have clearly indicated that the rate at which Irish as a community language is being eroded, continues unabated.[45] Accordingly, we find it difficult to conclude without stating that this certainly seems to imply it is most likely that those commencing schooling in Gaeltacht districts in both the immediate and the long-term future will be bilingual, with Irish being more dominant than English in some cases, and English being more dominant than Irish in others. In other words, the days of the young monoglot speakers of Irish, about whom we have written much in the early chapters of this book, including on their problems related to curriculum, teaching and learning on commencing school, has passed. Relatedly, whether this situation and broader developments in the Gaeltacht continue to follow a trajectory such that there may be no subject matter in 50 years' time for engagement in a study aimed at producing a follow-up companion volume to this book remains to be seen.

Notes

1. D. Mac Giolla Chríost. *The Irish Language in Ireland: From Global to Globalisation* (London: Routledge, 2005), p. 235.
2. A. Marwick. *The Nature of History* (London: The Macmillan Press, 1970), p. 13.
3. https://www.counterpunch.org/2018/11/02/irelands-gaeltacht-regions-transitioning-into-oblivion/.
4. Ibid.
5. N. Ó Gadhra. 'Irish Government Policy and Political Developments in the Gaeltacht', *Language, Culture and Curriculum*, Vol. l, No. 3, 1988, p. 251
6. Ibid. For an exposition on the many complexities related to this rather general pattern see A. Doyle. *A History of the Irish Language: From the Norman Invasion to Independence* (Oxford: Oxford University Press, 2015).
7. On this, see also A. Kelly. *Compulsory Irish: Language and Education in Ireland 1870s–1970s* (Dublin: Irish Academic Press, 2002).
8. Ibid.
9. Ibid.
10. Ibid.
11. T. J. Ó Ceallaigh and Á. Ní Dhonnabháin, 'Reawakening the Irish Language Through the Irish Education System: Challenges and

Priorities', *International Electronic Journal of Elementary Education*, Vol. 8, No. 2, 2015, pp. 179–198.

12. Ibid.
13. T. Ó hIfearnáin. 'Raising Children to Be Bilingual in the Gaeltacht: Language Preference and Practice', *International Journal of Bilingual Education and Bilingualism*, Vol. 10, No. 4, 2007, pp. 510–518.
14. Ibid.
15. Ibid.
16. https://www.irishexaminer.com/breakingnews/sport/gaa/the-kieran-shannon-interview-fifty-years-a-talking-with-sean-ban-breathnach-914292.html.
17. https://www.youtube.com/watch?v=6-QdBQ_9o-0.
18. https://www.irishtimes.com/news/politics/from-russia-with-gr%C3%A1-muscovite-appointed-to-promote-irish-in-kerry-1.3800740.
19. https://www.irishtimes.com/culture/move-over-ring-and-dingle-the-pop-up-gaeltacht-is-here-1.3232314.
20. For a recent work dealing with this see C. De Barra. *Gaeilge. A Radical Revolution* (Dublin: Currach Books, 2019).
21. https://www.teachingcouncil.ie/en/Registration/Registration-with-Conditions/.
22. D. Ó Giolláin. *Locating Irish Folklore: Tradition, Modernity, Identity* (Cork: Cork University Press, 2000).
23. http://www.ogmios.org/blog/austerity-and-resistance-in-irelands-gaeltacht-2008-18-by-ben-o-ceallaigh/.
24. Ibid.
25. https://www.counterpunch.org/2018/11/02/irelands-gaeltacht-regions-transitioning-into-oblivion/.
26. Ibid.
27. Ibid.
28. Ibid.
29. https://www.thejournal.ie/tory-island-ferry-protest-3850363-Feb2018/.
30. A. Mac Póilín. 'The Universe of the Gaeltacht'. In A. Higgins Wyndham (Ed.). *Re-imagining Ireland* (Charlotsville: University of Virginia Press, 2006), pp. 99–101.
31. http://www.irishnews.com/news/northernirelandnews/2019/02/16/news/tributes-to-unstoppable-vision-and-commitment-of-families-who-established-first-urban-gaeltacht-in-west-belfast-on-50th-an-1553305/?param=ds12rif76F.
32. https://en.wikipedia.org/wiki/Gaeltacht_Quarter,_Belfast. See also Fionntán de Brún. *Belfast and the Irish Language* (Dublin: Four Courts Press, 2006).
33. Ibid., p. 103.

34. https://www.pri.org/stories/2013-04-10/new-protestant-beginning-irish-language-belfast.
35. https://discoversociety.org/2017/06/06/learning-the-irish-language-of-reconciliation-in-protestant-east-belfast/.
36. T. Ó hIfearnáin. 'Raising Children to Be Bilingual in the Gaeltacht: Language Preference and Practice'.
37. Ibid.
38. Ibid.
39. https://www.maynoothuniversity.ie/sites/default/files/assets/document/GaeltachtAreaProfileEnglish_Online_0.pdf.
40. For details on this see http://www.leeds.ac.uk/educol/documents/172488.pdf. See also S. Warren. 'Private Sentiment and Public Issues: Irish Medium Education and Complex Linguistic and Political Identification'. In A. Pilch Ortega and B. Schröttner (Eds.). *Transnational Spaces and Regional Localization Social Networks, Border Regions and Local-Global Relations* (Munster, Germany: Waxman, 2012), pp. 167–178.
41. https://www.irishtimes.com/news/education/irish-medium-schools-continue-to-outperform-on-feeder-lists-1.3719834.
42. https://www.chg.gov.ie/app/uploads/2015/07/20-Year-Strategy-English-version.pdf.
43. https://www.education.ie/en/Press-Events/Events/Gaeltacht-Education-Policy-Proposals/Policy-Proposals-for-Education-Provision-in-Gaeltacht-Areas-May-2015.pdf.
44. https://www.irishtimes.com/news/education/irish-medium-teacher-training-places-announced-in-7m-push-1.3444375.
45. https://pure.uhi.ac.uk/portal/en/publications/nuashonru-ar-an-staidear-cuimsitheach-teangeolaioch-ar-usid-na-gaeilge-sa-ghaeltacht-20062011(680629be-fcac-4342-a123-4cb8a2a4e14e).html.

Appendix: Irish-Speaking Districts in 1911

T. O'Donoghue and T. O'Doherty, *Irish Speakers and Schooling in the Gaeltacht, 1900 to the Present*,
https://doi.org/10.1007/978-3-030-26021-7

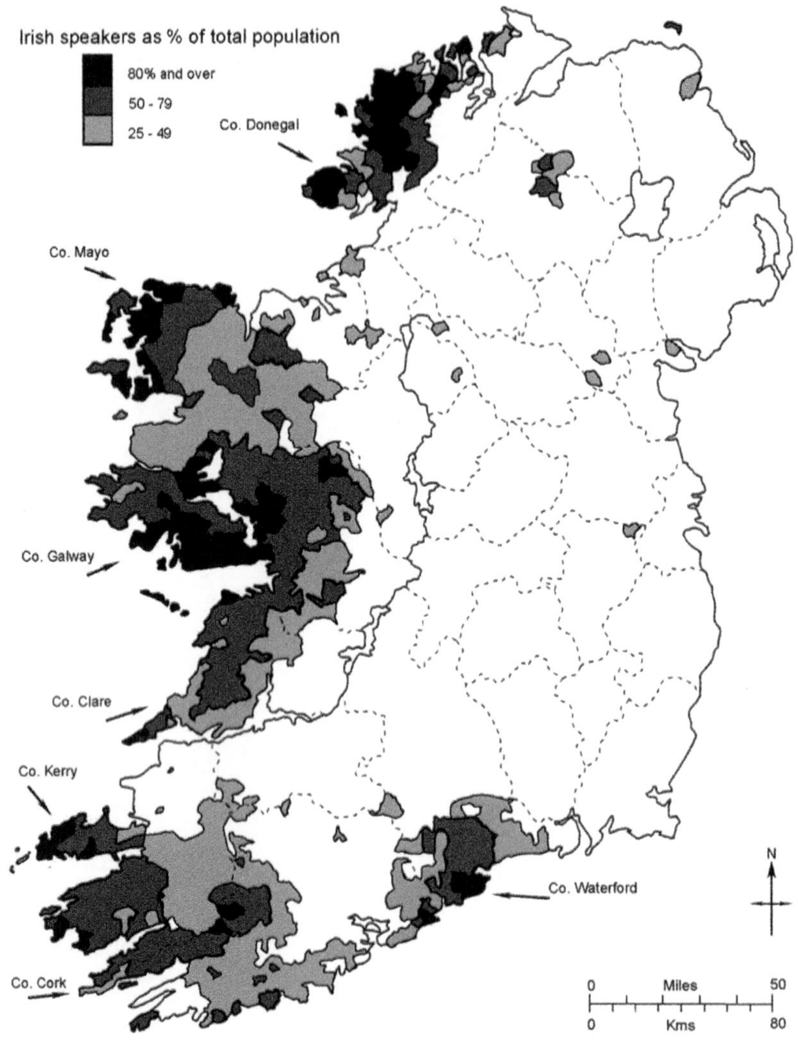
Irish speakers as % of total population
80% and over
50 - 79
25 - 49
Co. Donegal
Co. Mayo
Co. Galway
Co. Clare
Co. Kerry
Co. Cork
Co. Waterford
N
0 Miles 50
0 Kms 80

Bibliography

Manuscript Material

Department of Irish Folklore,
University College, Dublin
Main Manuscript Collection: Mss. 153, 275, 1157.
Schools' Collection: Mss. 641, 642.

National Library of Ireland
Conradh na Gaeilge, Minute Book of the Executive Committee 1897–98.
M. Fogarty, Bishop of Killaloe, Speech in 1919. ILB. 300. p. 4, item 64.
Gaelic League, Minutes of the Education Committee, Ms. 9798.
Minutes of the Meetings of the Commissioners of National Education 1900–1921 (printed).
Redmond Papers, Ms. 15,230.
Inspectors' Report

Books held in Schools
Doaghbeg National School, Co. Donegal; Clydagh National School, Headford, Co. Galway; Inisheer Isl. National School, Co. Galway; Scoil an Chnoic, Lettermullen, Co. Galway; Rosmuck National School, Co. Galway; Cromane National School, Co. Kerry; Glin National School, Co. Kerry; Lispole National School, Co. Kerry; Minard National School, Co. Kerry; Clonpriest National School, Gortroe, Co. Cork; Coomhola National School, Co.

T. O'Donoghue and T. O'Doherty, *Irish Speakers and Schooling in the Gaeltacht, 1900 to the Present*,
https://doi.org/10.1007/978-3-030-26021-7

Cork; Kilbrien National School, Co. Waterford; Modeligo National School, Co. Waterford; Ring National School, Co. Waterford; Tooraneena National School, Co. Waterford; Whitechurch National School, Co. Waterford.

Privately Owned

Archives of the Archdioces of Dublin, Clonliffe, Co. Dublin. Walsh Papers, including letters to various individuals and groups on education.

Micheál Ó Dómhnaill, *Stair Choláiste na Rinne* (unpublished typescript in Ring College, Dungarvan, Co. Waterford).

National Archives, Dublin

National School Records, Ed. 9. This collection includes the files on the various schools that introduced the Bilingual Programme of Instruction.

Official Papers

Hansard Debates

Hansard's Parliamentary Debates, 4th. S., 86, 20 July 1900, Col. 675, 679; 4th. S., 94, 19 May 1901, Col. 848.

Reports of the Commissioners of National Education in Ireland (C.N.E.I)

C.N.E.I. Report 1855. Appendix to the *Twenty Second Report of the Commissioners of National Education in Ireland for the year 1855* (2142-1), H.C. 1856, XXVII, pp. 11, 75–76.

———. 1856. Appendix to the *Twenty Third Report*...(2304), H.C. 1857-58, XX, pp. 144–145.

———. 1857. Appendix to the *Twenty Fourth Report*...(2456-11), H.C. 1859, VII, p. 135.

———. 1857. Appendix to the *Twenty Fifth Report*...(2593-1), H.C. 1860 XXV, p. 180.

———. 1879. *Forty Second Report*...(C. 2592), H.C. 1881, XXXIV.

———. 1893. *Sixtieth Report*...(C. 7457), H.C. 1894, XXX.

———. 1894. *Sixty First Report*...(C. 7796), H.C. 1895, XXIX.

———. 1895. *Sixty Second Report*...(C. 8142), H.C. 1896, XXVIII.

———. 1896–97. *Sixty Third Report*...(C. 8600), H.C. 1897, XXVIII.

———. 1897–98. Appendix to the *Sixty Fourth Report*...(C. 9038), H.C. 1898, XXVII.

———. 1899–1900. Appendix to the *Sixty Sixth Report*...(Cd. 285), H.C. 1900, XXIII.

———. 1900. Appendix to the *Sixty Seventh Report*...(Cd. 704), H.C. 1901, XXI.

———. 1901. Appendix to the *Sixty Eight Report* ...(Cd. 1198), H.C. 1902, XX, 403.

———. 1904. Appendix to the *Seventy First Report*...(Cd. 2567), H.C. 1905, XVII, 389.
———. 1905–06. Appendix to the *Seventy Second Report*...(Cd. 3154), XXIX, 635.
———. 1906–07. *Seventy Third Report*...(Cd. 3699), XXII, 1075.
———. 1907–08. *Seventy Fourth Report*...(Cd. 4291), XXVII, 841.
———. 1908–09. *Seventy Fifth Report*... (Cd. 4873), H.C. 1909, XX, 627.
———. 1909–10. *Seventy Sixth Report*...(Cd. 5340, H.C. 1910, XXV, 537.
———. 1910–11. *Seventy Seventh Report*...(Cd. 5903), H.C. 1911, XXI, 319.
———. 1911–12. *Seventy Eight Report*...(Cd. 6986), H.C. 1913, XXII, 507.
———. 1912–13. *Seventy Ninth Report*...(Cd. 7141), H.C. 1914, XXVII, 607.
———. 1914–15. *Eighty First Report*...(Cd. 8341), H.C. 1916, VII, 687.
———. 1915–16. *Eighty Second Report*...(Cd. 8495), H.C. 1917–18, IX, 713.
———. 1916–17. *Eighty Third Report*...(Cd. 9097), H.C. 1918, IX, 963.
———. 1917–18. *Eighty Fourth Report*...(cmd. 299), H.C. 1919, XXI, 705.
———. 1918–19. *Eighty Fifth Report*...(cmd. 1048), H.C. 1920, XV, 821.
———. 1919–20. *Eighty Sixth Report*...(cmd. 1476), H.C. 1921, X, 447.

Other Reports

Royal Commission of Inquiry into Primary Education (Ireland), (Powis Report). Minutes of Evidence, (C. 6-11), H.C. 1870, XXVII, Pt. III.
Report of the Commissioners on Intermediate Education (Ireland)—Final Report H.C. 1899 (C. 9511), XXII. First Report, Appendices and Evidence in H.C. 1899 XXII, XXIII, XXIV.
Report from the Commissioners on University Education (Ireland)—Final Report H.C. 1903 (Cd. 1483-4), XXXII, I, First, Second and Third Reports in H.C. 1902, XXXI, XXXII.
Report of Vice-Regal Committee of Inquiry into Primary Education (Ireland) 1913—Final Report H.C. 1914 (Cd. 7235) XXVIII, 1081. Other Reports and Appendixes H.C. 1913, XXII; H.C. 1914, XXVIII.
Report of Vice-Regal Committee of Inquiry into Primary Education (Ireland). 1918—Final Report H.C. 1919. (Cmd. 60) XXI, 741. Evidence, Memoranda etc. in H.C. 1919 (Cmd. 178) XXI.

Official Publications Since 1922

An Coimisiún um Athbheochan na Gaeilge. *An Tuarascáil Deiridh* (Dublin: Stationery Office, 1965).
An Roinn Oideachais. *Notes for Teachers: Irish* (Dublin: Stationery Office, n.d.).
An Roinn Oideachas. *Tuarascáil an Chomhchoiste um Oideachas sa Ghaeltacht* (Baile Átha Cliath: Oifig an tSoláthair, 1982).
Coimisiún na Gaeltachta. *Coimisiún na Gaeltachta Report* (Dublin: The Stationery Office, 1926).

Commission on the Restoration of the Irish Language. *Athbheochan na Gaeilge: The Restoration of the Irish Language* (Dublin: The Stationery Office, 1965).

Committee on Language Attitudes Research. *Report* (Dublin: The Stationery Office, 1975).

Curriculum and Examinations Board. *Language in the Curriculum: A Curriculum and Examinations Board Discussion Paper* (Dublin: Curriculum and Examinations Board, 1985).

Department of Education. *Report of the Department of Education for the School Year 1924–25 and the Financial and Administrative Years 1924–25–26.* Dublin: Stationery Office, 1926.

Department of Education. *Irish Folklore and Tradition* (Dublin: Stationery Office, 1937).

Department of Education. *Revised Programme for Infants* (Dublin: The Stationery Office, 1948).

Department of Education. *Terms of Reference to the Council of Education and Inaugural Addresses* (Dublin: Department of Education, 1950).

Department of Education. *Notes for Teachers: Infants* (Dublin: Stationery Office, 1951).

Department of Education. *Report of the Council of Education on (1) The Function of the Primary School and (2) The Curriculum of the Primary School* (Dublin: The Stationery Office, 1954).

Department of Education. *Report of the Council of Education: The Curriculum of the Secondary School* (Dublin: The Stationery Office, 1962).

Department of Education. *Primary School Curriculum: Teacher's Handbook: Part 1* (Dublin: The Stationery Office, 1971).

Department of Education. *White Paper on Educational Development* (Dublin: Stationery Office, 1980).

Department of Education. *Report of the Committee on Primary Schools Inspection* (Dublin: The Stationery Office, 1981).

Department of Education. *Programme for Action in Education 1984–1987* (Dublin: The Stationery Office, 1984).

Department of Finance. *Second Programme for Economic Expansion* (Dublin: Stationery Office, 1958).

Department of Finance. *Programme for Economic Expansion* (Dublin: Stationery Office, 1958).

Government of Ireland. *Investment in Education: Report of the Survey Team Appointed by the Minister of Education in October 1962* (Dublin: The Stationery Office, 1962).

Government of Ireland. *Statement of Government Policy on Recommendations of the Gaeltacht Commission* (Dublin: The Stationery Office, 1928).

National Programme Conference. *National Programme of Primary Instruction* (Dublin: Browne and Nolan, 1922).

National Programme Conference. *Report and Programme* (Dublin: Stationery Office, 1926), p. 27.

Review Body on the Primary Curriculum. *Report of the Review Body on the Primary Curriculum* (Dublin: Department of Education, 1990).

Sáorstát Éireann. *Report of the Commission on Technical Education* (Dublin: Stationery Office, 1927).

Sáorstát Éireann. *Memorandum V.40, 1942. Organisation of Whole-time Continuation Courses in Borough Urban and County Areas* (Dublin: Department of Education).

The Survey Team. *Investment in Education: Report of the Survey Team* (Dublin: Stationery Office, 1966).

Newspapers

An Claidheamh Soluis.
Clare Journal.
Connaught Telegraph.
Cork County Eagle.
Cork Examiner.
Donegal Vindicator.
Freeman's Journal.
Irish Independent.
Irish Times.
Irish School Weekly.
Kerry Searchlight.
Southern Star.
The Gaelic Journal.

Books, Book Chapters, Articles and Unpublished Theses

Akenson, D. H. *The Irish Education Experiment: The National System of Education in the Nineteenth Century* (London: Routledge and Keegan Paul, 1970).

Akenson, D. H. *A Mirror to Kathleen's Face* (Montreal: McGill-Queen's University Press, 1975).

Anderson, C. *The Native Irish* (London: n.p., 1816).

Anderson, C. *A Brief Sketch of Various Attempts Which Have Been Made to Diffuse a Knowledge of the Holy Scriptures Through the Medium of the Irish Language* (Dublin: Graisberry and Campbell, 1818).

Anderson, C. *Ireland, but Still Without the Ministry of the Word in Her Own Language* (Edinburgh: Oliver and Boyd, 1835).

Anderson, H. *Life and Letters of Christopher Anderson* (Edinburgh: Oliver and Boyd, 1854).

Association for Discountenancing Vice. *A Brief View of the Association for Discountenancing Vice and Promoting the Knowledge and Practice of the Christian Religion* (Dublin: Association for Discountenancing Vice, 1801).

Atkinson, N. 'Educational Construction in Malta.' *The Irish Journal of Education*, Vol. 3, No. 1, 1969, pp. 32–39.

Baker, C. 'Bilingual Education in Ireland, Scotland and Wales.' In C. Baker and S. P. Jones (Eds.). *Encyclopedia of Bilingualism and Bilingual Education* (Avon: Multilingual Matters, 1988), pp. 127–141.

Beard, R. M. *An Outline of Piaget's Developmental Psychology* (London: Routledge and Keegan Paul, 1969).

Betts, C. 'Irish: Scarce Better Off Under the British.' In *Culture in Crisis: The Future of the Welsh language* (Upton Wirral: Ffynnon Press, 1957), pp. 226–235.

Bilingual Teacher. *Bilingual Arithmetic for Standard III* (Dublin: Educational Company of Ireland, n.d.).

Breathnach, C. *The Congested Districts Board, 1891–1923* (Dublin: The Four Courts).

Breathnach, T. 'Social and Economic Problems of Western Ireland.' *Christus Rex*, Vol, 20, No. 2, 1966, pp. 125–133.

Brennan, M. 'Agriculture and Our School System, Irish Ecclesiastical Record.' Vol. 60, 1942, pp. 6–8.

Browne, T. *Ireland: A Social and Cultural History, 1922–1985* (London: Fontana Books, 1985).

Cahill, S. 'The Politics of the Irish Language Under the English and British.' In *The Proceedings of the Barra Ó Donnabháin Symposium, 2007* (New York: New York University, 2007).

Carnie, A. 'Modern Irish: A Case Study in Language Revival Failure.' In J. D. Bobaljik, R. Pensalfini, and L. Storts (Eds.). *Papers on Language Endangerment and the Maintenance of Linguistic Diversity* (New York: The MIT Working Papers in Linguistics, 1996, Vol. 28), pp. 99–116.

Carter, R. W. G., Carter, B., and Parker, A. J. (Eds.). *Ireland: Contemporary Perspectives on a Land and Its People* (Oxford: Routledge, 1989).

Chenevix French, D. *What Is the Use of Reviving Irish* (Dublin: Maunsel, 1909).

Cleary, A. E. 'Gaelic Colleges.' *Studies*, Vol. 6, No. 2, pp. 470–475.

Collins, M. *The Path to Freedom* (Dublin: Talbot Press, 1922).

Comhairle na Gaeilge. *Implementing a Language Policy* (Dublin: Comhairle na Gaeilge, 1974).

Comhar na Múinteoirí Gaeilge. *Bunoideachas trí Ghaeilge sa Ghaeltacht: Tuarascáil* (Baile Átha Cliath: Comhar na Múinteoirí Gaeilge, 1981).

Connolly, S. *Religion and Society in Nineteenth Century Ireland* (Dundalk: Dundalgan Press, 1985).

Conradh na Gaedhilge. *An Treas Leabhar* (Baile Átha Clíath: Conradh na Gaedhilge, 1906).

Conradh na Gaedhilge. *An Chéad Leabhar* (Baile Átha Clíath: Conradh na Gaedhilge, 1911).

Conradh na Gaeilge. 'The Language and the National Identity.' *An Múinteoir Náisiúnta*, Vol. 11, No. 11, January 1967, pp. 30–31.

Coolahan, J. *Irish Education: History and Structure* (Dublin: Institute of Public Administration, 1981).

Coolahan, J. *The ASTI and Post-Primary Education in Ireland 1909–1984* (Dublin: Cumann na Meanmhúinteóiri, 1984).

Coolahan, J. 'Imperialism and the Irish National School System.' In J. Mangan (Ed.). *Benefits Bestowed? Education and English Imperialism* (Manchester: Manchester University Press, 1998), pp. 76–93.

Corcoran, T. *Some Lists of Catholic Lay Teachers and Their Illegal Schools in the Later Penal Times* (Dublin: Gill, 1932).

Cremin, P. 'The Irish Language as a Medium of Instruction and as a School Subject, 1800–1921' (Unpublished M.Ed. Thesis, University College, Cork, 1977).

Crowley, J. W., Smyth, J., and Murphy, M. (Eds.). *Atlas of the Great Irish Famine* (Cork: Cork University Press, 2012).

Davis, V. *Our National Language* (Dublin: Gaelic League, 1945).

De Barra, C. *Gaeilge: A Radical Revolution* (Dublin: Currach Books, 2019).

De Búrca, M. *The G.A.A.: A History of the Gaelic Athletic Association* (Dublin: Gill and Macmillan, 1980).

De Paor, L. 'Ireland's Identities.' *The Crane Bag*, Vol. 3, No. 1, 1979, pp. 354–361.

Devine, E. 'The Connacht Irish College at Tourmakeady.' *Catholic Bulletin*, Vol. 11, January 1912, pp. 9–14.

Dowling, P. J. *The Hedge Schools in Ireland* (Dublin: Talbot Press, 1935).

Doyle, A. *A History of the Irish Language: From the Norman Invasion to Independence* (Oxford: Oxford University Press, 2015).

Duffy, P. *The Lay Teacher* (Dublin: Fallon, 1967).

Dunn, S. 'Education, Religion and Cultural Change in the Republic of Ireland.' In W. Tulasiewicz and C. Brock (Eds.). *Christianity and Educational Provision in International Perspective* (London: Routledge, 1988), pp. 89–116.

Durkacz, V. E. *The Decline of the Celtic Languages* (Edinburgh: John Donald, 1983).

European Research Centre on Multilingualism and Language Learning. *The Irish Language in Education in the Republic of Ireland* (Ljouwert/Leeuwarden, The Netherlands: Fryske Akademy Doelestrjitte, 2016).

Fahey, T. 'Catholicism and Industrial Society in Ireland.' In J. H. Goldthorpe and C. T. Whelan (Eds.). *The Development of Industrial Society in Ireland* (Oxford: Oxford University Press, 1994).

Fennell, D. 'The Last Years of the Gaeltacht.' *The Crane Bag*, Vol. 5, 1981, pp. 8–11.

Fenton, S. *It All Happened* (Dublin: M.H. Gill and Son, 1948).

Ferriter, D. *The Transformation of Ireland 1900–2000* (London: Profile Books, 2005).

Ferriter, D. *On The Edge: Ireland's Off-Shore Islands: A Modern History* (London: Profile Books, 2018).

Fischer, S. R. *A History of Language* (London: Reaktion Books, 2018).

Fishman, J. 'The Social Science Perspective in the Centre for Applied Linguistics.' In *Bilingual Education: Current Perspectives* (Arlington: Centre for Applied Linguistics, 1977).

Fitzgerald, G. *Estimates for Baronies of the Minimum Level of Irish Speaking amongst Successive Decennial Cohorts: 1771–1781 to 1861–1871* (Dublin: Royal Irish Academy, 1981).

Fitzpatrick, B. 'Bilingualism as a Factor in Education, with Application to the Language Question in Ireland' (Unpublished M.A. Thesis, University College, Dublin, 1918).

Foster, R. *Modern Ireland 1600–1972* (London: Allen Lane, 1988).

Foster, R. *Vivid Faces. The Revolutionary Generation in Ireland* (London: W. W. Norton, 2014).

Fullerton, R. 'The Place of Irish in Ireland's Education.' *Irish Educational Review*, V, 1911–12, pp. 456–466.

Gadhra, N. Ó. 'Irish Government Policy and Political Developments in the Gaeltacht.' *Language, Culture and Curriculum*, Vol. 1, No. 3, 1988, pp. 251–261.

Genesee, F., and Lindholm-Leary, K. 'Two Case Studies of Content-Based Language Education.' *Journal of Immersion and Content-Based Language Education*, Vol. 1, No. 1, 2013, pp. 3–33.

Granville, G. 'Politics and Partnership in Curriculum Planning in Ireland.' In C. Sugrue (Ed.). *Curriculum and Ideology: Irish Experiences: International Perspectives* (Dublin: The Liffey Press, 2004), pp. 67–99.

Greene, D. 'The Founding of the Gaelic League.' In S. Ó Tuama (Ed.). *The Gaelic League Idea* (Cork and Dublin: Mercier Press, 1972).

Harris, J. *Spoken Irish in Primary Schools* (Dublin: Institiúid Teangeolaíochta Éireann, 1984).

Harris, E. 'Prince Charles Not the Only One Who Needs a History Lesson.' *Sunday Independent*, 17 June 2018.

Harris, J., Forde, P., Archer, P., Nic Fhearaile, S., and O' Gorman, M. *Irish in Primary Schools: Long-Term National Trends in Achievement* (Dublin: Government Publications, 2006).

Harris, J., and Murtagh, L. 'Irish and English in Gaeltacht Primary Schools.' In G. Mac Eoin, A. Ahlqvist, and D. Ó hAodha (Eds.). *Third International Conference on Minority Languages: Celtic Papers. Multilingual Matters* (Clevedon: Multilingual Matters., 1988), pp. 104–124.

Hickey, R. 'Language Use and Attitudes in Ireland: A Preliminary Evaluation of Survey Results.' In B. Ó Catháin (Ed.). *Sochtheangeolaíocht na Gaeilge, Léachtaí Cholm Cille* (Maigh Nuad: An Sagart, Vol. 39, 1998), pp. 62–89.

Hickey, T. *Luathoideachas Trí Ghaeilge sa Ghaeltacht* (Galway: Údarás na Gaeltachta, 1999).

Hindley, R. *The Death of the Irish Language: A Qualified Obituary* (London: Routledge, 1990).

Hovdhaugen, E., Karlsson, F., Henriksen, C., and Sigurd, B. *The History of Linguistics in the Nordic Countries* (Helsinki: Nordic Research Council for the Humanities, 2000).

Irish National Teachers' Association. *Report of the Committee of Inquiry into Irish as a Teaching Medium* (Dublin: Irish National Teachers' Association, 1941).

Irish National Teachers' Organisation. *The Irish National Teachers' Organisation and the Irish Language: Discussion Document* (Dublin: Irish National Teachers' Organisation, 1985).

Irish National Teachers' Organisation. 'The Irish National Teachers' Organisation and the Irish Language.' *Tuarascáil*, Vol. 44, No. 3, March 1989, pp. 29–31.

Jenkins, D. E. *The Life of the Reverend Thomas Charles of Bala* (Denbeigh: n.p.).

Johnson, N. C. 'Nation-Building, Language and Education: The Geography of Teacher Recruitment in Ireland, 1925–55.' *Political Geography*, Vol. 11, No. 2, 1992, pp. 170–189.

Johnson, N. C. 'Building a Nation: An Examination of the Irish Gaeltacht Commission Report.' *Journal of Historical Geography*, Vol. 19, 1993, pp. 157–168.

Jones, T. W. (Ed.). *A True Relation of the Life and Death of William Bedell, Lord Bishop of Kilmore in Ireland* (London: Camden Society, 1872), pp. 26–44.

Jones, M. G. *The Charity School Movement in the Eighteenth Century* (Cambridge: Cambridge University Press, 1938).

Jones, W. R. *Bilingualism in Welsh Education* (Cardiff: University of Wales Press, 1966).

Jones, V. *A Gaelic Experiment—The Preparatory System 1926–61 and Coláiste Moibhí* (Dublin: The Woodfield Press, 2006).

Kavanagh, Rev. P. E. 'The History of Ireland.' *Catholic Bulletin*, Vol. I, February 1911, pp. 69–73.

Kearns, K. C. 'The Resuscitation of the Irish Gaeltacht.' *Geographical Review*, Vol. 64, No. 1, 1974, pp. 82–110.

Kelly, R. J. 'The Congested Districts.' *Journal of the Statistical and Social Inquiry Society of Ireland*, Vol. IX, 1891, pp. 492–498.

Kelly, J. 'Educational Print and the Emergence of Mass Education in Ireland, c.1650–c.1830.' In J. Kelly and S. Hegarty (Eds.). *Schools and Schooling 1650–2000: New Perspectives in the History of Education* (Dublin: Four Courts Press, 2017).

Knirck, J. *Afterimage of the Revolution. Cumann na nGaedheal and Irish Politics, 1922–1932* (Madison: University of Wisconsin Press, 2014).

Lewis, G. *Bilingualism and Bilingual Education* (Oxford: Pergamon Press, 1981).

Logan, W. J. P. 'An Aspect of Rural Reconstruction: The Work of the Congested Districts Board, with Specific Reference to County Donegal, 1981–1923' (Unpublished M.A. Thesis, Queen's University, Belfast, 1976).

London Hibernian Society. *Summary of the Proceedings of the Hibernian Society* (London: London Hibernian Society, 1812).

Mac Aodha, B. S. *The Galway Gaeltacht Survey: 1968–69* (Galway: Social Sciences Research Centre, University College Galway, 1971).

Mac Aodha, B. S. 'Was This a Social Revolution.' In S. Ó Tuama (Ed.). *The Gaelic League Idea* (Cork and Dublin: Mercier Press, 1972), pp. 20–30.

Mac Aonghusa, P. *Ar Son na Gaeilge: Conradh na Gaeilge 1893–1993* (Baile Átha: Connradh na Gaeilge, 1993).

MacClean, M. 'The Protestant Gael.' In A. Higgins Wyndham (Ed.). *Re-imagining Ireland* (Charlotsville: University of Virginia Press, 2006), pp. 102–105.

MacDonagh, O. *O'Connell: The Life of Daniel O'Connell 1775–1847* (London: Weidenfeld and Nicolson, 1991).

Mac Donnacha, S., Ní Chualáin, F., Ní Shéaghdha, A., and Ní Mhainín, T. *Staid Reatha na Scoileanna Gaeltachta* (Baile Átha Cliath: An Chomhairle um Oideachas Gaeltachta agus Gaelscolaíochta, 2005).

Mac Gabhann, M. *Rotha Mór on tSaoil* (Baile Átha Clíath: Foilseacháin Náisiúnta Teóranta, 1968).

Mac Giolla Chríost, D. *The Irish Language in Ireland: From Goídel to Globalisation* (London: Routledge, 2005).

Mac Giolla Chríost, D. 'Micro-level Language Planning in Ireland.' In A. Liddicoat and R. B. Baldauf (Eds.). *Language Planning in Local Contexts* (Bristol: Multilingual Matters, 2008), pp. 75–94.

Mac Mathúna, S., and Mac Gabhann, R. *Conradh na Gaeilge agus An t-Oideachas Aosach?* (Co. na Gaillimhe: Cló Cois Fharraige, 1981).

Mac Póilin, A. 'The Universe of the Gaeltacht.' In A. Higgins Wyndham (Ed.). *Re-imagining Ireland* (Charlotsville: University of Virginia Press, 2006), pp. 99–101.

Madaus, G. F., and McNamara, J. *Public Examinations: A Study of the Irish Leaving Certificate* (Dublin: Educational Research Centre, 1970).

Magner, K. 'Ballingeary.' *Catholic Bulletin*, Vol. 11, 1912, pp. 640–645.

Mallinson, V. *The Western European Idea in Education* (Oxford: Pergamon Press, 1980).

Marwick, A. *The Nature of History* (London: The Macmillan Press, 1970).

Mhic Mhurchú, D. 'Phillip Barron: Man of Mystery.' *Decies: Journal of the Old Waterford Society*, May 1976, pp. 10–15.

Monck Mason, H. J. *The Life of William Bedell, D.D., Lord Bishop of Kilmore* (London: Seeley, 1843).

Moran, D. P. *The Philosophy of Irish Ireland* (Dublin: University College Dublin Press, 2016).

Murphy, J. A. *Ireland in the Twentieth Century* (Dublin: Gill and Macmillan, 1975).

Murphy, D. *Education and the Arts: The Educational Autobiographies of Contemporary Irish Poets, Novelists, Dramatists, Musicians, Painters and Sculptors* (Dublin: School of Education, Trinity College Dublin, 1987).

NA. 'Buntús Gaeilge and Buntús Cainte.' *An Múinteoir Náisiúnta*, Vol. 12, No. 7, 1967, p. 3.

NA. 'Linguistic Research and Its Application.' *An Múinteoir Náisiúnta*, Vol. 12, No. 7, 1967, p. 27.

Nic Craith, M. 'Primary Education on The Great Blasket Island 1864–1940.' *Journal of the Kerry Archaeological and Historical Society*, Vol. 28, 1995, pp. 77–137.

Ní Chinnéide, M. (Ed.). *Peig* (Baile Átha Clíath: Cómhlacht Oideachais na hÉireann, n.d.).

Nic Pháidín, C., and Ó Cearnaigh, S. (Eds.). *A New View of the Irish Language* (Dublin: Cois Life, 2008).

Ní Fhearghusa, J. *Gaelscoileanna. Stair na hEagraíochta. 1973–1988* (Unpublished M.Ed. Thesis, University College Dublin, 1998).

Ní Luasa, E. 'Scoláire bocht na seascaidí.' *Cumann Staire Bhéal Átha'n Ghaorthaidh*, Vol. 1, 1999, http://ballingearyhs.com/journal1999.html.

Ní Néill, B. 'Cúrsaí Oideachais ar an Bhlascaod Mór' (Unpublished B.A. Thesis, Thomond College of Education, Limerick, 1984).

Ní Rouirc, C. 'Mo smaointí ar Mheánscoil Mhuire.' Vol. 1, 1999, http://ballingearyhs.com/journal1999.html.

Nowlan, K. B. 'The Gaelic League and Other National Movements.' In S. Ó Túama (Ed.). *The Gaelic League Idea* (Cork: The Mercier Press, 1972), pp. 41–51.

Ó Buachalla, S. *Education Policy in Twentieth Century Ireland* (Dublin: Wolfhound Press, 1988).
Ó Catháin, G. C. *The Loneliest Boy in the World: The Last Child of the Great Blasket* (Dublin: The Collins Press, 2014).
Ó Ceallaigh, T. J., and Ní Dhonnabháin, Á. 'Reawakening the Irish Language Through the Irish Education System: Challenges and Priorities.' *International Electronic Journal of Elementary Education*, Vol. 8, No. 2, 2015, pp. 179–198.
Ó Céidigh, P. *Socio-economic Profile of the Seven Gaeltacht Districts in Ireland* (Dublin: Irish Research Council, 2018).
Ó Coileáin, An Bráthair. 'No Good Purpose Would Be Served.' *Cómhar*, Nollaig 1949, p. 5.
Ó Comhraí, C. (Ed.). *Scoil Chuimsitheach Chiaráin: Caoga Bliain ag Fás* (Indreabhán, Conamara: Cló Iar-Chonnacht, 2016).
Ó Conaill, S., and Ó Duilearga, S. *Leabhar Sheáin Uí Chonaill: Scéalta agus Seanchas Ó Ui Rathach* (Dublin: Educational Co. of Ireland for the Folklore of Ireland Society, 1948).
Ó Cuív, B. 'Irish Language and Literature, 1845–1921.' In W. E. Vaughan (Ed.). *A New History of Ireland: Ireland Under the Union, 11, 1870–1921* (Oxford: Oxford University Press, 1996), pp. 374–422.
Ó Danachair, C. 'The Gaeltacht.' In B. Ó Cuív (Ed.). *A View of the Irish Language* (Dublin: The Stationery Office, 1969), pp. 112–121.
Ó Dómhnaill, M. *Stair Choláiste na Rinne* (Unpublished Typescript, Coláiste na Rinne, Dungarvan, County Waterford).
Ó Domhnalláin, T. 'Buntús Gaeilge: Cúlra, cur le chéile, cur i bhfeidhm.' *Teangeolas*, Vol. 13, 1981, pp. 24–32.
O'Donoghue, T. A. *Bilingual Education in Ireland, 1904–22: The Case of The Bilingual Programme of Instruction* (Perth: The Centre for Irish Studies, Murdoch University, 2000).
Ó Duibhir, P. 'The Spoken Irish of Sixth Class Pupils in Irish Immersion Schools' (Unpublished Ph.D. in Applied Linguistics, Dublin, Trinity College, 2009).
Ó Fiaich, T. 'The Language and Political History.' In B. Ó Cuív (Ed.). *A View of the Irish Language* (Dublin: Stationery Office, 1969), pp. 101–111.
Ó Fiaich, T. 'The Great Controversy.' In S. Ó Tuama (Ed.). *The Gaelic League Idea* (Cork: The Mercier Press, 1972), pp. 63–75.
Ó Fiannachta, P. *Stair na Gaeilge ó Thús* (Corcaigh: Mercier Press, 1974).
Ó Flatharta, P. *A Structure for Education in the Gaeltacht: Summary* (Dublin: An Chomhairle um Oideachas Gaeltachta agus Gaelscolaíochta, 2007).
Ó Gadhra, N. 'Irish Government Policy and Political Developments in the Gaeltacht.' *Language, Culture and Curriculum*, Vol. 1, 1988, pp. 251–261.

Ó Giollagáin, C. *Comprehensive Linguistic Survey of the Use of Irish in the Gaeltacht* (Maynooth: National University of Ireland Maynooth, 2007).

Ó Giollagáin, C. *Stair Sheanchais Mhicil Chonraí* (Indreabhán, Co. Galway: Cló Iar-Chonnachta, 1999).

Ó Giolláin, D. *Locating Irish Folklore: Tradition, Modernity, Identity* (Cork: Cork University Press, 2000).

Ó Grádaigh, S. 'Who Are Qualified to Teach in Second-Level Irish-Medium Schools?' *Irish Educational Studies*, Vol. 34, No. 2, 2015, pp. 165–182.

Ó hAilín, T. 'Irish Revival Movements.' In B. Ó Cuív (Ed.). *A View of the Irish Language* (Dublin: Stationery Office, 1969), pp. 91–100.

Ó hÁodha, C. 'An Phíarsach agus múineadh na Gaeilge.' *Inniu*, 12 Deireadh Fómhair 1979, p. 15.

Ó hIfearnáin, T. 'Raising Children to Be Bilingual in the Gaeltacht: Language Preference and Practice.' *International Journal of Bilingual Education and Bilingualism*, Vol. 10, No. 4, 2007, pp. 510–528.

Ó Laoighre, P. *Leabhar Núa ar Áireamh* (Baile Átha Clíath: Brún agus Ó Nóláin Teor, n.d.).

Ó Laoire, M. 'The Language Planning Situation in Ireland.' *Current Issues in Language Planning*, Vol. 6, No. 3, 2005, pp. 251–314.

Ó Loingsigh, P. 'The Irish Language in the Nineteenth Century.' *Oideas*, Vol. 14, Spring 1975, pp. 5–21.

Ó Luasaigh, D. 'Ceardscoil Bhéal Átha'n Ghaorthaidh.' *Cumann Staire Bhéal Átha'n Ghaorthaidh*, Vol. 1, 1999, http://ballingearyhs.com/journal1999.html.

Ó Mainín, S. 'Scoileanna an Oileáin.' In A. Ó Muircheartaigh (Ed.). *Oidhreacht an Bhlascaoid* (Dublin: Coiscéim, 1989), pp. 1–35.

Ó Munghaile, T. *Ó Bharr Thrámh go Baile Ghib* (Baile Átha Cliath: Coiscéim, 2008).

Ó Sé, M. D. *A Thig ná Tit Orm* (Dublin: C. J. Fallon, 2011).

Ó Searcaigh, C. *Light on Distant Hills* (London: Simon and Schuster, 2009).

Ó Síocháin, C. *The Man from Cape Clear* (Cork: Mercier Press, 1992).

Ó Siochrú, M. *God's Executioner—Oliver Cromwell and the Conquest of Ireland* (London: Faber and Faber, 2008).

Ó Snodaigh, P. *Hidden Ulster* (Baile Átha Clíath: Clódhanna Teo., 1973).

Ó Snodaigh, P. *Hidden Ulster, Protestants and the Irish Language* (Belfast: Lagan Press, 1995).

Ó Súilleabháin, S. 'An béaloideas agus and t-oideachas.' *Oideas*, Vol. 2, Earrach 1969, pp. 44–49.

Ó Torna, C. *Cruthú na Gaeltachta 1893–1922* (Baile Átha Clíath: Cois Life Teoranta, 2005).

Ó Tuathaigh, G. *The Development of the Gaeltacht as a Bilingual Entity* (Dublin: Linguistics Institute of Ireland, 1990).

Ó Tuathaigh, G. *I mBéal an Bháis: The Great Famine and the Language Shift in Nineteenth Century Ireland* (Hamden, CT: Quinnipac University Press, 2015).

O'Connell, T. J. *One Hundred Years of Progress* (Dublin: Irish National Teachers' Organisation, 1966).

O'Connor, J. 'The Teaching of Irish.' *The Cappuchin Annual*, 1949, pp. 205–220.

O'Connor, S. *A Troubled Sky: Reflections on the Irish Educational Scene 1957–68* (Dublin: Educational Research Centre, St. Patrick's College, Drumcondra, 1968).

O'Donoghue, T. *The Catholic Church and the Secondary School Curriculum in Ireland, 1922–62* (New York: Peter Lang, 1999).

O'Donoghue, T. (2000). *Bilingual Education in Ireland, 1904–22: The Case of the Bilingual Programme of Instruction* (Perth: The Centre for Irish Studies, Murdoch University).

O'Donoghue, T. 'Patterns of Attendance at Irish Secondary Schools from the Establishment of the Independent Irish State to the Introduction of the 'Free Education' Scheme in 1967.' In Judith Harford (Ed.). *Reflecting on Fifty Years Since the Advent of 'Free Post-Primary Education'* (London: Peter Lang, 2017), pp. 9–26.

O'Donoghue, T., and Harford, J. *Secondary School Education in Ireland: History, Memories and Life Stories, 1922–1967* (London and New York: Palgrave Macmillan, 2016).

O'Donoghue, T., Harford, J., and O'Doherty, T. *Teacher Preparation in Ireland: History, Policy and Future Directions* (Bingley, UK: Emerald Publishing, 2017).

O'Donovan, P. *Stanley's Letter: The National School System and Inspectors in Ireland 1831–1922* (Galway Education Centre, 2017).

O'Hickey, Rev. M. P. *Irish in the Schools* (Dublin: The Gaelic League, 1902).

O'Leary, Fr. *Eolas ar Áireamh* (Dublin: Irish Book, 1902).

O'Leary, P. K. 'The Development of Post-primary Education in Ireland Since 1922, with Special Reference to Vocational Education' (Unpublished Ph.D. Thesis, QUB, 1962).

O'Malley, V. 'An Account of the Growth of the Lay Schools in Ireland, 1922–1970, the Motives of the Lay founders, the Demise of the Lay Schools, and the Impact of Lay Education During That Period.' Paper presented at the History of Education Society Conference, Trinity College Dublin, Dublin, November 2004.

O'Riordan, M. 'Technical-Vocational Education, 1922–52: The Cultural Emphasis.' In *The Proceedings of the Education Conference Held in University College Cork*, 24–26 March 1977, pp. 194–199.

O'Rourke, K. 'Independent Ireland in Comparative Perspective.' *Irish Economic and Social History*, Vol. 44, 2017, pp. 19–45.

Pegley, S. M. 'The Development and Consolidation of the Gaeltacht Colony Ráth Cairn, Co. Meath 1935–1948' (Unpublished M.Litt Thesis, Department of Modern History, National University of Ireland Maynooth, 2007).

Redmond, J. E. 'The Policy of Killing Home Rule by Kindness.' *The Nineteenth Century: A Monthly Review*, Vol. 38, No. 226, 1895, pp. 905–914.

Selleck, R. J. W. *The New Education* (London: Pitman, 1968).

Shils, E. A., and Finch, H. A. (Eds.). *Max Weber on the Methodology of the Social Sciences* (Glencoe, IL: The Free Press, 1949).

Spolsky, B. 'Speech Communities and Schools.' *TESOL Quarterly*, Vol. 8, 1974, pp. 17–26.

Stewart, A. T. Q. *The Narrow Ground: The Roots of Conflict in Ulster* (London: Faber and Faber, 1989).

The Christian Brothers. *The Educational Record* (Dublin: The Christian Brothers, 1927), p. 284.

The Gaelic League. *Bilingual Education* (Dublin: The Gaelic League, 1900).

The Gaelic League. *The Bilingual Instruction in National Schools: The Prize Programmes* (Dublin: The Gaelic League, 1900).

The Gaelic League. *The Case for Bilingual Education in Irish-speaking Districts* (Dublin: The Gaelic League, 1900).

Thomas, N. 'Education in Wales.' In R. Bell, G. Fowler, and K. Little (Eds.). *Education in Great Britain and Ireland* (London: Routledge and Kegan Paul, 1973), pp. 14–18.

Thompson, A. M. *A Brief Account of the Rise and Progress of the Change in Religious Opinion Now Taking Place in Dingle and the West of the County of Kerry* (Dublin: Burnside and Seeley, 1846).

Tierney. M. *Education in a Free Ireland* (Dublin: Martin Lester, 1919).

Ua Maoileóin, P. *Na hAird Ó Thuaidh* (Baile Átha Cláith: Sáirséal agus Dill, 1970).

Uí Chearnaigh, S. S. *An tOileán a Tréigeadh* (Baile Átha Cláith: Sáirséal agus Dill, 1974).

Uí Mhurchú, M. B. 'An máistir. Cérbh é?' *Cumann Staire Bhéal Átha'n Ghaorthaidh*, Vol. 1, 1999, http://ballingearyhs.com/journal1999.html.

Waldron, K. *Out of the Shadows: Emerging Secondary Schools in the Archdiocese of Tuam* (Barnaderg, Tuam, Co. Galway, 2002).

Wall, M. 'The Decline of the Irish Language.' In B. Ó Cuív (Ed.). *A View of the Irish Language* (Dublin: Stationery Office, 1969), pp. 81–90.

Walsh, J. *Díchoimisiúnú Teanga: Coimisiún na Gaeltachta 1926* (Dublin: Cois Life, 2002).

Walsh, T. 'Conceptions of Childhood in Ireland in the Twentieth Century: A View from the Primary School Curriculum 1900–1999.' *Child Care in Practice*, Vol. 11, No. 2, 2005, pp. 253–269.

Walsh, T. A. 'Critical Analysis of Curricular Policy in Irish Primary Schools 1897–1990' (Unpublished Ph.D. Thesis, National University of Ireland Maynooth, 2006).

Warren, S. 'Private Sentiment and Public Issues: Irish Medium Education and Complex Linguistic and Political Identification.' In A. Pilch Ortega and B. Schröttner (Eds.). *Transnational Spaces and Regional Localization Social Networks, Border Regions and Local-Global Relations* (Munster, Germany: Waxman, 2012), pp. 167–178.

Watson, I. 'The Irish Language and Identity.' In C. Nic Pháidín and S. Ó Cearnaigh (Eds.). *A New View of the Irish Language* (Dublin: Cois Life, 2008), pp. 66–75.

Whitaker, T. K. 'Capital Formation, Saving and Economic Progress.' *Journal of the Statistical and Social Inquiry Society of Ireland*, Vol. 19, 1955–1956, pp. 185–188.

Whitaker, T. K. 'Economic Development: The Irish Experience.' *The Irish Times*, 20 September 1982.

Withers. C. *Gaelic in Scotland, 1698–1981: The Geographical History of a Language* (Edinburgh: John Donald, 1984).

Wolf, N. 'The National-School System and the Irish Language in the Nineteenth Century.' In J. Kelly and S. Hegarty (Eds.). *Schools and Schooling: 1650–2000: New Perspectives on the History of Education. The Eight Seamus Heaney Lectures* (Dublin: Four Courts Press, 2017), pp. 72–92.

Index

T. O'Donoghue and T. O'Doherty, *Irish Speakers and Schooling in the Gaeltacht, 1900 to the Present*,
https://doi.org/10.1007/978-3-030-26021-7

Printed by Printforce, the Netherlands